Elizabeth Spencer

Twayne's United States Authors Series

Warren French, Editor

Indiana University, Indianapolis

TUSAS 488

ELIZABETH SPENCER
(1921–   )
Photograph by Piroska Mihalka

Elizabeth Spencer

By Peggy Whitman Prenshaw

University of Southern Mississippi

Twayne Publishers • *Boston*

Elizabeth Spencer

Peggy Whitman Prenshaw

Copyright © 1985 by G. K. Hall & Company
All Rights Reserved
Published by Twayne Publishers
A Division of G. K. Hall & Company
70 Lincoln Street
Boston, Massachusetts 02111

Book Production by Elizabeth Todesco
Book Design by Barbara Anderson

Printed on permanent/durable acid-free
paper and bound in the United States of
America.

Library of Congress Cataloging in Publication Data

Prenshaw, Peggy Whitman.
  Elizabeth Spencer.

  (Twayne's United States authors series ; TUSAS 488)
  Bibliography: p. 174
  Includes index.
  1. Spencer, Elizabeth—Criticism and interpretation.
2. Mississippi in literature. I. Title. II. Series.
PS3537.P4454Z83 1985   813'.54   85–5546
ISBN 0–8057–7442–4

Contents

About the Author
Editor's Introduction
Preface
Acknowledgments
Chronology

Chapter One
A Life of Storytelling   1

Chapter Two
Mississippi Hill Country   16

Chapter Three
From the Hills to the Delta   32

Chapter Four
Voices of Mississippi   49

Chapter Five
Italian Departure   66

Chapter Six
Two Women Adrift   78

Chapter Seven
Angels in a Gray World   91

Chapter Eight
The Life Snare   112

Chapter Nine
The Short Fiction   131

Chapter Ten
After the Storm   151

Notes and References   165
Selected Bibliography   174
Index   179

About the Author

Peggy Whitman Prenshaw is dean of the Honors College and professor of English at the University of Southern Mississippi. Since 1973, she has been editor of the *Southern Quarterly: A Journal of the Arts in the South.* She has edited *Eudora Welty: Critical Essays* (1979), *Conversations with Eudora Welty* (1984), and *Women Writers of the Contemporary South* (1984), and she has coedited *Sense of Place: Mississippi* (1979) and *Order and Image in the American Small Town* (1981). She has published articles on Welty, Tennessee Williams, Elizabeth Spencer, and others, her research and scholarship having centered especially upon the literature and culture of Southern women. A native Mississippian, she holds the B.A. and M.A. degrees in English from Mississippi College (1957, 1959) and the Ph.D. in English from the University of Texas at Austin (1970).

Editor's Introduction

Of the sixty-odd books that I have edited for this series about our distinguished contemporary writers, this one has a very special significance for me as the realization of a long-cherished intention.

When I began my full-time teaching career at the University of Mississippi in September 1948, Elizabeth Spencer was one of my three office mates in a spacious, sunny room with a fine view of Ole Miss's picturesque campus. During our first year there, Elizabeth's first novel, *Fire in the Morning*, was published, occasioning many local celebrations that gave me a completely erroneous idea of how glamorous academic life would continue to be. I admired the novel tremendously; and I thought—correctly, I still believe—that Elizabeth Spencer was going to be one of the important novelists of my generation. She was not only a fine writer, but an inspiring teacher who attracted many devotees among the students.

I left Mississippi to return to graduate work at the University of Texas in 1950, and several years later Elizabeth left the country on a Guggenheim Fellowship to Italy. A quarter century passed before we met again, although I followed her career with consuming interest. Then in the 1970s when I began spending summers in New Hampshire, I had the opportunity to visit several times with her and her husband in Montreal and New England. Just about the same time I assumed editorial responsibilities for this series, and I determined that it must include a book that would do justice to Elizabeth's distinguished career. In the meantime I had written a short preliminary sketch about her work for James Vinson's *Contemporary Novelists,* and I had commissioned an article about her by one of our other Mississippi colleagues from 1948–50, David Pugh, for a book that I was editing about American literature of the 1950s.

About the same time that I became reacquainted with Elizabeth, I also got to know Peggy Whitman Prenshaw, the editor of the *Southern Quarterly,* who was gathering essays for a tribute to Eudora Welty. Peggy was pleased enough with an essay that I wrote on one of my favorite novels, *The Robber Bridegroom,* to ask me to edit a special issue of the magazine on the South and film that subsequently was published in book form by the University Press of

Mississippi. While working on these projects, I learned that Peggy was particularly interested in writing a book about Elizabeth Spencer, so that the arrangements were made for the book that is now before you.

The odds of one distant day arranging for and editing a book about a chance office mate must be incalculable, as it is also a pleasure beyond expression, binding together nearly forty years of my enthusiasm for the writings of Elizabeth Spencer and my dedication to the service of contemporary American writing.

Warren French

Preface

Elizabeth Spencer has written a distinguished body of fiction that critics have widely reviewed and admired, beginning with her first novel in 1948. To date, she has published eight novels and nearly forty short stories. In view of her critical success and this considerable canon, it is remarkable that this should be the first book-length study of her work.

Spencer's first three novels were all set in the twentieth-century South, in fact, in her native Mississippi, and inevitably critics expected to find looming over them the shadow of William Faulkner. Not surprisingly, her earliest work does to some extent show traces of the Faulkner influence, but ultimately her separate vision and extraordinary craftsmanship have revealed in her work a penetrating and original voice.

Spencer has not lived in the South since 1953, although she has often returned for visits. In stories and novels she has continued to write about the South, although her fiction since the late 1950s has increasingly reflected the international settings she has come to know from residences in Italy and Canada. The later fiction also shows changes in focal characters, particularly a shift from the male protagonists of the Mississippi novels to female protagonists in most of the subsequent works. Not until the 1984 novel, *The Salt Line*, does she return to a central male figure and a Mississippi setting. In all of her fiction, however, she reveals an acute understanding of men and women, and she writes about contemporary life not only as a perceptive observer of the infinite detail through which a society expresses itself, but as a woman who understands the subtle psychological patterns webbing throughout society.

In this study of Spencer's fiction I have sought not only to give the pertinent facts of the author's life in the first chapter, but to suggest some of the interactions between her life and work throughout the chapters on the novels and stories. My method of discussing the fiction is chiefly descriptive and explicative, and insofar as it is possible in a survey of an entire canon, I have tried to suggest the nuances of style and structure that reflect Spencer's mastery of the forms of fiction.

As for the arrangement, I have discussed the novels in order of publication, devoting a chapter to each of seven books and a chapter to the novella *Knights and Dragons* and a linked story, "Ship Island." I have discussed all other stories collected in *The Stories of Elizabeth Spencer* in a single chapter, a necessarily abbreviated treatment of Spencer's remarkable achievement in the short story. In a brief conclusion I have tried to identify the pattern of Spencer's development as a writer and to suggest the significance of her contribution to twentieth-century American fiction.

Peggy Whitman Prenshaw

University of Southern Mississippi

Acknowledgments

I am chiefly indebted to Elizabeth Spencer, who has graciously given interviews on a number of occasions, corresponded with me on matters of family history and publication of her fiction, and who even generously consented to read portions of the manuscript to save me from factual errors and inadvertencies. I am also indebted to the editors at Twayne, especially Warren French, for their patience and assistance.

I should like to acknowledge the support of the administration and staff of the University of Southern Mississippi. The University library staff have been unfailingly supportive. I am particularly indebted to Joyce Phillips Sanders and Patti White Dearman, whose skillful assistance and cheerfulness made my work much easier than it otherwise would have been.

For his patience, endurance, and unstinting support, which often included doing most of my share of the chores at home, I am grateful to my husband, Richard Prenshaw.

Finally, I should like to acknowledge the following: McGraw-Hill for permission to quote from *Fire in the Morning, This Crooked Way, The Voice at the Back Door, The Light in the Piazza, Knights and Dragons, No Place for an Angel,* and *The Snare;* Doubleday for permission to quote from *The Stories of Elizabeth Spencer* and *The Salt Line;* the *Southern Quarterly* for permission to reprint material from my article "Mermaids, Angels and Free Woman: The Heroines of Elizabeth Spencer's Fiction," 22 (Fall 1983):13–31.

Chronology

1921   Elizabeth Spencer born 19 July, in Carrollton, Mississippi, second child of James Luther Spencer and Mary James McCain Spencer, both of families who had lived and farmed in Carroll County since the 1830s. Prominent among the McCain family were military heroes from West Point and Annapolis.

1921–1938   Childhood and youth spent in Carrollton and at the McCain family plantation, Teoc, bearing the Choctaw name, Teoc Tillala (Tall Pines). Graduated as class valedictorian from J. Z. George High School in Carrollton, Spring 1938.

1938–1942   Attends Belhaven College, Presbyterian college for women, in Jackson, Mississippi. Second place winner for short story at the Southern Literary Festival. During senior year invites Eudora Welty to speak to the literary society.

1942–1943   Attends Vanderbilt University, studies with Donald Davidson. M.A. in English, thesis, "Irish Mythology in the Early Poetry of William Butler Yeats."

1943–1944   Instructor at Northwest Junior College, Senatobia, Mississippi.

1944–1945   Teaches at Ward-Belmont, private school for girls, Nashville, Tennessee. Takes class in short story writing taught by Raymond Goldman, Watkins Institute, Nashville. *New Yorker* rejects "The Little Brown Girl" in 1945 (published the story in 1957).

1945–1946   Reporter for the Nashville *Tennessean*. Summer 1946, resigns to work full-time on novel.

1948   *Fire in the Morning*. Manuscript recommended by D. Davidson to David M. Clay of Dodd, Mead. Fall, joins English faculty at University of Mississippi in Oxford.

1949   April, participates in the Southern Literary Festival at University of Mississippi, with H. H. Kroll, John Crowe Ransom, and Stark Young, who was a distant relation of Spencer. Meets William Faulkner at party given for Young. Awarded the Women's Democratic Committee Award. August, visits Italy.

1950   "Pilgrimage," *Virginia Quarterly Review,* Summer. Story given honorable mention in Martha Foley's collection of year's best short stories.

1951–1952   On leave from University of Mississippi; for part of year, lives in Pass Christian, on Mississippi Gulf Coast, writing full-time.

1952   *This Crooked Way.* Visited in March on the Gulf Coast by Eudora Welty and Katherine Anne Porter, and on another occasion by Welty and Elizabeth Bowen. Receives Recognition Award from the National Institute of Arts and Letters.

1953   Guggenheim Fellowship; leaves for Italy, settles in Rome.

1954   February, attends a party in Rome given for William Faulkner. Spends five months in Florence, returning to Rome in September. In Florence, meets John Arthur Blackwood Rusher (b. 1920), an Englishman who teaches in a language school.

1955   Summer, returns briefly to Mississippi; spends remainder of year in New York, revising new novel.

1956   *The Voice at the Back Door.* Returns to Italy; marries John Rusher, 29 September, at St. Colomb Minor in Cornwall, England.

1957   Rosenthal Award of the American Academy of Arts and Letters; Kenyon Review Fellowship.

1958   The Rushers move to Montreal, Canada.

1960   *The Light in the Piazza,* published originally in the *New Yorker* (18 June). Movie rights sold to MGM. McGraw-Hill Fiction Award of $10,000; O. Henry Award for "First Dark."

1962–1963   Donnelly Fellow, Bryn Mawr College.

1964   Spencer papers deposited at the University of Kentucky, Lexington.

1965   *Knights and Dragons,* published originally in a shortened version in *Redbook* (July). "The Visit" included in Martha Foley's *Best American Short Stories.* May, guest writer, Mississippi Arts Festival, Jackson.

1966   O. Henry Prize for "Ship Island."

1967   *No Place for an Angel.* September, visits Eudora Welty in Mississippi, en route from Key West to Montreal; the evening's visit described in an essay by Charlotte Capers.

1968   *Ship Island and Other Stories.* Bellamann Award. Litt. D., Southwestern University, Memphis, Tennessee.

1970   Moves from the suburban Lachine into Montreal. March, visiting writer at Gulf Park College in Mississippi.

1972   *The Snare.* Writer in residence for a month at Hollins College, Roanoke, Virginia.

1974   Death of Mary James McCain Spencer.

1976   Begins teaching at Concordia University, Montreal; subsequently has held positions as writer in residence and adjunct professor. Death of James Luther Spencer.

1981   *The Stories of Elizabeth Spencer,* and *Marilee* ("A Southern Landscape," "Sharon," "Indian Summer"). Spends spring at Yaddo. Lectures at summer Faulkner conference, University of Mississippi. Gives reading in August at the Old Capitol in Jackson, introduced by Eudora Welty. Guest of Governor and Mrs. William Winter. Visits the Gulf Coast and Walker Percy in New Orleans before returning to Montreal.

1982   Spring at Yaddo, working on new novel.

1983   Award of Merit Medal for the Short Story, American Academy and Institute of Arts and Letters. Visits Italy in late summer.

1984   *The Salt Line.* Manuscripts and papers deposited at the National Library of Canada, Ottawa.

1985   Elected to the American Academy and Institute of Arts and Letters.

Chapter One
A Life of Storytelling

From the beginning Elizabeth Spencer's life has been richly infused with stories, stories springing from a literary and oral tradition that formed an important part of her childhood in Mississippi. She grew up amid an active tradition of storytelling and reading, listening to tales told by family and friends and to stories read aloud by her mother and teachers. "Being a Southerner, a Mississippian," she wrote in a 1972 essay on storytelling, "had a good deal to do . . . with my ever having started to write at all." She explained that her impulse to create fiction traced in part from the communal tradition of storytelling that she had known ever since she was old enough to "understand speech."[1]

To the world at large, the tradition Spencer describes is perhaps more familiar from the example of William Faulkner, her neighbor of sorts, his Oxford (and Yoknapatawpha) lying just sixty miles northeast of her own Carrollton. The proximity to Faulkner, as Flannery O'Connor once noted, was often harrowing for a young Southern writer just beginning to write in the 1940s and 1950s. In Spencer's case it was especially so because the people and places she knew firsthand and wanted to write about were inevitably close to Faulkner's "postage stamp," his fictional Yoknapatawpha County, based on Lafayette County, Mississippi. Also, she was reading Faulkner at a formative time in her life, during the years she was at Vanderbilt University and while working in Nashville just prior to the publication of her first novel in 1948.

In the essay "Emerging as a Writer in Faulkner's Mississippi" Spencer has written with great insight about the literary tradition in which she came of age.[2] By her account, the Faulkner model was a mixed blessing, a galvanizing influence on her career and a slightly intimidating one. In an interview conducted in August 1972, she described the literary climate in which she began writing as "both a very good and a very bad time," in that "the giants in literature were people who were dealing with the same people she wanted to deal with."[3] Given the force of Faulkner's influence and prominence,

1

as well as the proximity of Spencer's settings to his, it is not surprising that many critics found a Faulkner strain in her first two novels. This early strain was minor, however, and was ultimately mediated by her talent and originality, which would be fully manifest in her third novel, *The Voice at the Back Door,* as an independent, mature vision of the South.

Despite all the lines of attachment—literary and personal—that bound Spencer to the South and gave her much of her material for the first three novels, nonetheless a turning point did come for her in the 1950s when she needed distance and perspective and when she sought new directions for her work. She left the South for a sojourn of several years in Italy and, after her marriage in 1956, for a residence in Canada, where she has lived since 1958. One finds a sure movement toward literary achievement throughout these various periods of her life—her Mississippi beginnings, the years of college and the early novels, the Italian stay, and the lengthy Canadian residence, during which she has published her later five novels and several collections of short stories. Each of these stages has given Spencer a varied store of personal experience that she has transmuted through imagination and craft into distinguished, memorable fiction.

Mississippi Beginnings

Elizabeth Spencer was born on 19 July 1921, to James Luther Spencer and Mary James McCain Spencer in Carrollton, Mississippi, a town with a population of about five hundred in the north central hills section of the state. Both her parents came from families who had lived and farmed in Carroll County since the 1830s. The Spencers had one older child, a son, James L. Spencer, who later became a physician. Among Spencer's mother's family, the McCains, were a number of military heroes, including a great uncle, Pinckney McCain, who served as a general in World War I with the Allied Expeditionary Force; an uncle, William Alexander McCain, a West Point graduate who served in World War I; and another uncle, J. S. McCain, named for his father, who was an admiral during World War II, serving under Admiral William Halsey in the Pacific. His son, the third in the John Sidney McCain line, was also an admiral, serving as commander of the Pacific fleet in the 1960s.[4]

The McCains were a Scots Presbyterian family, and though Spencer has commented that one may not accurately describe them as "bookish," they did place much emphasis upon education and "made ready reference to books" (*EW*, 121–22). Spencer's aunt, Katie Lou McCain, taught Latin for many years in McComb, Mississippi, and before her marriage Mary James McCain, called Jimmie, gave piano lessons. As a child, Elizabeth Spencer was particularly close to her maternal grandfather, John Sidney McCain I (1851–1934) and frequently visited the nearby family plantation, Teoc, which bore the Choctaw name (Teoc Tillala) for "tall pines." It lay on the margin of the rich Mississippi delta near Malmaison, the estate of the Choctaw chieftain, Greenwood Leflore. Spencer's grandfather, a lifelong resident of the area and at one time county sheriff, provided her with a reservoir of stories about the people and places of Carroll and surrounding counties. In fact, he even remembered and told of events of the Civil War period, though he had been too young to serve in the war. It was her grandfather McCain upon whom she modeled the character Daniel Armstrong in her first novel, *Fire in the Morning,* and the grandfather in the largely autobiographical stories "The Day Before" and "A Christian Education."

On the paternal side of the family, Spencer's grandfather had actually fought at Gettysburg, but he had died before she was born. Unlikely though it seems, Spencer is only two generations removed from the Civil War, her father having been the youngest in his family and she the younger child in hers. James Luther Spencer had come from the little crossroads of McCarley when he was a young man setting out to start a business of his own. He met Mary McCain when she came to McCarley to teach music, and they were marrried later in Carrollton. They bought a large frame house on the outskirts of town, the house where their daughter was born and where they lived for the rest of their lives. In her early story "The Little Brown Girl," Spencer rather clearly draws upon details of her childhood home and the surrounding acreage in her portrayal of the child Maybeth.

Spencer has spoken at length of her childhood in Carrollton in an interview with John Griffin Jones and has written of it in even greater detail in such essays as "Valley Hill" and "Emerging as a Writer in Faulkner's Mississippi." Older than Faulkner's Oxford, Carrollton has antebellum houses and gardens that in recent years have been opened to tourists during an annual pilgrimage season, and indeed in many respects the town is not much changed from what it was in earlier times. If anything, it is perhaps less flourishing than it once was, as was indicated by the decision to film the movie version of Faulkner's *The Reivers* in Carrollton. The filmmakers found Oxford "too modern" to provide a convincing image of Faulkner's Jefferson at the turn of the century (*EW,* 123).

A quiet little town during the 1920s and 1930s of Spencer's childhood, Carrollton nonetheless had something of a mysterious past, made evident in the existence of a North Carrollton, which lies just across the Big Sand Creek. "North Carrollton got mad at Carrollton once, back in the mists of time," Spencer writes, "or Carrollton got mad at North Carrollton, I forget which. At any rate, we had, between us, never more than 1,000 souls, but two separate 12-year high schools, two separate post offices, two mayors and boards of aldermen, and any number of separate reasons to feel different and superior, each to the other. I think, though, that since Carrollton had the courthouse and the county records, we quite possibly were more successful snobs, if this is any distinction" (*EW,* 123). Spencer's fictional towns of Tarsus in *Fire in the Morning* and Lacey in *The Voice at the Back Door* both closely resemble in topography and other detail the county seat town of Carrollton.

From her interviews, essays, and fiction one would judge that Spencer's immediate and extended family were a source of affection and support in her childhood. She remembers her father as a conscientious man, ambitious to support his family. He had numerous business interests, which included the Chevrolet agency, the Standard Oil franchise, a cotton gin, a farm, and at one time some stores, though in the face of hard times it was not until later, after he sent her brother to medical school and her to college that, in Spencer's words, "he had any kind of affluence."[5]

Spencer's recollections of her mother have most often focused upon Mary Spencer's love of books. As a young child, Spencer had bouts of poor health when her mother frequently read aloud to her, clearly with much enjoyment and skill. Despite Spencer's disclaimer about her family's bookishness, a love of storytelling and a rich legacy of reading came to her almost as a birthright. She has herself made the point of how the oral tradition of her Southern culture was at every turn complemented and informed by the strong literary tradition. "It was no interruption in small town social life, or family life or church-going or hunting or fishing," she writes, "to have your mother read to you every night out of Greek and Roman myths, the story of the Bible, Robin Hood, Arthurian legend, Uncle Remus, Hawthorne, Aesop, Grimm, Robert Louis Stevenson, George MacDonald, Louisa May Alcott, and all those others, who followed naturally after Mother Goose and Peter Rabbit." She remembers a little later reading and speaking of characters from Dickens, Thackeray, Austen, George Eliot, and Victor Hugo as if they were persons all known well to her family (*EW*, 122).

In the same essay Spencer remembers, too, her uncle's urging her to read a favorite novel, *Les Miserables,* and her cousin's and brother's recitations. "A cousin of mine from up the street who often used to play with the rest of us at my house in the summer, used to quote Swinburne by the yard, and even before that, my brother, whose bent was certainly not 'literary,' would recite long stanzas from Macaulay along with Robert W. Service." In addition to teaching Latin, her aunt "relished reading fiction," and "long scraps of original poems were to be found in the notebooks of some of the family members." Looking back on her family's enjoyment of books and their easy familiarity about reading them and talking of what they had read, Spencer has said that the literary activity was regarded by them all as a "kind of liveliness. It made life more enjoyable, expanded it, to have feelings for somebody in New England, or France or England, or for never-never characters out of myths" (*EW*, 122).

On various occasions Spencer has said that her own interest in writing stories began when she was quite young, with the writing of adventure stories and fairy tales for her parents and teachers. Of her very first impulse to write, she has given a vivid account in an interview: "I remember when I first got this terrible urgency. I stayed awake all night with a kind of excitement about something or other. There was a fire in the room burning and casting shadows. The next day I tried to paint that . . . but I had no talent for painting, so I wrote a poem." The writing, she says, was a way of releasing the "inner excitement." As for anyone's "explaining" the cultural forces that produce a writer, Spencer is dubious, noting that finally "Mississippi doesn't explain it; nothing explains it. Being read to as a child doesn't explain it. It's a kind of chemical excitement you feel, and you're drawn toward one sort of expression or another. As I couldn't draw, I wrote."[6]

Spencer's early literary efforts were aided considerably by some memorable teachers, including several in elementary school who loved poetry and frequently read aloud to their classes. She began the study of Latin in the seventh grade and studied Shakespeare in high school with a teacher who brought her training at Vanderbilt under Walter Clyde Curry to Carrollton. Spencer recalls reading the plays aloud, "sitting around an iron stove with our knees toasting and our backs cold and hunks of plaster threatening to fall down on our heads, taking parts in *Romeo and Juliet*, *The Merchant of Venice*, or *As You Like It*," building up to grade twelve, when they moved "full-scale into *Macbeth*" (*EW*, 125).

Spencer's varied exposure to literature from her earliest years and her deeply felt connections to a vast network of family and community gave her experiences that in many ways were ideally suited to the making of a writer. Partaking of the oral tradition of Southern storytelling, she also grew up with a sharp sense of how stories take shape in books, and with the ambition to create such stories herself. "I believe that making books springs from a love of books," she has written, "and that many cultural forces, some of the literary nature, were at work around those small, dusty, obviously 'backward,' apparently asleep, possibly dead, little old Southern towns" (*EW*, 125–26.).

In 1938 Spencer graduated as valedictorian of her class from J. Z. George High School, named for a U. S. senator from Carroll County. The following fall she left home to attend a small Presbyterian college in Jackson. Though she had wanted to attend the University of Mississippi at Oxford, she went to Belhaven College because of her family's Presbyterian ties with the school and her having been awarded a scholarship. At Belhaven she majored in English, her studies following a traditional curriculum, and she actively participated in many campus activities. She served as class president, editor of the campus paper, and president of the literary society. It was in the latter role that during her senior year she first met Eudora Welty, whose home stood just across the street from the college. Welty recounts the 1941 meeting in her foreword to *The Stories of Elizabeth Spencer*. "Elizabeth made a telephone call to ask if I'd please step over to a session of the Literary Society so they could meet a real writer and seek my advice." Since it would have been "unneighborly," according to Welty, to refuse, she accepted the invitation. "I met then a graceful young woman with a slender, vivid face, delicate and clearly defined features, dark blue eyes in which, then as now, you could read that Elizabeth Spencer was a jump ahead of you in what you were about to say. She did as nice

Southern girls, literary or unliterary, were supposed to do in the Forties—looked pretty, had good manners (like mine, in coming when invited), and inevitably giggled (when in doubt, giggle). But the main thing about her was blazingly clear—this girl was serious. She was indeed already a writer."[7]

The meeting initiated a lifelong friendship between the two writers, the warmth and ease of which in later years is shown in Charlotte Capers's account of a visit Spencer made to Jackson in 1967, in the essay "An Evening with Eudora Welty and Elizabeth Spencer."[8] Welty's reference in the foreword to *Stories* to Spencer's having come to think of herself as a writer while in college suggests something of Spencer's serious determination in her ambition to be a writer. In college she had written steadily, though there was only one creative writing class offered at Belhaven at the time. It was mainly as a member of the literary group that she worked at her craft, and through the association she achieved some measure of recognition. She was awarded the Chi Delta Poetry award, and one of her short stories won second place in the Southern Literary Festival. As she approached graduation in 1942, she began to look beyond Mississippi in her effort to further her education and find more personal freedom than had been possible as a college girl in a small Presbyterian college. In the fall of that year she left Mississippi for Nashville and Vanderbilt University, which for decades had been a major literary center in the South.

Nashville and a Career Underway

Spencer has said that the most memorable course she had at Vanderbilt was one in the modern British and American novel taught by Donald Davidson. In a 1961 interview in the Nashville *Tennessean* she spoke of it as "more formative in my thinking, in my approach to literature, than any other I've ever had."[9] Although the glory days of the Fugitives at Vanderbilt had long passed by 1942, the literary ferment persisted, giving a young writer from the hinterlands a sense of what it was like to be part of an active writing tradition.[10] Davidson, an important member of this tradition, was a major influence on Spencer. He read and criticized her fiction, directed her master's thesis on William Butler Yeats and Irish mythology, and introduced her to Faulkner and other modernist writers. The discovery of Faulkner, Spencer said, was particularly affecting. "Very few people can ever make that kind of discovery because very few people have a novelist of genius living right up the road. Oh, I'll never forget the experience. Here was life as I knew it rendered in the highest literary form. Everything I've heard all my life, people I've seen, types I've seen all my life, speech I've heard all my life."[11]

Despite the galvanizing effect, the Faulkner connection presented certain problems, too. Once she had entered "Faulkner Country," she was stuck with the quandary of how, as a writer, to get out. Her antidote to his infectious style was to read, voraciously, other modern writers who could give her different models and thus serve as "counter-influences, neutralizers" (EW, 132). Writers as varying as Turgenev, Chekhov, Mansfield, Cather, Porter, and Hemingway all gave some relief. Her habit of prescribing for herself the reading of certain authors as a means of correcting some imbalance or eccentricity in her stylistic development is a strategy she has mentioned on several occasions. In an interview with Elizabeth Pell Broadwell and Ronald Wesley Hoag in 1980 she recalled that in college she had "a natural inclination to write a little like Katherine Mansfield. So it seemed to me that if I was ever going to firm things up and be the kind of writer I wanted to be, I needed to escape a feminine sort of hovering over things, an overly-sensitive poetic prose like Mansfield's or Virginia Woolf's. To get away from that, I read a lot of Hardy and Conrad—excellent writers with a very firm, controlled style. This was the way I wanted to write, and in my early novels I deliberately forced myself to avoid a more feminine style."[12]

Spencer's effort to avoid a "feminine style" doubtless reflects the traditional attitude of the literary establishment during the period of her undergraduate and graduate studies. She understandably reacted pragmatically to distance herself from a style that critics, almost without exception, regarded pejoratively as typifying most female writers. Interestingly, even in the face of her determined use of a vigorous, straightforward style in the early novels, some reviewers still described it, as if automatically responding to the author's name, as "feminine."

In 1972 Spencer discussed the fact that she "came very late to Jane Austen and to women writers generally." As a bright college student, her "snob attitude toward women writers" grew out of her notion that they were "oversensitive" and tended to flutter over details. Not until later did she come to read and appreciate Virginia

Woolf, whom she speaks of as having "a very hard intelligence." And it was later still that she read Jane Austen and George Eliot with a full appreciation of what they had accomplished. "I began to see that women writers were right in there when the novel was first being formed, and now they rank very high in my estimation, and I'm proud to call myself a woman writer; I used to insist that I wanted to be considered as A WRITER not as a woman writer. But now my later judgment has taken over, and I begin to see that there is a difference."[13]

During her Vanderbilt days and in the years immediately following, however, Spencer concentrated chiefly on such modernist writers as Joyce, Proust, Yeats, Faulkner, and such other active Southern contemporaries as Robert Penn Warren. She continued to read and work at her writing despite the pull of several teaching jobs and a stint on the Nashville paper, the *Tennessean*. In 1943–44 she taught English at Northwest Junior College in Senatobia, Mississippi, and then returned to Nashville to teach at Ward-Belmont, a private girls' school. Increasingly, she found teaching not to her liking, and in the summer of 1945 she took the job with the newspaper. The work on the *Tennessean* staff taught her to compose at the typewriter and showed her for the first time something of the underside of life in a city.

At this time Spencer also began taking an evening course in short-story writing at Watkins Institute. The instructor, Raymond Goldman, proved to be an enthusiastic teacher and a strong supporter of Spencer's writing, urging her to try her hand at a novel. When she did at last decide to give up her job at the *Tennessean* and try writing full-time, she took a small, spare apartment in Nashville and set herself a disciplined writing routine. To supplement the $500 savings she had to live on, she occasionally assisted Donald Davidson at Vanderbilt by pinch-hitting in the classroom and grading papers. It was Davidson who introduced her to David Clay, a representative from Dodd, Mead publishers who was interested to see the manuscript she was working on. With Clay's and others' support *Fire in the Morning* was published in 1948.

For a first novel, *Fire in the Morning* enjoyed widespread critical success, though Spencer's income from it was small. In the fall of 1948 she took a position on the English faculty at the University of Mississippi and set about working on her next novel. At first she was assigned the usual freshman composition and sophomore literature classes, but the following year she was given a reduced teaching load that included one creative writing class.

During the spring of her first year at the university the Southern Literary Festival was held at "Ole Miss," and among the speakers invited were John Crowe Ransom and Stark Young, both of whom had admired *Fire in the Morning*. At one of the social events given in Oxford for Young, who was a distant cousin of Spencer's, she met William Faulkner for the first time, although she had roomed at his mother's house since her arrival at the university in the fall. The meeting hardly went beyond introductions, however, and it was not until later, in 1954 when Spencer was in Italy, that she got to know Faulkner at all. Stark Young was particularly helpful to Spencer, reading her fiction, corresponding with her, and recommending her after the publication of her second novel for a Guggenheim Fellowship. Following his visit to Oxford in April 1949, he wrote in December to his hostess, Ella Somerville, asking her to pass along his encouragement to Spencer in her work on the new novel. Of *Fire in the Morning,* he added that "there was a scene in her book that was done so well that I think it has cut a gash in me for the rest of my life, it is unforgettable. That is where the mean boy leads the little dog to his death in the water. It is quite powerful, and therefore full of talent."[14]

With the continued encouragement of these and many other literary friends, including David Clay, who for several years acted as Spencer's agent and mentor, she kept at her writing, publishing the short story "Pilgrimage" in the *Virginia Quarterly Review* in 1950 and her second novel, *This Crooked Way,* in 1952. In order to devote more time to her writing, she took leave from her faculty position in 1951–52, spending part of her year living on the Mississippi Gulf Coast. In March Katherine Anne Porter and Eudora Welty drove to Pass Christian to visit her, a trip Welty recalls with obvious pleasure in a 1978 interview.[15] On another occasion Welty and Elizabeth Bowen, who was visiting from England, paid Spencer a visit. The months of residence on the Gulf Coast bespeak the lifelong attraction the coast has held for Spencer, who has set several of her works in this region, including the title story of her first story collection, "Ship Island: The Story of a Mermaid," and the 1984 novel *The Salt Line*.

The school session of 1952–53 was to be the last year Spencer would teach at the University of Mississippi or live in the state, except for extended visits. With recommendations from various literary sponsors and university officials, she submitted the outline of a new novel to the Guggenheim Foundation, and with the award granted her she left for a year in Italy. The departure from the South marked a pivotal turn in her personal life and in her literary career.

Italian Sojourn and Canadian Residence

In Italy Spencer began work on *The Voice at the Back Door,* her third novel set in Mississippi and in many ways her final "Mississippi novel." Writing gave her the experience of taking stock of her youth. At some distance from the family and community values she had grown up accepting, she found herself questioning much about the life she had known, especially the racial attitudes and social arrangements of the South. Like many writers before her, she began to see her homeland with different eyes and to understand it more deeply, once she was removed from it. It was as if she could see the South more sharply from the vantage of Italy. She has said that she regards her style as having come "to maturity" with the writing of *The Voice at the Back Door,*[16] and most critics agreed when the book was published in 1956 that the novel reflected a distinctive voice.

During her first year in Italy, Spencer settled in Rome, though she later made trips to Florence and traveled about the country. It was during this year that she met and talked with William Faulkner at a party given by the head of the U.S. Cultural Service in Rome, and it was also during this stay that she met John Rusher, a handsome young Englishman who was directing a language school in Rome. In 1955 Spencer returned home for a brief visit in the summer and then went on to New York, where with the aid of David and Justine Clay she completed *The Voice at the Back Door.* She continued to correspond with Rusher and at last decided to return to Europe. "I didn't want to marry a foreigner," she said, "but the farther away I got from him the more I missed him. . . . Then I went back to see him and we decided this separation was ridiculous, so we got married."[17] The ceremony took place on 29 September 1956, at St. Colomb Minor in Cornwall, England, which was the nearest parish church to Porth Veor estate, where Rusher's parents lived.

Her marriage and the publication of *The Voice at the Back Door* in 1956 marked a kind of final leave-taking of Mississippi. Her parents had long felt ambivalent about her decision to be a writer; what they had hoped for her, Spencer says, was that she would get married and give up the writing, "as if somehow marriage was going to change all that."[18] They had in mind, of course, marriage to a Southerner of a background like hers, not a foreign marriage that would keep her abroad. Finally, in 1958, five years after arriving in Italy for an anticipated stay of a year, Elizabeth Spencer Rusher moved with her husband to Montreal, Canada. It was the couple's compromise solution to Spencer's wish not to live permanently in Europe and Rusher's not to move to the United States. In addition, Rusher's sister was living in Canada at the time, and in fact many of his mother's family were Canadian. During the 1960s and 1970s Spencer made many visits south to see her parents and other family members and friends, sometimes for several months at a time, particularly during the years of her parents' declining health, but she has maintained her permanent residence in Canada since 1958.

Understandably, the years in Italy and Canada have amply expanded Spencer's perspective on the world and have greatly affected the direction her later work has taken. In 1979, writing the preface to her collected *Stories,* Spencer looked back to the middle 1950s as a time of transition in her life and literary career, noting that the separation from home in the South had meant "the breaking up of those long tides of existence in one locale that have yielded up countless novels, out of which the novel seems to unfurl so naturally, so rhythmically, so right." At that time she found her experience "broken into pieces, no less valid, perhaps no less interesting— perhaps even more relevant . . . to the restless life of the world." She turned then for a time to writing short stories, some with Southern locales, others set in Italy. *The Light in the Piazza,* which began as a story and grew to novella length, was her fourth work to be published by the *New Yorker,* which has published well over a dozen of her stories since 1957. The novella was also issued separately in 1960 to enormous critical and commercial success, and it is the only one of her works to have been filmed. It is one of the ironies of fate that a work on which she spent hardly more than several months should turn out to be the novel that has brought her greatest recognition.

Throughout the 1960s and early 1970s Spencer wrote and published much of her major work. Following *The Light in the Piazza* came another novella about an American woman in Italy, *Knights and Dragons,* in 1965. About this time she began work on two different novels, which she worked on alternately until the publication of *No Place for an Angel* in 1967. With its publication Spencer demonstrated her mastery of larger subjects and more expansive settings than she had written about before. She found her Canadian vantage "a sort of counterpoint to American society as a whole," and for her a useful position from which to view contemporary society.[19] After *No Place for an Angel,* with its large cast of characters and a setting that includes a half dozen locales in the United States and Italy, she published in 1968 *Ship Island and Other Stories,* a collection of ten short stories, which she dedicated to her friend Eudora Welty. Among other departures from the style of her early novels, the stories show Spencer's growing use of mythic characters and structures as background to contemporary situations. In 1972 she published the other long novel that she had been at work on for years, *The Snare,* set in New Orleans and, unlike most of her earlier work, having a strong, independent woman as its central protagonist.

These fruitful years of writing also produced a number of literary awards and prizes for Spencer. In addition to a fellowship in the 1950s from the Guggenheim Foundation, a recognition award from the National Institute of Arts and Letters, and the *Kenyon Review* fiction fellowship, she received the $10,000 McGraw-Hill Fiction Award in 1960 for *The Light in the Piazza* and in the same year an O. Henry prize for "First Dark." Several times Martha Foley chose Spencer's stories for inclusion or honorable mention in her annual collection of best American short stories, and in 1966 Spencer received her second O. Henry prize for her story "Ship Island." She was granted the Bellaman award in 1968 and was honored the same year by Southwestern University in Memphis with an honorary doctorate in literature. Frequently invited to college campuses to read and discuss her work, she has visited Bryn Mawr College as a Donnelly Fellow, the University of North Carolina at Chapel Hill, Gulf Park College in Long Beach, Mississippi, Hollins College, and the University of Mississippi, to mention a few.

After the publication of *The Snare,* Spencer continued to work steadily at her short fiction, but it would be twelve years before she next published a novel. Of her writing schedule at this time she told Hunter Cole in 1973 that she tried to write for three or four hours a day, at the most five, which was about as long, she said,

as she could put into "prime creative time." She started in the
morning at about 9:30 or 10:00, after her husband left for work,
and stayed at her desk until about two, when she stopped for lunch
and other chores.[20] Later, in 1983, she commented upon the difficulty of writing "without clear quiet space around me." She described her solution to interviewer Laurie L. Brown, "I rent a small
studio—only one large room really—over in East Montreal where
I know scarcely anyone."[21]

In 1981 Spencer published with Doubleday *The Stories of Elizabeth
Spencer,* thirty-three stories that date from her earliest work, going
back to 1944 and including the *Ship Island* stories and *Knights and
Dragons.* The critical reception was very favorable, reviewers responding especially to the rich variety in style and subjects that
distinguishes the collection. Among the later stories are several in
which for the first time Spencer portrays Canadian characters and
settings. These hint of her appropriation finally of her Canadian
home as territory known well enough to inform the imagination.
In an interview in 1965 she said she had been unable to write about
Canada because she "hadn't been able to reach it,"[22] but in a story
such as the 1976 "I, Maureen" she writes of Montreal and the
surrounding townships with sympathetic identification and obvious
familiarity.

Also included in the 1981 collection are three stories related to
one another by a shared central character, a young Mississippian
named Marilee Summerall. The University Press of Mississippi published the three stories separately in 1981 in a book entitled *Marilee.*
In her foreword to this book Spencer writes that she is sometimes
asked whether Marilee is a reflection of the author herself. "No,
she's not me," Spencer says. "If I'd stayed put, there's a bare possibility, I like to imagine, that I might have been something like
her." The Marilee stories, among others, give evidence of Spencer's
continued connectedness, through imagination and understanding,
with the Southern subjects and settings of her youth. Indeed, the
range in Spencer's subjects from the sunny Marilee to the dark,
disturbed Maureen reflects at once the range of her interest in contemporary life and the flexibility of her extraordinary craftmanship
as a storyteller.

In the 1984 novel *The Salt Line,* Spencer returns to the present-
day South, depicting as she had in *The Snare* a setting that in some
ways reflects a stable, earlier South, but increasingly is also marked

by the transience and drift of the postmodern world. She has said of the novel that it is "a book of an after-the-storm feeling, when revival and renewal are necessities,"[23] and she has appropriately set the action on the Mississippi Gulf Coast a few years after the devastating 1969 hurricane Camille.

The Salt Line shows Spencer's effort to come to grips with her time and place, which have been vastly enriched and complicated for her by the experience of living literally and imaginatively for the past thirty years in several different countries. Having grown up in the American South, and having spent much of her adult life in Italy and Canada, she understands in a distinctive way the forces that have shaken the post—World War II world. With her protagonist Arnie Carrington, she invokes the persevering human spirit that generously and willingly, if somewhat decrepitly, contends with a world of spiritual assault.

Spencer has said of her years in Italy and Canada that they showed her a world other than that of the "fixed geography" that formed the background of her early novels. Still, true to the storytelling tradition in which she grew up, she sees "the world and its primal motions as story, since story charts in time the heart's assertions and gives central place to the great human relationships." In recent years, she writes, the challenge "to wring" the world's stories from it has become "more difficult" at the same time it has become "more urgent" that she and other writers should attempt to do so. "A story may not be the only wrench one can hurl into the giant machine that seems bent on devouring us all, but it is one of them." It is the mark of Spencer's considerable literary achievement that she has rarely gone for the easy story, the kind she describes as "tooled, shaped, and slicked up." She has sought and made, rather, "the real creature," the kind of story that is "touchy and alive, dangerous to fool with."[24] The search for such stories as these has distinguished a life of storytelling for Elizabeth Spencer.

Chapter Two
Mississippi Hill Country

Elizabeth Spencer's first novel, *Fire in the Morning*, attracted wide praise when it appeared in 1948. Doubtless the sponsorship of Robert Penn Warren, Eudora Welty, her editor David Clay, and others spurred reviewers to read the book, but it was Spencer's talent and control of her material that elicited the favorable reviews. Many critics, like Hubert Creekmore for the *New York Times Book Review*, commented upon the novel's similarity to recent Southern fiction and drama, specifically to the writings of Faulkner, Warren, and Lillian Hellman.[1] Nonetheless, reviewers found many original elements in *Fire in the Morning*, with its involved plot of four generations of hill-country Mississippians, and they admired it for the verve of its narrative line and its delineation of character.

A Journey to Dark Corners

Fire in the Morning, like Warren's *All the King's Men*, portrays a young man who makes a roundabout journey into the past in an effort to discover and expose the roots of an evil afflicting his community. Kinloch Armstrong, son of the respected, plain-living farmer Daniel, has since childhood hated the Gerrards, the main family of Tarsus. His particular hatred of Lance Gerrard, who is his own age, dates from an incident when Lance cruelly drew Kinloch into a prank that led to the drowning of Kinloch's dog. At the time, and for weeks afterward, Kinloch fought the bully Lance and finally overpowered him, but as an adult he has not forgotten or forgiven the incident.

Kinloch dimly perceives that his nagging antipathy for the Gerrards results not only from their deceit and evil, but from their having forced upon him the discovery of his own capacity for violence and destruction. After striking Lance at the swimming hole, he realizes with a child's incipient perception "that the other thing was born." The "thing born" is, of course, a seductive partnership in violence, which can victimize the defender of the good as well as the evildoer. Fighting Lance and the other boys involved in the dog's drowning, Kinloch "knew he was fighting what he could not see and what he could not see was turning him blind."[2] Resembling the biblical Saul of Tarsus, Kinloch makes an arduous journey of the spirit before he achieves true sight into the Gerrards and Tarsus and into himself.

The novel opens in June 1935 during Kinloch's first year of marriage to Ruth Shaffer, an outsider who had come to Tarsus to work in the local office of a New Deal agency. Ruth's friendship with Lance Gerrard and his wife, Elinor, draws Kinloch unwillingly back into the old entanglement with the Gerrards. The complication is further heightened at the end of part 1 when Ruth, like Kinloch years before, is drawn into a childish escapade with the Gerrards, including the younger sister Justin, that leads to the death of Ben Gardner, the town drunk. Although largely blameless, Ruth is nonetheless driver of the car that pushes Gardner into the ravine and to his death. When she lets the Gerrards persuade her to remain silent about the accident, she sets the stage for future complications at the hands of Lance's unscrupulous father, Simon.

The thick web of relationships grows more dense in part 2 when Kinloch's garrulous cousin, the lawyer Randall Gibson, decides that Kinloch should at last have a full accounting of the Gerrards' long history of treachery. Goaded by his revulsion for Simon and the haughty daughter, Justin, and outraged by the Gerrards' latest injustice—the "theft" of a marble statue from his yard—Gibson begins his long tale one afternoon over several beers at the Melrose Cafe, six weeks after the death of Ben Gardner.

Shortly after, he completes his story of how the Gerrards thirty-five years earlier had managed to invalidate the will of Kinloch Walston, whose closest friends were Daniel Armstrong and another neighbor, Felix McKie. At his death Walston had bequeathed the mansion, Walston Cedars, and the large tract of surrounding land to Armstrong and McKie, but the land had been effectively stolen by Simon and his older brother, Wills Gerrard. Charging in court that Walston was insane, they had gotten the land from the heirs once the will was broken. Three days after the trial, as Gibson tells Kinloch, "Felix McKie was covered with blood, lying in the doctor's office in back of the drug store with his eyes blown out. Simon Gerrard's brother was dead in the court hallway. A hunted Negro was shot down in Kosciusko and would have been lynched even in

death along with his living wife and child but for Dan Armstrong
. . ." (83).

To finish the story to his satisfaction, Kinloch goes to his father,
who cautions him to let the old wrongs lie, and he refuses to say
more of how the Gerrards accomplished their treachery. Kinloch
persists, going back to the trial records, and finds that the testimony
of one Dr. Derryberry was crucial in the evidence establishing Walston's insanity. Infused with a knight's noble motives, Kinloch sets
out in part 3 for Dark Corners, the physician's backwoods home,
where he expects to gain final answers to old mysteries, expose the
Gerrards' evil, and put an end to their lying and stealing. Above
all, he is determined to destroy their false front of respectability
and gentility. The young man's journey to Dark Corners, with its
obvious tag name, leads to discoveries Kinloch never expected and,
eventually, to revelations about the moral ambiguity that marks
most human action. In the final pages of the novel two central
themes merge. The individual's effort to know and establish himself
in this world, embodied in Kinloch's plight, and the burden of
history that unfailingly impinges on the individual's effort to be
independent and honorable, represented in the legacy left by Tarsus's
older generations, come together when Kinloch returns to Tarsus
to confront the Gerrards.

The Legacy of the Past

Spencer draws the portrait of earlier generations of Southerners
in this novel not only from her own experience as a Mississippian
but quite obviously from the rich tradition of Southern fiction of
the 1930s and early 1940s. Her respect for the agrarian origins
of Tarsus also doubtless owes something to the Agrarians of
Vanderbilt, a presence in influence if not in fact during the years
she was living in Nashville. The attitude toward the past of most
of the writers of the Southern Renaissance, particularly that of Faulkner and Warren, was an intense respect for the complexity of history,
comprising, as it did, human courage and cowardice, generosity
and avarice, nobility and ignominy. Such writers, in sharp diver-
gence from the popular American myth of individualism and its
freedom from the past, regarded history as inescapable: the mistakes
and achievement of the past cannot be abrogated by the man or
woman of the modern world.

The nineteenth- and early twentieth-century characters who form the social legacy Kinloch inherits are presented chiefly through Randall Gibson's interpretation of Tarsus's history. Although we have no reason to discount the accuracy of the main details of his story, he almost certainly embroiders it to heighten the irony and melodrama. He begins his account of the Gerrards by going back one generation, then finds that he must go back two generations, at least, to explain the interlocking network of past and present. He begins, as he says, with the "king," Marshall Walston, who was murdered on an election night in 1875 while he and a group of white citizens, including Kinloch's grandfather, Ernest Armstrong, intimidated the Negroes who had come to vote and thereby wrested the election from the carpetbag officials who had been in office. Walston's son, Kinloch, named for his friend Kinloch McKie, patriarch of a neighboring Scots Presbyterian clan, inherited his father's land and position. Unfortunately, Kinloch Walston was not a man who would be king, and so by default of leadership, and an integrity partly manifest as a shy aloofness from the community, he lived at a distance from Tarsus, close only to Daniel Armstrong and Felix McKie, both sons of his father's friends.

Kinloch Walston's one show of respect for the community's expectations of him, his decision to settle down sensibly and marry the sister of his friend Armstrong, founders with the arrival from New Orleans of a fluttery belle named Cherry Bell LeGarde. Their brief romance, which quickly goes awry, leads to Walston's entering the forces of the Spanish-American War and dying in it, and to Cherry Bell's dependence upon her kin, Charlie Gibson and his wife, formerly Beatrice Armstrong, the spurned fiancée of Walston. Ultimately Cherry Bell becomes the invalid charge of their son Randall. By 1935, weak and dying, her one solace is the marble figure of the minstrel that she had brought to the Gibson yard from the Walston estate. It is Henrietta Gerrard's demand for the statue that triggers Randall's monologue to his cousin Kinloch Armstrong and, indirectly, brings on the death of Cherry Bell and Randall's departure to New York.

In depicting the legacies and burdens bequeathed by the old families of Tarsus, Spencer is evenhanded in pointing up their strengths and weaknesses. The Walstons, Armstrongs, McKies, and Gibsons could be counted on for honesty and integrity, but they maintained these qualities largely by holding themselves apart from the larger community. When they go into the world to oppose the wrongs they see, as Marshall Walston did in 1875 or as Kinloch Armstrong does in 1935, they inevitably risk moral compromise. On the other hand, aloofness and disdain for moral compromises may result in one's simply handing over the world to rapacious "little foxes." Kinloch and Felix McKie both suspect, despite their respect for Daniel Armstrong, that something of his shrinking from a confrontation with the Gerrards accounts for Daniel's decision not to pursue Simon Gerrard after the infamous insanity trial of Kinloch Walston. Nonetheless, they do not have the full story, and their ignorance of its complexity leads to naïveté and self-righteousness.

Spencer's persistent theme regarding the legacies of the past is that the most responsible and admirable actions of men and women are those undertaken with a sympathetic knowledge of the past. Still, excessive sympathies for the traditions of the past can be corrupting. One such example is the "protection" of Cherry Bell at the time of the Walston trial. She was the person who could have conclusively explained the letters, remarks, and other behavior offered as evidence of Kinloch Walston's insanity, but she was not called as a witness because of the Victorian disposition to regard any such public exposure of woman as a disgrace. The loss of her testimony led to the land loss and ultimately to the blinding of one man and the deaths of three others, including Old Tuck, the black beneficiary of a small strip of Walston land who was murdered by the Gerrards. The falsity of such protection of womanhood is underscored by Spencer's portrait of Cherry Bell first as flirtatious and simple-minded and, as an older woman, whining and alcoholic.

Spencer's expansive and intricate plot that traces Tarsus's history back to the middle nineteenth century is given focus by the arrival of the Gerrards about 1870. Bearing resemblance to Faulkner's Snopeses and even to the Bundrens of *As I Lay Dying,* they had appeared one day from the country community of Dark Corners—sixty-year-old Wills, his sixteen-year-old second wife, Lily, and Young Wills, the only one of Gerrard's large family of children who accompanied him to town. Over the years they had kept an eerie silence and separateness, shrewdly biding their time, according to Randall Gibson, until they could make their move upwards. To Gibson, their silence is "the central point of horror" (111), for it signals their rejection of communal values and loyalties. During these years the son Simon was born, and Young Wills went to work at the hardware store, which he in due time purchases. Gibson credits Young Wills with a malevolent intuition that guides him to possession of the Walston estate. It is left to Kinloch Armstrong's detection, however, to discover how the Gerrards coerced good people to serve their acquisitiveness.

Kinloch finds the key to the Gerrard story in Dark Corners. Dr. Derryberry, who had been guardian of a young niece courted and impregnated by Young Wills Gerrard, falsely attested to Walston's insanity in exchange for Young Will's agreement to marry her. Despite a good education and noble ambitions, the physician becomes "entangled" in family obligations that entrap him in moral compromise. Long since released from these by the deaths of the niece and later of her son, Derryberry agrees to give Kinloch a statement admitting the perjury and the Gerrards' involvement.

Spencer approaches the story of the Gerrards of Dark Corners with the same realism and evenness with which she portrays the old families of Tarsus. Although Randall Gibson and Kinloch tend to regard anyone named Gerrard as absolutely evil, Spencer exposes the error of their judgment. In a vivid, lively episode in which Kinloch makes his way to the backwoods community he encounters the comic, but menacing, Guptons. He gains information from them about the whereabouts of Dr. Derryberry, pays for the use of a horse to make the trip, and parks his truck at their place. Riding away, he is attacked by the two gangly sons who want the keys to his truck. Only the intervention of a friendly young horseman saves him from harm. His name is Tom Gerrard, as he tells Kinloch just before disappearing into the woods.

Spencer underscores the point in several ways that one's name or one's past does not determine one's character. When Kinloch earlier quizzes his father about the Gerrards, he is rather clearly seeking a shortcut to a code of moral behavior. But Daniel, with a prophet's sight, rejects Kinloch's easy equating of the name Gerrard with evil: "It means nothing . . . Through the years I have argued with Felix, You cannot hate a man, you cannot kill a man because of his last name" (148). A particularly ironic casting of the human tendency to ascribe reprehensible behavior to one's "blood," or one's nature, comes in the conversation between Tom Gerrard and Kinloch. The talkative, obliging young man tells Kinloch of a job he had in Chicago and of the couple who employed him—"mean and low-down for no reason, but by nature." He asks Kinloch, "Have you ever knowed such folks?" (215), but not knowing the young man's name, Kinloch, who holds this very view of the Gerrards, misses the irony of the exchange. In fact, his moral certainty that he has correctly interpreted the legacy of the past is not challenged until he is faced with the same conflict between love and honor, or loyalty and justice, that the older generations faced.

One final legacy that shapes the moral landscape that Kinloch and his generation inhabit is a haunting and prophetic story that dates back to the Civil War. A story of the callous destruction of a house that had been a Tarsus landmark, it furnishes a central symbol as well as the title of the novel. One morning after a family had fed breakfast to a group of Yankee soldiers, the colonel in charge had methodically piled kindling wood about the stove, setting the house afire and burning it to the ground. The gratuitous evil of the burning is vexing to Randall Gibson and Kinloch alike, both of whom take it as a symbol of the kind of treachery represented by the Gerrards. Despite the familiarity of the story, it is difficult for the community's imagination to take hold of: "It happened and people still talked about it, because they had heard the old ones talk about it, but nobody was ever really convinced of it. Fire in the morning burns as thoroughly as another fire, but it has no efficacy in the memory which must evermore look upon it through a veil, unreasoningly conscious that here is something which should not be" (17–18).

The source of this central image of the fire comes from Spencer's own experience, as she has explained: "As a child, I once saw a house burn down in the morning, and the flames didn't seem to exist. It was an unreal occasion—this house turning to ashes in front of my eyes and the flames almost absorbed into the sunlight. You could hardly see the fire as an outrage at all, as the cause of this destruction." She goes on to comment on the symbolism of the fire and its relation to the title: "In the book, the Gerrards have done a grievous wrong to the Armstrongs and to other people, but society now accepts them as a leading family. . . . That's what maddens the young man, Kinloch. . . . He's about the only one who perceives the continuing outrage of what the Gerrards have done. The fire in the morning is an image of this situation."[3] Of course, Spencer chiefly employs Randall Gibson's perspective in developing the symbolism of the fire. It is Gibson who links the pivotal crime of the Gerrards' land grab to the universal evil signified by the Civil War violence. He sees that the destructive events of the past and present are "all of a piece" (132).

Gathering knowledge about the legacies of the past forms the central action of the protagonist Kinloch throughout much of the novel. This is a traditional plot, of course, with strong roots in the nineteenth-century novel. The young man setting forth in the world uncovers old secrets—crucial knowledge that forces choices determining his future.

Knowledge versus Action

What one *does* when one confronts evil is the central ethical question running throughout the book, and it is debated at length by Kinloch and his older cousin Randall Gibson. Their relationship recalls that of Faulkner's Ike McCaslin and Cass Edmonds, except that it is the younger Kinloch in *Fire in the Morning* who thinks the duty of a good man is to *do* something with the knowledge he acquires. Remembering an episode years earlier when Kinloch had revealed his disposition to act when faced with cruelty or hurt, Randall Gibson points out that his rescuing Milly Cabot from ridicule at a teenage party typifies Kinloch. "You aren't content simply to comprehend; you also have to act" (70).

Gibson is an interesting if somewhat stereotyped character who plays the role of observer, or seer, in contrast to Kinloch's active role. Gibson triggers reflection, truth telling, and emotional energy in others. He is also a catalyst for action and a reflector for the author. His language, particularly in the long monologue in the middle section, is extremely elevated and rhetorical, though according to Spencer his type comes directly from the culture of the American South. "There were many people in my parents' generation who were awfully good at that sort of speech, especially small-town drinking lawyers like a Randall Gibson. . . . The ornate speech, the long rolling sentences, seemed to flow out of their considerations of the times, especially over a glass of bourbon with a friend. They had read a great deal and often drew from literature in their conversation; they knew how to weigh events and heighten them with their speech." Spencer sees the Gibson narrative as important in giving resonance and universality to the plot. "He has the poetic vision necessary to lift that story up to the plane of consideration it needs. His presence makes of the whole retribution theme something higher and grander than it otherwise would be."[4]

Gibson is saved from pomposity only by his self-knowledge and sense of irony. As he says, "I was born at dead center where I remain, cross-legged as Buddha but I can't ever keep quiet about it" (235). He's not quite accurate in assessing himself at "dead center," however, for he does move himself to act in defense of Cherry Bell's statue by telling Kinloch the Walston-Gerrard story and eventually by leaving Tarsus after her death. Like Dr. Derryberry he is "entrapped" by a sense of duty to his invalid charge as much as by his passivity. Still, one cannot entirely explain away the failure of nerve, or cynicism, implicit in his refusal to engage the world. "I abdicate," he tells Kinloch. "Confronted with heaven and hell, I choose neither" (70).

The two central female characters also face decisions about what to do about their knowledge of moral transgressions. Ruth leaves Tarsus with her visiting brother, Scott, following the weeks of confusion and unhappiness after Ben Gardner's death. She returns, however, to deal with the legal and domestic consequences that confront her, persuaded to act by her sense of responsibility and nudged by advice from Randall Gibson.

Elinor Gerrard, who clearly despises her husband's family, nevertheless stays with her marriage until the day that Lance betrays her friend Ruth and, in doing so, his own marriage as well. With the knowledge of her husband's cowardice and perfidy, Elinor leaves him, returning to her family in the Delta.

Neither Ruth nor Elinor has to contend with moral dilemma, though, in the way that Kinloch does. His decision about what to do with the evidence of the Gerrards' evil nearly duplicates the situation of his father thirty-five years earlier. Like Daniel, he discovers at the physician Derryberry's that undoing evil is a sticky business. The innocent inevitably get caught in the middle—a theme as old as history—though Kinloch, unlike his father, refuses to acknowledge that protecting the innocent and punishing the guilty often work at cross purposes. He angrily dismisses Derryberry's philosphical comment on such dilemmas: "It's getting late and I can't waste time. If you start fumbling and fooling around in a mess of words, first thing you know you've got the devil on the throne of God" (226).

After leaving Dark Corners, Kinloch returns to Tarsus to confront Simon with the proof of perjury, only to find that Simon too has "a piece of paper," a document signed by Lance and Justin accusing

Ruth of the accidental death of Ben Gardner. Daunted but not stopped by this threat to Ruth, Kinloch sees the depth of Simon's villainy and begins to understand his power. "It's me you're striking at now," he says to Simon, "same as you struck at the others, every one, you and Young Wills, getting them to protect what they love by giving you what you want" (248). When he leaves Simon, he is determined to enact the retribution that he feels the past evils require.

In the dramatic climax of the novel Kinloch at last confronts the egotism implicit in his willful pursuit of justice. In a vivid scene, in which the strands of plot are perhaps a little too neatly tied, Simon meets his death in an accidental fall from the bluff behind Felix McKie's house, and Daniel Armstrong dies of a heart attack trying to save him. Arriving minutes after the accident, Kinloch "put his hands to his eyes to blind them from the sight of his own guilt, for his whole life seemed about to be swept away into it" (265). Here, as elsewhere, Spencer employs the motif of sightedness versus blindness to express the opposition between knowledge and impetuous or ill-informed action.

In the concluding chapter she brings together the two central motifs of the novel: the individual's quest for knowledge and self-vindication and the community's (and family's) barriers to independence, especially to one's moral autonomy. The chapter begins with a flashback to the inquest, months earlier. In the scene Kinloch corrects the false interpretation of events given by McKie and then tells the young lawyer presiding: "You may say I killed them. . . . You may say I killed them both" (269). Kinloch thus discovers his moral and mortal limits in a classic encounter with the father. Feeling that his vengeful actions led to the death of his father, he accepts his guilt and, in doing so, decides to get on with his life. Unlike Lance Gerrard, who likewise matures during the eventful summer of disclosure and violence, Kinloch chooses to remain in Tarsus and accept the legacy of the past, which has become part of his own personal past.

In the present time of the last scene, November 1936, Kinloch pays a visit to Lance, who tries to exorcise some of his own guilt by offering Kinloch a strip of land adjoining the Armstrong farm. Refusing the land he had once wanted to own, Kinloch reveals his mastery over the acquisitiveness that formerly begot so much dishonesty and conflict. This mastery, together with his and Ruth's anticipation of the birth of their child, furnishes the upbeat, predictable resolution to the Armstrong-Gerrard conflict. Thus Spencer reasserts the values of individual integrity and family continuity.

The Achievement of the Novel

When Spencer resigned from the *Nashville Tennessean* to write *Fire in the Morning,* she had the novel "securely in mind," she once told a reporter. "Getting it written down was another matter, a long task, full of its own special kind of punishment and reward." She went on to describe the rigorous writing schedule she set for herself—from 8 A.M. to 4 P.M. daily in her small apartment near the Vanderbilt campus.[5] In a later interview she returned to the subject of how she had planned and written the novel: "I was very much aware that I was writing a first novel, so I tried to outline the whole book in advance. Initially, I wanted it to be the story of Ruth, the young wife; that's how I had it planned. But so much of her life had been spent away from the local scene, in places that I knew nothing about and could not successfully imagine, that I was forced either to condense or to eliminate much of that material. Finally, the story came to be concentrated on the one small town of Tarsus and on Ruth's husband, Kinloch."[6]

It is largely Spencer's success in protraying the intricate relationships of the characters in the small town that accounts for the enthusiastic critical response to the novel. Hubert Creekmore, despite his charge that the several plots are loosely connected and that the book shows some stereotyping and blurring of character, nonetheless concludes that it is, "on the whole, a good novel." He writes, "It is not so much a study of the character or people (a misconception fostered by thinking always 'hero-heroine') as of the character of a complex of people—the moral relationship of the citizens of a community."[7]

For a first-time novelist, Spencer demonstrates remarkable skill and control in managing this portrait of a "complex of people." The plot is many-layered and elaborate, as we have seen. In only a few instances do the turns and twists invite disbelief and weaken the credibility. For example, Ruth's decision to go to New York with her brother and Kinloch's decision to pursue the Walston-Gerrard story come as a result of misunderstandings on both sides. The manipulation of their conversation, in which neither one ex-

presses or apprehends crucial information, seems forced and melodramatic. But this scene is clearly an exception to the rule. What
remains in memory after one has finished the novel is the vitality
of the characters and the grounding of motivation for their action
through the subtle, slow accretion of details. These are recognizably
the attributes of the traditional novel, and Spencer shows her mastery
of them in writing this realistic novel of action.

In addition, the novel shows the unmistakable influence of mod-
ernistic technique. The structure, although more traditional than
experimental, is marked by irregular chronology, flashbacks, flashbacks within flashbacks (most notably in the first part in the account
of the dog's drowning and the events that led to it), and the employment of multiple points of view. The novel is narrated through
an omniscient view (as in the scene of the deaths of Simon and
Daniel), but in various scenes Spencer shifts to the limited omniscient views of Kinloch, Ruth, and Daniel, and even to a first-
person reflection by Elinor (185 ff.), and the long monologues of
Randall Gibson. These structural shifts in voice and time, which
link the numerous consciousnesses in the novel, embody the theme
of interrelatedness, suggesting the close connection between hero
and community, past and present, stranger and native.

Spencer's skill in handling symbols and figurative language is
also notable for a first novel. For example, the description of Lance
and Elinor Gerrard's bungalow (9–11), contrasting with the great
house of Marshall Walston that once occupied the same valley, gives
a sharp, vivid symbol of the decline from flamboyant grandeur to
mediocrity that marks the change of leadership in Tarsus from
Walston to Gerrard. Similarly, in a telling metaphor of flesh, Spencer draws a clear portrait of the Armstrongs and the Gerrards. From
Kinloch's perspective, "the Armstrongs were of big solid bone, the
skin over it showing the vein, inclined to blemish and rough-
ness. . . . But about the Gerrards there was a thickness that had
nothing to do with measurement, as marked in Lance's tall frame
as in heavy Simon. It seemed that flesh, vein, muscle and bone,
instead of finding a separate life and play within the larger, living
body, each defining the other, were in them all matted and solidified
together, affecting an imperceptible shortening or concealment of
joint and tendon, a layered depth of skin" (77–78).

Literary allusions, which sometimes seem a bit self-conscious in
the mouth of Randall Gibson, nonetheless add resonance to the

novel and give the reader the pleasure of recognition. Quoting Hardy ("Neutral Tones"), Keats ("Ode on a Grecian Urn"), Tennyson ("The Lotos-Eaters"), and others, Gibson anchors his philosophical musings about ambiguity, impermanance, and world-weariness in classic English poetry. As we have already seen, Spencer herself views Gibson's role as one of the book's strengths. In a 1975 interview she discussed the barriers to the other characters' understanding or explaining the events they were caught up in. Kinloch and his father were "the strong, silent type," and Ruth was a stranger to the community. "So somebody had to get in there who could really talk." As she says, once she got Gibson going, "he practically took the book because he was so articulate. I think that he loosened it up and opened it up much better than the people that I had put in motion could because they were involved in the action. I think that's how literary devices are born."[8] Gibson's love of poetry and his frequent recitations both heighten his commentary and delineate his personality.

The dominant literary allusion in the novel comes not from Gibson, however, but from the epigraph on the title page. It is a quotation from Djuna Barnes's *Nightwood:* "All through the night Rome went burning. Put that in the noontide and it loses some of its age-old significance, does it not? Why? Because it has existed to the eye of the mind all these years against a black sky."[9]

The passage from *Nightwood* comes in the section, "Watchman, What of the Night?" from the monologue of Dr. Matthew O'Connor. Randall Gibson bears some resemblance to the brilliant, talkative doctor, who sees and tells everything there is to know about the world and the people around him, only to be utterly exhausted by their imperception and indifference. In the Barnes novel Dr. O'Connor's disquisition on the symbolic significance of daylight and darkness, night and day, bears directly on the insidiousness of evil represented by the Gerrards in *Fire in the Morning*. As the philosopher Hannah Arendt and others have pointed out, it is frequently the banality of evil that is most horrifying. In her description of the burning of the Delbrook mansion, Spencer writes an evocative lyric variation on the quotation from *Nightwood*. It suggests that the citizens of Tarsus are confounded by a "fire in the morning," that in the case of the Gerrards, wealth and respectability have masked their greed and violent behavior. How it is that evil can flourish in a good world is the implicit question she raises in the conclusion of the passage: "he who is enemy or vandal is expected to take his prerogative from the night, and the spoiler who will not, troubles a vaster sphere than thought would choose to enter, and something unreconciled is here" (18).

Although the Walston-Armstrong-Gerrard plot conflict is finally resolved, the philosophical quandary about the relation of good and evil is only slightly developed in the novel. It is an issue that Spencer returns to in subsequent novels, however, and develops with much subtlety and insight. In her allusive use of *Nightwood* in this first novel Spencer suggests something of the subtle insight to come.

Critical response to the achievement of the novel was unusually favorable. Nash K. Burger summarizes the critical consensus in his 1964 retrospective essay on Spencer's first three novels, praising the vitality and order of *Fire in the Morning* while noting its debt to Faulkner and other predecessors:

If the Gerrards are inevitably reminiscent of Faulkner's Snopeses, they are, for all their wrongdoing and ruthlessness, somewhat more recognizable, less caricatured. . . . There is notable variety in this long narrative spanning half a century; episodes of violence and emotional tension are followed by quietly ironic scenes of social comedy. Small-town romance, rural folkways and boisterous humor, lechery and brawling, politics and Reconstruction, the idyllic Southern rural scene and the slow passage of the seasons—all find a place in this tumbled, yet well-managed tale.[10]

Most of the reviewers note the Faulknerian influence, although R. W. Flint writes that the novel falls "almost in the genre of the 19th century historical romance." He concludes that Spencer owes almost as much to Scott as to Faulkner.[11] Worth Tuttle Hedden praises the novel's depiction of Southern social lines—"finer than that of most regional novelists"—and elements that are "charmingly reminiscent of the glass-front bookcase with its nineteenth century classics." Overall, Hedden finds the novel more original and interesting than derivative and concludes the review with a strong recommendation: "For discrimination in choice of material, economy in its use, poetic feeling and keen, unpredictable flashes of humor Miss Spencer is indebted to no predecessor in her mastery of the novel's technique."[12] Harrison Smith, writing for the *Saturday Review*, likewise finds the characters to be "alive and vital," not stock Southern figures. He concludes that Spencer's manner of writing reveals "true talent," and that "if her next novel is as admirable in delineation of character and in dialogue, she can afford to drop the complications of an involved and conventional plot."[13]

Although there is evidence that Spencer's Tarsus from time to time overlaps Faulkner's Yoknapatawpha (various characters and episodes recall John Sartoris, Joe Christmas, and Gavin Stevens, as well as the Snopeses), there is also striking evidence that it is often raw rather than literary material that Spencer shares with Faulkner. There is, for example, a remarkable resemblance between Spencer's Guptons and the Gowries of *Intruder in the Dust,* but there is little question of influence since both novels were published in 1948.

Recommended by the *Library Journal,*[14] *Fire in the Morning* was praised by reviewers for the *New Yorker* and *Time,* though some rather obvious biases subverted the reviews. A paragraph note in the *New Yorker* begins with mention of "a quiet first novel of considerable understated power" and then continues with more than a little regional arrogance: "Despite the locale, Miss Spencer's men and women speak and act with high intelligence. . . ."[15] The *Time* reviewer admires her skillful handling of theme, finding that "the things this young writer can do with the novel form are astonishing." The reviewer concludes, however, by berating Spencer's "frenzied style of the sort of 'woman novelist' who worries her subject and prose to death by merely vibrating portentously when she should be letting her narrative move along."[16] The comment is amazing, considering that this reviewer, like the others, praised in particular Spencer's pacing and control of the narrative. In his article Nash Burger also mentions Spencer's "feminine sensibility," though he never explains what he means by the phrase.[17]

Interestingly, the most serious critical reservations about the novel have to do with Spencer's cool, detached control of the plot. Flint finds the tone "elegiac" and hopes Spencer will "move on to subjects that can engage her more seriously."[18] Henrietta Buckmaster is more pointed: ". . . there is something which talent in the accepted sense is often reluctant to face—that is, the fire, the compassion, the heart which gives the only substance there is to a story, even if sometimes inchoate or faultily mechanized. And heart and compassion are missing from *Fire in the Morning,* although talent is recognizedly evident."[19]

On balance, the reception of Spencer's first novel was strongly favorable. Critics found its strengths in its energy and controlled artistry and predicted an important career for the young novelist.

In her next novel Spencer would return to her Mississippi setting to explore further the legacies of the past that shape and define one's life. And in telling the story of Amos Dudley, she would find a subject to engage her deeply.

Chapter Three

From the Hills to the Delta

Elizabeth Spencer has said of her second novel, *This Crooked Way* (1952), that it was "a hard book to write."[1] The difficulty arose partly from the demands of her teaching schedule at the University of Mississippi during the years of the book's composition, 1948– 51, and partly from the demands of the experimental form she devised for the novel. In fact, one may surmise that she arrived at the form, five discrete sections involving multiple viewpoints, not only as a means of giving perspective to the portrayal of the dream-obsessed protagonist, Amos Dudley, but also of accommodating her available writing time ("in spurts"). If so, necessity mothered an invention of form that serves the novel well. In an interview conducted in 1980 Spencer maintained her opinion that *This Crooked Way* is her most original book. "In fact," she said, "I think I might like it better than any of the other Mississippi books. And of all my characters, Amos is probably the largest in heroic stature."[2]

Amos is unquestionably a compelling character, a wonder to himself and to most of the family and friends he moves among in his trek from the Mississippi hills to a plantation in the Delta. He first appears in *Fire in the Morning* in Elinor Dudley Gerrard's succinct but dramatic account of her father's rise in the span of thirty-three years from the new owner of a swamp of uncleared land to proud patriarch of "the Dudley estate" (180). Speaking of her decision to place Amos Dudley at the center of *This Crooked Way,* Spencer said to John Griffin Jones: "I remember that what started that book off was my uncle sitting and talking one twilight down at Teoc. Somebody asked him about two brothers who'd gone over into the Delta and made what amounted to a lot of money at that time. Somebody said, 'Where did they come from?' And he said, 'Just like a lot of Delta folks, they came from out of the hills dragging a cotton sack, and in ten years they had a fortune.' That sort of stuck in my mind."[3]

Presumably, the remark of Spencer's uncle furnished the kernel of the story of Amos Dudley for both novels. It is clear that the story of the rise of the hill country boy to rich planter—Elinor's story of her father—continued to claim Spencer's attention after *Fire in the Morning*. She said in the Bunting interview, for example, that after she completed her first novel, the Dudley story seemed "to have a good deal of kick in it." As she explained, "I began to wonder what kind of people, where did they live, what were they like, and that unsolved, unexplored part of the first novel led me to the second. . . ."[4]

Tangled up with God

Amos Dudley's story begins in 1900 when at the age of 16, on the Yocona River at a camp meeting known as "Tabernacle," he has a vision of God. One of nine children of a poor hill country family, Amos might have had a fate like that of his older brothers Ned or Ephraim, one a wanderer frequently on the wrong side of the law, the other a fundamentalist homebody squeezing pennies from the small store he owns in the Yocona community. But one traumatic night after Amos has heard a fiery sermon on God's dealings with Jacob, he himself has a visionary encounter with God as dramatic as Jacob's vision of the ladder of angels. Leaving the brush arbor meeting site during the swelling hymns and prayers of the congregation, Amos heads toward the river: "Because Amos Dudley had to listen to the voice. He had to listen because he was afraid to think. It was the first and last voice he ever paid close attention to in his life, and it took hell itself to make him listen."[5] Aroused not only by the sermons and songs but by the daily musings of his father and the older men about the world's last days, ominous signs and times—the second coming—Amos goes to the river in search of God.

Spencer's depiction of Amos's vision is one of the high marks of the novel. In vivid imagery she creates the sensuous experience of Amos walking the path to the water, gazing at three pine trees that loom like holy markers on the distant bank, moving finally from the shallow edge toward the deepening midstream. The young man's baptismal search for revelation beneath the water's surface is a familiar motif in literature, certainly in the literature of the American South where rivers and religion are bountiful. In different but related circumstances, a river serves as the site where Robert Penn Warren's Seth in "Blackberry Winter" and Eudora Welty's William Wallace

Jamieson in "The Wide Net" both mark a new direction in their lives. In one of Flannery O'Connor's best-known short stories, "The River," first published in the *Sewanee Review* in the summer of 1953, the year after *This Crooked Way,* the child Harry Ashfield drowns in his effort to baptize himself in his pursuit of the Kingdom of Christ. There are, in fact, some striking parallels (and reversals) in the portrayals of Amos's vision and Harry's plunge into the river at the conclusion of "The River."

In Spencer's novel an undercurrent catches Amos and pulls him downward, at which point he feels betrayed by God. "Cheat, he thought bitterly, spitting the water, the thin muddy taste, from his mouth. And that included not only the river but the preacher's words that had stirred him, the singing that had comforted him, and the men who casually talking of the day of fire had made him afraid. Nothing to it, he thought. Nothing to any of it" (11). Suddenly, God's presence is real, palpably so, in the form of "One" whom he feels is close and has heard him. "Whatever came to him came from behind, unseen by him forever, a hand stretched down from behind to lift him up. He felt the strike and pull of fiery pain in his right shoulder, the lightening and lift of his whole body" (12). In Amos's eyes he is quite literally saved by the hand of God that snatches him from drowning in the river.

By contrast, O'Connor's child protagonist momentarily feels betrayed because the river "rejects" him: "The river wouldn't have him. He had tried again and came up, choking. This was the way it had been when the preacher held him under. . . . He stopped and thought suddenly: it's another joke, it's just another joke. He thought how far he had come for nothing and he began to hit and splash and kick the filthy river." Like Amos, Harry Ashfield feels the current's pull downward, but to him the forceful pull is the hand of God. "He plunged under once and this time, the waiting current caught him like a long gentle hand and pulled him swiftly forward and down."[6]

Whereas O'Connor's theological interest centers on the question of the child's spiritual salvation, Spencer's interest is in the psychological complexity involved in a young man's effort to validate and fulfill a religious experience in the secular world. Interestingly, the origin of his American dream of success is the evangelical rebirth at the river. His setting out in the world is like that of the Old Testament Jacob, who held a clear contract with God that required obedience and delivered wives, children, wealth. In speaking of her characterization of Amos, Spencer has in fact commented that "a great many things in that book were played off against biblical stories," and she notes the literal parallel between Jacob and Amos.[7]

There are also some resemblances to Faulkner's Thomas Sutpen and F. Scott Fitzgerald's Gatsby in Amos's progress toward worldly success, although Amos Dudley sets out, unlike them, with an inciting vision not quasi- but quite religious. It sprang not from a platonic conception of himself derived from the plantation world or from Gatsby's vast, vulgar midwestern and eastern worlds, but from his literal view that God chose him for a special destiny. His religious obsession, like Sutpen's innocence, leads him, however, to equate his own willful ambition with God's will.

Amos presents a fascinating study of a kind of Protestant evangelical ideal described by Donald G. Mathews in his study of religion in the nineteenth-century South: "the free individual's wrestling with the demons of his own soul until set free by a mighty surge of the will." The evangelical experience is sometimes thought of, as Mathews says, as the "religious mood of individualism." Amos also fits the model of Southerners who Mathews notes were most likely to undergo evangelical conversions— "honest, hardworking folk, who aspired to become more esteemed by their fellows than they had been, but who had neither the family connections nor the wealth to enable them to do so. This is not to ascribe to them ulterior motives nor to cast any doubt at all on the sincerity and depth of their faith, but to suggest why they were more likely to be converted than people who had already achieved or inherited an enviable place in society."[8]

In one important way Amos differs from the evangelicals described by Mathews; he does not seek the community of fellow converts. And it is precisely in his denial of communal ties and obligations that Amos expresses his pride and defiles his vision. Like his many forerunners in American literature, he isolates himself from the community because he aspires to something higher than the commonplace world. Perhaps, finally, it does not much matter whether his sense of separateness and destiny comes from the revival meeting or from the wonder and ambition aroused by a plantation mansion or a yacht. For Amos, like Sutpen and Gatsby, does yoke his Old-Testament-style vision to his own romantic yearnings for distinction in the world, which in the Mississippi society of the early 1900s, like that virtually anywhere in the country after 1607, meant land, wealth, power.

Spencer's Amos, unlike many of Melville's heroes who brood over the difficulties of satisfying the often conflicting demands for success with God and man, is rather like a throwback to the type of Puritan discussed by Martha Banta in *Failure and Success in America: A Literary Debate*. Although he bypasses entirely the Puritans' mission to establish a godly new world in the wilderness, he does possess their supreme assurance as he goes about establishing his own world in the Delta wilderness. Banta explains:

One word which nicely approximates the total confidence required to drive toward success that is possessed by any settlers of a howling wilderness is *chutzpah*. Roughly translated as outrageously nervy assertiveness, American *chutzpah* is a legacy from that other Chosen People in the Wilderness, also adept at survival, and more, during their own flight from Whorish Babylon. The Pilgrims and Puritans had, and needed, *chutzpah* in abundance. This word—one which may imply comic arrogance to us—would have meant to them an iron-strong humbleness before God and the itch to do great things in His name.[9]

Amos Dudley never doubts that God has great things in store for him, but for a short time after he leaves Yocona with his friend Arney to pick cotton in the Delta, he is unsure what these things are. Earlier he had a glimpse of worldly success when he made $96.84, taking over his brother's store during Ephraim's illness and stocking it with an array of cheap nostrums and trinkets. But Ephraim censured him, telling him he should hand over the entire amount as a tabernacle offering, and his father reacted only by saying he owed the Lord at least a ten percent tithe. Clearly, in Amos's view Yocona offered no destiny for one of God's chosen.

Amos's wandering, which constitutes the first section of the novel, at last gains direction when he has a second vision, less otherworldly but no less traumatic. He beholds success and earthly fulfillment in the face of Miss Ary Morgan, daughter of the estimable planter Ross Morgan. When he sees Ary riding her bay mare at the mule auction in Leland, where he has bought a small grocery store, he finally has a clear idea of what his special destiny might be. Just as Daisy embodies success for Gatsby, and Ellen Coldfield respectability for Thomas Sutpen, Ary represents to Amos a world elsewhere that he is trying to reach. Specifically, she ignites in this young man from the hills a burning desire to transform himself into an "aristocrat," and thus Amos sets forth to play a late version of an old, familiar ideal—the Southern Cavalier. He thinks, "In order to get in where you didn't belong you had to be good enough first, and next you had to be sure enough. She was good and she was sure. . . ." In that instant he fastened his visionary dream upon the possession of Ary, imagining that her assurance and success would become his own: "He became the face, whirled as the face was whirled, immediate with all speed, skill and rightfulness" (39).

In the latter half of the opening section of the novel Spencer portrays Amos's unrelenting drive to establish himself as a Delta landowner in one of the most vivid and interesting passages in the novel. Trading his grocery store to a Chinaman named Wang Tu Jones for six hundred acres of uncleared Delta canebrake, Amos throws himself against heat, mosquitoes, and a resisting gang of black laborers in his frenzy of land clearing and planting. He is helped in his enterprise by a woman, Thelma Dubard, who appears unexpectedly one day at the logging site, pregnant and deserted by her husband. In her self-containment and complacency she resembles Lena Grove of Faulkner's *Light in August,* though her eventual fate is more ominous than Lena's for those around her.

Thelma comes to live with Amos in the old house set back in the cane wilderness. She cooks for him and in a strange way marshals the labor of the black workers, who are convinced she possesses conjuring power. After an accident resulting in her miscarriage, Amos buys an iron bed and they sew "the two mattresses together," but six months later their routine life is halted abruptly when Amos's old friend, Arney Talliafero, arrives with the news that Amos's father has died. As it turns out, Amos's return to his home in the hills marks the final stage of his preparation for the rise to worldly success he dreams of.

Harboring some guilt over having left his family, he returns to Yocona, seeking a clear sign from God that what he has done is "right." In a solitary moment he addresses his father's corpse, "My land was given to me, out of high heaven where they know about me for sure. The time's not come for her, for Ary Morgan; but if I get her too, wouldn't you take it for a Sign? A Sign I was right to leave, that I worked well, that Ephraim was wrong?" (76). No miracle occurs; no sign is given. Amos leaves his family a second time, refusing his mother's pleas to go in search of the absent brother

Ned. Back in the Delta, recounting to Arney what happened at home, Amos justifies himself by claiming that his family "all wished ill to me." He construes their every action as a sign of ill will, and he turns his face toward the private dream of success that will further separate him from them.

Multiple Voices of Indictment

In each of three subsequent sections a witness to Amos's life indicts him for failures of loyalty and love. They know nothing of his religious vision, seeing rather a man driven to hold power and wealth for his own prideful self-satisfaction. In creating the multiple narrators of the long middle section of the novel Spencer sought to broaden the perspective that defines Amos for the reader. She explained to Charles Bunting that she was aware of earlier uses of multiple narrators (notably in Faulkner's *As I Lay Dying*), but that she employed the device because it answered her novel's need. In fact, at the time she was writing *This Crooked Way*, Shelby Foote published *Follow Me Down*, which comprises a series of monologues by various speakers who reveal their views of the character Luther Eustis. Spencer reviewed the book for the Greenville (Miss.) *Delta Democrat Times* (25 June 1950) and wrote of its "tricky technique, reminiscent of Browning's *The Ring and the Book* and Faulkner's *As I Lay Dying*." Years later, when she discussed her own use of the form with Bunting, she said: "I wasn't trying to imitate, but it just seemed to me that a person obsessed as this man was, possessed by an inner vision, if he told it all himself, one would lose perspective totally. . . . The point of the book was a process of bringing this vision into perspective; therefore, one needed the viewpoint of other people, the witness of other people, on this person who almost seemed to be at times demonic."[10]

To Arney Talliafero, the first of the three speakers, Amos's great failing is disloyalty—to his own family, to Thelma Dubard, and to Arney himself. "I was friend to a fellow onct," Arney begins, and then reveals in a description of the year he spent with Amos and Thelma, helping "lift a whole plantation out of the swamp," how he came to think, "Amos Dudley is an evil man" (97). At first Arney dismisses Amos's disloyalty to his family, reasoning that he didn't really mean all the accusations he raised against his brother Ephraim and others in the family. But he cannot forgive Amos's ill treatment of Thelma. During the year after Amos's return from Yocona, Arney and Thelma both came to see their life with Amos as like that of a family, but for Amos the year of plantation building is nothing more than a marking of time until he can make his bid for Ary Morgan. When Ary arrives in a flashy buggy one day, it is clear that Amos is ready for Thelma to leave. Like a biblical patriarch, he is ready to put aside one woman for another. Both Thelma and Arney have too much pride to plead with Amos, and so they go, each a separate way.

Thelma heads for Arkansas, pregnant with a child Amos accuses her of "tricking" him into conceiving. She is one who neither complains nor explains—"You and me's even, Amos, she says. I come with a baby and I'm leaving with a baby" (96). Arney's reaction is to take Amos's sack of money from its hiding place and offer it to Thelma, but, as Arney later tells Amos, "she said the money would be nice, but you would come and get it back from her" (97). Amos recovers his nest egg, all but the treasured sack of silver dollars left from his youthful Yocona venture, which he believes Arney has stolen. For Arney, the final disloyalty is Amos's betrayal of their friendship. He leaves while Amos bitterly yells accusations against him.

Arney's monologue is rendered in language appropriate to his character, from an unspecified vantage point distanced in time and place from the events narrated. Spencer employs Arney's section to advance the story of Amos's rise from poor boy to planter, and also to add further detail to the complex psychological portrait of Amos that slowly emerges. Arney's perplexity in trying to "figure out" Amos and his literal, plainly spoken observations about him heighten one's interest and belief in Amos as a larger-than-life figure, while offering convincing evidence that he is credibly human. The second monologue, narrated by Amos's niece by marriage, Dolly, serves a similar narrative and dramatic function.

Dolly's fifteen-page indictment, like Arney's, is delivered as a recollection of "long ago days," the days of her childhood, when she had visited Amos and Ary at their new house near Cypress Landing. To Dolly, daughter of Ary Morgan's beautiful sister Louise, dead since Dolly's fourth year, the house was "a heart of happiness." It is not clear whether Dolly's disaffection for Amos comes chiefly because of her fear or his pride. What had been unqualified trust in her uncle's benevolence and love turns to fear one day when Amos opposes the Morgan family's effort, aimed mainly at spiting him, to send Dolly off to finishing school. Pressed by Ary to explain his motives, Amos replies in Dolly's hearing that what he did was not for love of Dolly. "I did it for myself" (115–16). Hearing his blunt statement of self-assertion and seeing the answering fear in Ary's eyes, Dolly recoils into her own timidity, disillusioned and fearful. Amos's directness and power are overwhelming to the adolescent girl, who clings to childhood as a refuge. She says, "I stood there . . . wishing to go back to all things I renounced when I came to him—silence and understanding and endearment, to say what I wanted his heart to say, I am only a child." But Amos offers her no pity for childishness or excuse for her fear—"he spoke to me on equal ground, kindly and direct" (118).

From the conclusion we learn that Dolly eventually followed the comfortable path laid out by the Morgans—finishing school, college—but that it had led to the rather lonely life of a spinster schoolteacher. In Dolly's indictment, as in Arney's, we gain a further sense of the heroic proportion of Amos, who betrayed them both because they expected ordinary understanding and acceptance from him. Not until the third indictment is issued, that of Ary in the longest section of the novel, do we hear from an accuser who matches Amos in strength of character.

Ary's indictment is the classic questioning of romantic individualism. She is well matched to take the measure of Amos's nature, for by her own admission she too was "a romantic," like the Morgans, but she "craved a hardier kind of romance than they seemed to offer" (131). She discovers during the years of her marriage, however, that Amos's kind of hardy romanticism is not only beguiling, but taxing almost beyond endurance. And yet she continues to live with him because she senses that life with Amos is more vital and satisfying than any comfortable, respectable return to her family's way of life would be. Nonetheless, Ary's list of particulars against Amos is serious, and the fear Dolly has once seen on her face is real. As Ary says, "I was afraid . . . because I know that he is death. He has to possess and what he possesses he has to destroy. To all that I love, hide it as he will, he is sudden and ruthless death" (201).

Ary holds Amos responsible for the death of their son Winston, killed in a car crash that she indirectly blames on Amos. She charges him with Elinor's early embitterment, the result of his having sold his daughter's beloved horses as punishment for Elinor's high-handed treatment of a young, low-born trainer Amos had befriended. Elinor's subsequent bad marriage, one of the central plots of *Fire in the Morning*, constitutes for Ary the second "loss" of a child due to Amos's willfulness. In her account of Amos's past sins Ary relates the story of the years during which Amos rose to wealth and prominence, as well as gives her version of their married life. Despite her protestation that she lives in fear of Amos, she draws a portrait of the two of them as mighty opposites, who finally face nearly mortal conflict over their third child, the daughter Mary Louise.

After Ary has suffered a late-age miscarriage, Amos relinquishes his dreams of having a son who will continue a Dudley line that can match the Morgans. Significantly, Ary brings on the miscarriage as she attempts to establish the Morgan presence in her Dudley house—symbolized by her effort to move an antique rocker from Dellwood, the Morgan mansion, to Cypress Landing. After the miscarriage, Amos devotes himself to transforming his daughter from a Morgan into a Dudley. Named for Ary's sister, the child Mary Louise is renamed by Amos "Dinah Lee." Ary acquiesces to her husband's action and to his subsequent domination of Dinah, partly to appease Amos and partly to exorcise her guilt over the miscarriage. It is finally the courtship of the adolescent Dinah by an unlikely young stranger named Joe Ferguson that precipitates the showdown between Ary and Amos. She confronts him with an account of Ferguson's ignominious behavior—the seduction of Dinah and a tawdry affair with an albino black girl—and, the most damning accusation of all, that she knows Amos suspects Ferguson of being his and Thelma Dubard's son. Amos's resolution—"to have them marry, of course"—proves an ultimate provocation to Ary, and she shoots Ferguson to put an end to what she sees as a morass of sorrow and complication. She ends her long monologue as she awaits Amos's discovery of the crumpled body that lies on the floor near her. It is a tense moment that has all the literary earmarks of a turning point in a tragedy, giving rise to the expectation that a recognition scene will follow, that at last Amos will acknowledge the pain his ambition and pride have inflicted upon others. But this is not the resolution that Elizabeth Spencer plots in *This Crooked Way*.

The Problem of the Ending

In the last section of the novel, entitled "The Return: Amos," Amos narrates what is essentially a happy and comic—decidedly not tragic—resolution. The radical shift in tone and in the character of Amos was clearly a major risk for Spencer, and it drew strongly mixed reactions from reviewers, who responded not only to the unexpected comedic form but to the hurried pace of the narrative action. F. C. Flint, writing for the *Sewanee Review,* was so provoked by the conclusion that he proffered the generalization about the contemporary novel that "the ability to manage endings may be on the decline."[11]

Unquestionably, Spencer's plot, which turns upon intricate detail and numerous characters in the earlier sections, advances several degrees in intricacy and compression of space and time in the final part. In addition, she seems to manipulate the language forcefully and relentlessly in the twenty-six page conclusion to transform the intense, heroic Amos into an acquiescent family man who at last feels at peace with himself. The language has everything to do with the shift in tone—so entirely so that one might surmise that Spencer, deciding to write the final chapter from the first-person view of Amos, discovered in Amos's speech an undeniably comic tone that compelled the shift from the tragic direction. From the moment Amos begins to talk, the incipient tragedy turns into rueful humor.

According to Amos, he had wanted two things in life: "one was to see Ary's face again like I saw it first that day above the horse's mane . . . and the other sight I thirsted to see was a ladder of angels" (221). The two desires embody Amos's essential conflict, the desire for acceptance and success in the secular world and the longing for assurance that he has God's backing. Amos's easy, almost folksy language suggests, however, that the earlier intensity of his two desires is waning: "If anybody wants to know which is worse—to want a thing you had once, or to want a thing you never had—I'm here to say it's first one and then the other, and there's no telling which" (221). Of the two desires, what Amos gets is the first, that is, an act—followed by a look—from Ary that ultimately pulls him back into the world of family and community, the world of mutual dependence. He forsakes finally his obsessive, egoistic Protestantism and seeks the ordinary, human salvation offered in a ritualistic baptism witnessed by a congregation of his Yocona family.

Amos begins the section by quickly summarizing the events of his life leading to the discovery of Ary's murder of Joe Ferguson. When he sees Ary, he sees what he has longed for—"twice now she has showed me her face" (226). It is a signal that Ary has finally freed herself from caring about what the Morgans will think of her, and it is a sign to Amos that he can no longer live a separate, secret life. Taking the gun from her, he is discovered by members of the family, who thereafter assume him to be the murderer. This sequence of events initiates Amos's return from his "crooked way." Unlike a Thomas Sutpen or Captain Ahab, Amos Dudley discovers that his secret sense of destiny, derived from his boyhood vision of God, is bound to the lives of others whom he cares for and cannot disregard. Acceptance and resignation, not rebellion, mark his recognition of the limits of a man's will.

So it was over. I was left with a secret that had no more power, and with my heart, and where God had been there was nothing but a big silence. In the big silence, alone with his heart, what does a man do then? I can say that too, though it took no thought at the time. He does what he was brought up to do; he goes back to the way he was born knowing. He buries the dead as decent as he can; then he goes home. (226)

Amos finally is a reasonable rather than heroic man, and so it is not surprising that he does what is practical and generous and that he ends up satisfied.

Amos makes what is to be his final stand as the solitary individualist in an incongruous burial scene, in which his widower brother-in-law, Nathan, a Presbyterian minister, offers a memorial prayer as Amos sinks the body of Joe Ferguson in his 1928 coupe beneath the river. Amos demands to know of Nathan what proof he has of God's goodness, of God's existence. Clearly in Amos's eyes his own direct encounter with God outmatches Nathan's quiet assurance that "It is a question of faith" (229). The exchange incites Amos to acknowledge his frustrated rage for order. From the moment of his apocalyptic vision he had expected God miraculously to show him a "sign," and he had spent his life secretly concealing the vision and awaiting the sign. Seeing the disorder of his life, asking Nathan to "sort it out, good from bad," Amos for the first time tells another human being of his mystical experience. Breaking the long silence about what has been most central in his life is the first step of

Amos's return. The next step occurs in his discovery of the sack of money he mistakenly thought Arney had stolen and his subsequent recanting his doubt of his friend's loyalty. Finally, he sees the "look" on Ary's face, which in effect nullifies the bad years between them.

To atone for his willfulness, his having deserted his family and accused his friend, Amos returns to Yocona to put matters straight. Instead of Arney, however, he finds an avatar of friendship in the person of a stranger, Elmore Jordan, and instead of the Dudley homestead, he finds a great "empty waste of raw dirt" and a "deep hole blasted" where the house used to be. Nonetheless, these are sufficient for him to put his life back together. Amos meets and drinks with Jordan (who eventually carries news of him back to Ary) and tells him how he got "tangled up with God" (235). As a first act of atonement, Amos throws the worn sack of silver dollars, the old Yocona earnings that first charged his ambition, into the river. Later, he finds the Dudleys living with an elderly aunt, and he makes his peace even with brother Ephraim by consenting to be baptized in the river along with three young nephews. As if the government's installing a large reservoir on their land were not dispossession enough, the Dudleys return from the baptizing in a storm to find the winds demolishing the aunt's house. There is nothing for Amos to do but bring the caravan of sixteen Dudleys and one Baptist preacher back to live at Cypress Landing.

The reunion is made possible because Amos has forsworn his ambition to be a high-toned planter and Ary has let him know with her look that she has finally consented to be a Dudley. In bringing his whole family home to live with him and Ary, Amos concludes that "no matter how much I have done for her, taking away the gun, I guess we came out even, Ary and me. Because the time wasn't long in coming when I had to count on her not to plug me through the head with a .22 cartridge" (243–44). Ary holds up her end, letting Amos know by the sound of her greeting of his family that she will willingly take them in. Amos's return is complete, realized at last, he thinks, because he disentangled himself from God. As he says at the end when he thinks of all those who have played a part in his life and are now gone, "I wonder sometime if God will go too, like they have, because He sure-Lord knows something that He won't tell and it took me a long time to find out that the only way to believe in Him is to give Him His right to be worthless too. He showed me a heap; but He held out on me about that ladder" (246–47).

Nash K. Burger, writing of the conclusion, commented that "it took daring and skill to envisage and write that final scene, but Miss Spencer brings it off."[12] Others, along with F. C. Flint, have disagreed.[13] Answering a direct question by Charles Bunting about the conclusion, Spencer indicated that in her view the ending progressed inevitably from Amos's nature and the events of the novel.

Because he couldn't come to direct terms with the God that he thought he experienced, there's a partial disillusionment. But ritualistically he could fulfill that. When he went back and threw the money sack in the water, this was a ritualistic fulfillment. . . . The river's coming in on that family and so he has to bring them home, and his wife has to take it. So this is a social resolution, and it's also partially ritualistic. The book is a fulfillment, even though it presents a disillusionment: the major things he started with are really impossible.[14]

Spencer adds that, as she looks back on the book, it seems somehow "central to a sort of experience that Mississippians could have." The comment provides a crucial clue to understanding how the conclusion does work thematically and how it forcefully contributes to the power and originality of the novel. *This Crooked Way* is the story not of a tragic or romantic hero, but of a boy from Mississippi hill country society—a proletariat with fundamentalist religious beliefs—whose dream of rising in the world takes the only form he can possibly imagine: the direct intervention of God. When he speaks in his own voice in the final part, the reader discovers that previous narrators have all aggrandized his motives and mystery. What Amos Dudley is, ultimately, is an intense, intelligent man who takes the evangelical preaching literally just as long as the events of his life will let him. He is a man of his time and place, and the novel partakes chiefly of realism.

"Locally Sound and Yet Universal"

Just as Amos "corrects" his view of God, Spencer's bold conclusion corrects the reader's image of Amos, and so reader and character together discover that life has merely human dimensions. The merger of form and content here represents a considerable artistic achievement and completes Spencer's design of portraying Amos as a man

who emerges naturally and credibly from his culture. In speaking
of Amos to Bunting, Spencer calls him a "strange man," but one
whose inner conviction of his experience "with God Almighty Himself" was absolute. She adds that "if you look closely at Protestant
belief it means that there you are with God, just you two. That
was the way he felt, without very much rationalizing about it. . . .
I thought his story made a good basis for a novel because it was
basic in Mississippi experience. . . . When I had both the character
and the culture he existed in, I thought there was a possibility for
the novel to formalize itself."[15]

The development of *This Crooked Way* closely follows Spencer's
intention to portray the character and the culture he existed in. In
the first four sections of the novel Amos appears as the separate
hero, with a conventional heroic stature made possible by the distanced vantage from which the reader sees him—the omniscient
narration of the opening and the multiple voices of the onlookers
in the middle sections. In the conclusion Spencer returns Amos to
his roots.

To metamorphose the heroic character into a realistic one, Spencer
employs a number of narrative devices, including the important one
already mentioned—Amos's voice. She also employs the character
Elmore Jordan to temper Amos's flamboyance. Jordan's recital of
personal woes matches Amos's and more, and yet Jordan's account
of his churchgoing, his wife's death, and his shooting of his wife's
former lover comes across as a comic tale, the last line of which is
delivered as the punch line of a joke. The rapid shifts in setting
and chronology and the hurly-burly pace of events further impart
a fluid, organic, comedic aspect to his story. Amos tells his story
in the narrative past tense, as he looks back upon the several busy
days from the time of Ferguson's death to the arrival of the Dudleys
at Cypress Landing. His narration zigzags from his own eyewitness
account of his return to Yocona to a thirdhand account of events as
reported by Jordan to Ary, who later filters the story back to Amos.
The narrative line is complex in plot and tone, but with control
and ingenuity Spencer convincingly maneuvers the heroic Amos
home to a human community. "It is a story," as reviewer Frances
Gaither concluded, "locally sound and yet universal, about the failure at the heart of success, about the sin of lonely striving and the
saving grace of human love."[16]

Other reviewers, particularly Southerners, praised Spencer's vivid depiction of the Mississippi hills and Delta. Cid Ricketts Sumner called Spencer's characters "definitely regional," and then added, "but the regional is only the universal seen from a special angle, and she has been able to give her characters the depth and fulness necessary to make them believable, intensely interesting, and significant."[17] Even the *Times Literary Supplement* reviewer noted that "the background of the Mississippi agricultural region and, indeed, much of the detail of the domestic interiors, is very vividly done and holds the reader's interest throughout."[18]

Some reviewers, such as Worth Tuttle Hedden, wrote in detail of the vividness and accuracy of Spencer's depiction of locale, concluding that in *This Crooked Way,* as in *Fire in the Morning,* she made a reader care intensely about the characters. "Miss Spencer may use any method she likes in writing a novel of rural Mississippi and she will find an avid audience."[19] Other reviewers, however, were sharply hostile to the Southern idiom, if not the Southern setting. The *New Yorker* review, for example, cited the Dolly and Ary sections as instances where Spencer had done better than "a rough job of storytelling," but then added the qualification: "She writes a limpid and attractive prose, accurate and sharp about tastes, smells, appearances, and emotions, which is essentially Southern and which pleasingly enlarges one's picture of the South. In the persons of the other characters she adopts the slithery flow of piney-woods English. It is accurate so far as the phonetics of that debased and lazy-mouthed tongue are concerned, but an accurate report of a blur has little to recommend it."[20] Nancy Baker likewise began her review for the *Chicago Sunday Tribune* with the disclaimer that "stories peopled with sleepy southerners and set in sleepy southern locales usually put the reader to sleep." Then Baker issues her praise: "But here is the exception; here is a forceful, stimulating novel!"[21]

This Crooked Way was prominently reviewed by national magazines and major newspapers and, in general, was greeted with acclaim. The negative reviews, such as those in *Time* and the *Nation,* typically faulted the novel for what was claimed to be a too great reliance upon Faulkner's model.[22] But *This Crooked Way* grew out of the author's experience of a South that existed a generation after Faulkner's formative years. Spencer's assumptions about the Southern culture are closer to those of Robert Penn Warren in *All the King's Men* (1946) than to Faulkner's in *Absalom, Absalom!* (1936).

In his recent study of Southern cultural history D. J. Singal shows that, for many reasons, the shift from Victorian to modernist thought was compressed into a relatively short space of time in the South, roughly the years 1919–45.[23] When Spencer was engaged in writing *This Crooked Way* during the late 1940s, she drew upon precisely the span of years Singal discusses, her own formative years, in writing her version of the plantation South. Her early religious training, her firsthand knowledge of the rags-to-riches opportunities existing in the Delta well into the twentieth century, her acquaintance with the Victorian ideal of culture as the refined, respectable life of good manners and enviable possessions—all these, and more, shape her portrait of the Dudleys and the Morgans. But by the late 1940s the cavalier myth of the aristocratic South had been mortally challenged by novelists and other Southern intellectuals, despite the Agrarian defense, even the vehement defense of the old tradition by Spencer's teacher, Donald Davidson, at Vanderbilt. And despite the Dixiecrat effort in 1948, the absolute faith in the "Southern way," including faith in old-time religion, belonged irrevocably to the past. Writers like W. J. Cash in *The Mind of the South* (1941) and Frank Owsley in *Plain Folk of the Old South* (1949) had gone far to debunk the image of the benevolent, aristocratic planter. Whereas Faulkner's characters had embodied the tension generated by conflicting views of the old and new Souths, those tragic, heroic tensions were giving way to an ironical consciousness and acceptance of cultural relativism. Amos Dudley's special sense of destiny leads him on a search for "culture," in the Victorian sense. He discovers, instead, several cultures—the "ruck of folks," in fact, that Jack Burden finds in Warren's *All the King's Men*. Amos accepts his place among the folk, accepts his limits as a man before an unfathomable God, and settles down to cultivate his family and place at Cypress Landing. Spencer's fusion in Amos Dudley of a radical Protestant mentality with the cavalier myth and her convincing portrayal of how such a character makes an accommodation with a modernist world represent a striking and original achievement.

Chapter Four

Voices of Mississippi

Recipient of a Guggenheim Fellowship in 1953, Spencer left her teaching position at the University of Mississippi, as well as her family in Carrollton, to go to Italy to write her next novel. The two-year sojourn in Italy marked a turning point in her personal and artistic life. She met John Rusher, whom she would later marry, and she wrote what would turn out to be her third, and in many ways her final, "Mississippi novel." When she left Mississippi, she carried the outline of *The Voice at the Back Door* with her. Looking back in 1965 to the novel's composition, she said that the book was one she "had planned to write . . . long before but for one reason or another—a job to hold, poor health—had not been able to."[1] It is also likely that the subject of the book made its writing difficult, so difficult, in fact, that Spencer had to have the physical and psychic distance afforded by Italy to do it at all. The subject was race relations in the South, a topic fraught with ambiguity, controversy, and passion.

In a recent interview Spencer speaks of the "moral pressure" she felt to write the novel, despite her misgivings about attempting a contemporaneous novel on race. She judged the time was right for her to attempt a "considerable work," that she had served her apprenticeship with two beginning novels that had had good critical reception, and so she was ready for a more ambitious undertaking. Thus it was with a sense of "enormous risk" that she set out to write the novel, fearful, as she has said, that it might seem "polemical," like a "social tract," or just another piece of "timely fiction." Nonetheless, she felt she had to write the book: "I still felt obliged to explore my own thinking about the racial issue. I couldn't avoid it."[2]

Spencer chose as setting for her exploration into the tangled web of Southern racial relationships a fictional town resembling Tarsus in *Fire in the Morning* and very much like her native Carrollton. Lacey, Mississippi, though larger than Carrollton, which had a population in the 1940s of about 475, is a county seat in the

Mississippi hill country. Site of a bitterly contested race for sheriff in 1950 or 1951 (the date is ambiguous in the novel), a race that turns upon two issues—prohibition and equal rights for blacks— Lacey mirrors the mind of the South that Spencer knew at firsthand. *The Voice at the Back Door* is a deliberately, intricately plotted novel of ideas. As Spencer acknowledged in a 1968 interview, "Plot is the most important element. . . . Plot carries out the idea, and so do the characters—everything bears on the question of race, on the race issue."[3] In creating the multitude of characters, and voices, who grapple with one another and with their separate identities as black or white, Spencer searched her own experience to discover what truths she could find:

> I wanted to write a novel about the confrontation of races on the local level. I was not trying to stand up and announce that I was above these characters and could therefore write a sermon in the guise of a novel. In fact, I felt that the reactions of many of the characters were mine in a way. I was struggling through the whole thing with them. While I was working on that book, I would hear again in my mind whole conversations that had passed over me and that I had never really analyzed. I began to listen to these inner voices, to people saying things that I had accepted all my life without question; and suddenly I found myself questioning. I realized for the first time how outrageous these things were. It was a healing experience for me to write that book.[4]

When Spencer returned to Mississippi in 1955 with the rough draft of the novel completed, she was dismayed to find that racial tensions had sharply intensified in the two years. On 17 May 1954, the United States Supreme Court had ruled in *Brown* vs. *Board of Education* that racial segregation in the public schools was unconstitutional. In the South, and certainly in Mississippi, many whites reacted to the ruling with bitter, angry resentment. There followed the organization of the white Citizens' Council specifically to maintain segregation, as well as a number of cases of racial violence, including the murder of the young black man Emmett Till in 1955, which occurred not far from Carrollton. After only a short visit, Spencer saw the extent of calamitous social change. She later wrote, "I realized to my horror that in my absence from the state a precipitate moment had come and gone, and that the local scene which in my manuscript I had hopefully allowed to contain the action— with its many ramifications in love and blessing—had already as good as vanished." Thus Spencer saw the "painful irony" of what she had done: "that even while I wrote it down, the tenuous but vivid thread of hope that I thought to be there had been dissolving utterly" (xx).

Spencer left Mississippi for New York, where she spent a year revising the novel. Anticipating Willie Morris's *North toward Home* by several years, she describes the painful journey she made, "going North," like so many other Southerners, knowing the trip was "definitive and final," that the South was no longer where she belonged. Although her brief stay in Mississippi had at first made her doubt the validity of her vision, she decided to stick with her story, reasoning that she had been "nothing but a Mississippian" when she wrote it, and "had had no motive but to place things there in their truest and clearest light." If the character of Duncan Harper, the sheriff, seemed impossible in 1956, "then perhaps in a society gone deliberately blind, a person who has the honesty to see at all will always seem impossible" (xxi).

The Critical Reception: "All Praise"

Of all Elizabeth Spencer's fiction to date, *The Voice at the Back Door* received the most unqualified literary praise at the time of its publication. Her next work, *The Light in the Piazza,* would be more widely reviewed, but no subsequent work so far has evoked such an outpouring of admiration by critics. The *New Yorker* review, entitled "All Praise," pronounced it "a practically perfect novel," one of the "two or three finest novels of the year." The praise was almost grudging at times, however, for Brendan Gill, like Anthony West on *This Crooked Way,* clearly did not cherish the setting: "a small town in Mississippi, and the prospective reader is begged not to be put off by that perhaps gruesome-sounding fact." Gill found the novel free of the "unpleasant phosphorescence" of the cavalier strain of Southern novels and went on to compare Spencer's treatment of moral issues with that of James Gould Cozzens in *The Just and the Unjust.* Both, he writes, are "profoundly concerned with the mystery of accountability, which is as good a word as any for what novels are about."[5]

Orville Prescott, writing for the *New York Times,* describes the novel as a "terse, gripping and chillingly sardonic melodrama," Spencer's "finest work to date." He speaks at length of her skill in characterization and concludes that the novel is "a good, thoughtful book and a technically brilliant one."[6] Francis Hackett in the *New Republic* likewise points to the authenticity and piquancy with which Spencer creates the inhabitants of Winfield County. "Her absorption in her people, who are quite themselves in spite of the die-stamps that other Southern writers furnish, is her great distinction."[7] Many reviewers, particularly those who were native Southerners, praised her handling of humor and dialogue.[8] But other reviewers, like Brendan Gill, rather clearly disliked the Southern setting and voices and had to be won over from an initial hostility.

Caroline Tunstall, reviewing the novel for the *New York Herald Tribune Book Review,* speaks of its "elaborate plot involving many characters, bright, winning, yet finely shaded." She writes a little later that "there is some farce, some beautifully understated terror, much bitter satire, much tenderness. And there is always a compelling imagery, whether of place or season or mood." With these and other favorable comments, she nonetheless calls the novel a "Faulkner story in a Faulkner setting" (with the unmistakeable hint that "Faulkner" and "Southern" are interchangeable) and then adds a puzzling swipe at Spencer's sex, "It is written directly, with a nervous, very feminine strength."[9] She offers no explanation of the seeming contradiction between "directness" and "nervous feminine strength." Contemporaneous reviews always furnish interesting perspectives on the literary and social milieu of any period, and these are no exception. In general, reviewers initially cast a wary eye on the Southern setting and racial subject matter of *The Voice at the Back Door,* but they responded to the cautious hope for racial harmony implicit in the novel, and they found themselves drawn to the timeless appeal of its vivid characterization and engaging, suspenseful narrative.

Four Citizens of Lacey

At the center of the complex plot of *The Voice at the Back Door,* with its cast of over fifty characters, stand four men whose lives are hopelessly intertwined with one another and with the town of Lacey. These are Duncan Harper, respected as an ex–All American football player whose exploits as "the fastest running back of the year" at the state university are remembered and cherished; Jimmy Tallant, owner of the local roadhouse and bootlegging establishment, and a lifelong friend of Duncan and Duncan's wife, Tinker; Beck Dozer, a black man whose life is shaped by a burdensome legacy, the murder of his father thirty years earlier at the hands of a mob led by Tallant's father; and Kerney Woolbright, ambitious twenty-five-year-old politician, graduate of Yale Law School, and, unlike the three other men, too young to have served in World War II.

Social change, anathema to the small Southern town, is everywhere in the air, partly the inevitable consequence of the uprooting wrought by a world war, and partly the result of a local event, the unexpected death of Winfield County's sheriff, Travis Brevard. For a "precipitate moment," the six months intervening between the death of Brevard and the election of a new sheriff, Lacey and the surrounding county face the possibility of changing the old dispensation—the "Southern tradition" of hypocritical prohibition and violent racism. Spencer's narrative of this short span, and of the days following Duncan Harper's death, portrays a small-town Southerner who wants to do "the right thing," a man whose sense of decency puts him at odds with encrusted tradition.

The novel begins with an image of speed and urgency that foreshadows the social upheaval embodied in the hurried sequence of events about to unfold. Sheriff Brevard races his car in a whirl of dust and gravel into town to the grocery store of Duncan Harper, where he shortly dies of a heart attack. He knows that with him an old order is passing, and he senses that the young Duncan Harper, rather than his old sidekick, deputy Willard Follansbee, is the man to replace him. The manner and place of Brevard's dying point up the hypocrisies about race and refinement that lie at the root of much that passes as Southern tradition in the novel.

Brevard's public life and private life are radically split apart, and so at the moment when he most needs to go home, when he needs a place to die, he has no home to go to. He explains to Harper: "I been married to Miss Ada for thirty-odd year, but I couldn't ever age her. She's nothing but a little girl and, God forgive me, but I'd rather die in a gully than on her bedspread." Then he tells Harper of Ida Belle: "Her house is a place where I could go out quiet as a match. She's been my nigger woman for fifteen years and everybody knows it, but it would likely embarrass her to have my corpse on her hands. You can't tell what they're liable to do to a nigger. She might have to leave town" (8). The "they" Brevard refers to, of course, are his cohorts, including Follansbee, who found Ida Belle for Brevard in the first place.

Dying, Brevard reflects the emotional and moral impotence that ironically afflicts the man who acquiesces to a tradition in which mind and body, ideal and reality, are split apart and defined by "white woman" and "black woman." Whereas Ida is lover and mother of Brevard's children, Ada is the childish, asexual, pious Southern lady. Though Spencer does not draw Ida/Ada as a Freudian allegory, their portrayal does rather clearly suggest two parts of a psyche—libido and superego—perniciously divided from each other. Spencer's portrayal of Ada also recalls Lillian Smith's description of the enervated Southern Lady in *Killers of the Dream:*

The majority . . . convinced themselves that God had ordained that they be deprived of pleasure, and meekly stuffed their hollowness with piety, trying to believe that the tightness they felt was hunger satisfied. Culturally stunted by a region that still pays nice rewards to simple-mindedness in females, they had no defenses against blandishment. They listened to the round words of men's tribute to Sacred Womanhood and believed. . . .[10]

In *The Voice at the Back Door* Spencer shows that Ida, Ada, Brevard, and all the other inhabitants of Lacey are victims of a tradition harmful to soul and body. The split between public and private selves, between professing and feeling, leaves one spiritually homeless.

The citizen of Lacey who tries to bring together private belief and public act is Duncan Harper, who serves as acting sheriff during the months he is running for the elective office. Despite his long-standing friendship with Tallant and his generally apolitical, good-old-boy acceptance of the local mores, Harper as sheriff cannot accept the blatant legal violations evidenced in illegal whisky and racial discrimination. The simplicity and purity of his idealism ultimately do affect the town, despite its resistance, before he dies in an automobile accident trying to save Beck Dozer from a lynch mob. Harper is the focal protagonist in the book, but he is not so interesting to the reader (or to Spencer, for that matter)[11] as the other three male characters are.

Kerney Woolbright represents a foil to Harper's unself-conscious liberalism. A Yale graduate, he has returned to Mississippi full of "new South" ideology, certain that backward tradition will shortly give way to a progressive liberalism. As Tinker Harper describes

him to Jimmy Tallant, "He thinks all you have to do is get a few
people in a few towns to take a great big risk of being martyrs,
only it will seem like a bigger risk than it actually is because people
know deep down but won't admit that the old reactionary position
of the South has played out to nothing but a lot of sentiment. He
thinks the Dixiecrat movement was the last gasp of it" (30). Woolbright's naïveté quickly evolves into political savvy, however, when
he sees how deeply rooted Southern sentiment is. His mentor is
Jason Hunt, the leading citizen of Lacey and father of Cissy, whom
Woolbright has strategically courted. After Hunt tells him that
"the last thing we need to discuss openly in this county now is the
Negro question," Woolbright moves inevitably to desert idealism—
and Harper—in order to get himself elected to the state senate. A
more complex man than Harper, Woolbright understands evil in
the society, partakes of it, and lives with his troubled conscience.
In the novel's epilogue he seeks exoneration from complicity in
Harper's death—or at least some assuaging of his guilt—as he
attempts to discover who precisely was responsible for the automobile accident.

In their complexity and complicity with evil Beck Dozer and
Jimmy Tallant also serve as foils to Harper. From childhood they
had grown up knowing of the fragility of abstract justice and the
cost of ideals carried to the public act. As in Tarsus in *Fire in the
Morning,* there is buried in Lacey an old ineradicable shame. In 1919
Robinson Dozer, Beck's father, had led a delegation of black citizens
to the courthouse to discuss with the judge ways of restoring racial
harmony in the community. The return of black war veterans,
changed by their exposure to other cultures and faraway places, had
triggered several violent exchanges between blacks and whites, and
Dozer, the most educated and respected black in the community,
had sought peace by appealing to reason and justice. The murder
of Dozer and the other blacks in what is the foremost symbol of a
society built upon law, the courthouse, epitomizes the crime that
impeaches a Southern tradition built upon racism. When Acey Tallant and his mob break in upon the black delegation, seated around
a table awaiting the judge, he speaks the fateful code: "I'm white
and you're black, that's all that you and me need to know" (232).

The racial conflicts forming the central moral issue of the novel
are reflected not only in the 1919 episode, but in an even earlier
event, when old Senator Upinshaw during the earliest days of Re-

construction had started a school for the children of his former slaves. Indeed, Spencer's theme—the frustration of efforts of ethical black and white Southerners to establish lawful and humane relations between the races in 1950—resonates with episodes from the past. In one short chapter, "Robinson Dozer," Spencer renders a miniature portrait of the South since the Civil War. In her account of Dozer's boyhood, as elsewhere in the figure of the elderly black woman, Aunt Mattie, she suggests the loving impulse that connects the races. As she relates in her 1965 introduction, "The story really started in a moment of love. I saw that as I went along, burrowing further and further back into local history, back to the Civil War, which is a Southerner's A.D. It started in other words, when the old man, Senator John, looked . . . and saw and loved the little Negro boy who stood in the threshold—wide-eyed, frightened, but bursting with the nameless, ineffable hope which had brought him there" (xix). The initial act of an individual's love, followed by the betrayal of it by a hating society, marks three generations of Spencer's Winfield County.

Beck Dozer and Jimmy Tallant both bear the memory of their fathers' lives, and it has strangely yoked them together. They met as social equals for the first time in England during the war, and though back home in Lacey they return to the old distanced ways, they are deeply connected to each other. On occasion, Beck works for Tallant, who is involved in a profitable bootlegging business with his father-in-law, Bud Grantham, and, later, in a prospective gambling partnership with a New Orleans criminal ring. To protect his illegal business against the raids of Sheriff Harper, Tallant concocts a story with Dozer's aid to suggest that Dozer has attacked Grantham and drawn the ire of his backwoods family. Tallant anticipates that Harper will move to protect Dozer from a threatened lynching and that, in defending the black man, Harper will inevitably forfeit his chance to be elected sheriff. The melodrama is played out with many interesting twists of plot and character. When Tallant is shot and severely wounded by one of the New Orleans gang, the whole county assumes Dozer to be the assailant. Tallant's efforts to clear Dozer come late; Kerney Woolbright's ignominious concealment of a crucial telegram adds further pressure; and so at last a duel between lawlessness and justice is inevitable.

Spencer's handling of this ageless plot is notable, particularly when compared to other Southern novels treating similar subjects. She writes what is close to parody in a scene midway through the novel, when the Granthams, presumably seeking vengeance, come to the jail where Dozer has sought "protection" from Harper. Harper steels himself to face the "mob" and its gunfire, but faces instead a kind of boyish rowdiness and a camera's flash. There is no show-down, no brave standoff, no lynching. Harper is effectually shot down by a photograph incriminating his "liberal" racial views.

The telling act of citizenship for Harper is a much more muted gesture, and the incident leading to his death is, ironically, casual and accidental. Driving with his wife, Tinker, to a remote part of the county to pick up Dozer, Harper encounters two bored young country boys, veterans of the Korean war, in a grocery–filling station. As with all the preceding generations of veterans, war has obviously misfitted them for life as usual in Winfield County, and their readiness to violence is the result. The spectacle of Harper's taking in Dozer would have been no more than a diversion for the pair, except for one slight move that was weighted with violation of the community's deepest racial taboos. It evokes their outrage. "There's plenty of room in the front," Harper tells Dozer, and Tinker slides over to make room for him in the front seat of the car. In a short italicized section Harper comes nearer to understanding the complexity of his society than he has at any earlier time: *"So it comes down to this,* Duncan thought. *To the tiniest decision you can make. To the slightest action. In front of people daring you to do what you believe in and they don't"* (305).

Neither Woolbright nor the reader ever discovers with certainty whether the two men slashed the tires and thus caused the wreck that shortly killed Harper, or whether the blowout was the consequence of his speed, an accident, as he attempted to elude a pursuing mob from Lacey. All that is clear is that Harper's act of citizenship does have its impact on the community. Beck Dozer and Jimmy Tallant inch away from their cynical self-interest toward a more generous view of the human possibility for justice, and Kerney Woolbright is left with the knowledge of his betrayal of Harper and Tinker, whom he loved, but not so well as his ambition for prestige and power. None of them, however, offers the hope-

fulness signified by Harper. "Duncan Harper was a citizen of Lacey.
. . . It was his strongest and final quality" (186).

"In the South It's
Nothing but Family, Family"

An important element that distinguishes this novel as something
more than a glib, melodramatic plot of good versus evil is the fullness
of portraiture with which Spencer develops the characters and the
conflicting values that frustrate and enmesh them. It turns out that
the characters' struggles against burdensome memories and destructive traditions are as often an effort to flee responsibility and accountability as to accept these. Some of the most poignant examples
of the moral complexity of choices between conformance with tradition and assertion of an independent self are posed in conflicts
between various individuals and their families.

Duncan Harper's deliberate public act to redress racial discrimination is certainly laudable in any abstract sense, but the ironic
consequence is that in helping Dozer, he aids the man who cynically
conspired to gull him, and in doing so left his own family bereft
of husband and father. A more overt and significant example of
strain between family and self, however, centers upon Marcia Mae
Hunt, older daughter of Jason and Nan Hunt, and formerly the
childhood sweetheart and fiancée of Harper. Unlike the other women
of the novel—her sister Cissy; Jimmy Tallant's wife, Bella; Tinker
Harper; or Beck Dozer's wife, Lucy—Marcia Mae refuses to accept
the passive role of Southern wife, to stay in the domestic background
and leave public acts to father or husband. If one takes her story as
emblematic of the range of possibility for reconciling heart's desire
and social reality, then one must conclude that the chance of an
independent woman's finding fulfillment in the South of the 1950s
was even less likely than that of a black man's doing so. Recoiling
from a liberal-thinking, but powerless mother, a domineering father, a homosexual brother whose death was virtually a suicide, she
begged Duncan Harper in 1940 to leave Lacey—"to go West somewhere." As she explains to Harper ten years later, during an affair
between them that nearly wrecks Harper and Tinker's marriage,
"We couldn't stay in the South and be free. In the South it's nothing
but family, family. We couldn't breathe even, until we left" (176).

There is no opportunity in Lacey or Winfield County for Marcia Mae to free herself sufficiently from family to make a separate life for herself, and so she impulsively marries a Yankee who has "no consciousness of families, small towns, roots, ties, or any sort of custom" (179). Moving to California, Marcia Mae is hardly more successful in achieving selfhood, however, either before or after her husband's death in the war. After ten years' absence, she returns to Mississippi, in part because of the unfinished emotional business with Duncan and in part because of the ineffable tie of blood. The pull of the family is imaged in a symbolic episode during which Duncan and Marcia Mae find a dog at a backwoods house long deserted by owners who had left to work in the defense plants of Detroit. Why, they wonder, would the dog return to a house where there wasn't even a smell of food? "They say they don't forget. . . . It's the hound blood." With as little nurturance promised to Marcia Mae from the Hunts, she nonetheless returns, like the hound, drawn by the inexplicable family ties.

Once sees in the women characters in the novel, even in the rebellious Marcia Mae Hunt, a nearly absolute failure to imagine any other way of life than that they know as traditional Southern ladies, or, in the case of Lucy Dozer, as victimized, subservient black woman. On one occasion Marcia Mae ventures to Duncan her wish for a break with the dependent, reactive life, her desire for freedom from the tradition: "I wish . . . that I was anybody's secretary in some big city. And that every morning I got up and put on a gray suit and a clean white blouse and went to work in a beautiful soundproof air-conditioned office one hundred and one floors up, with streamlined filing cabinets and a noiseless electric typewriter. I wish I had a little apartment with a view from the window of nothing but skyscraper tops. Then I would be happy" (112). Duncan dismisses her thought, with the comment that she wouldn't like getting up early and, besides, she'd be bored.

Their exchange is extremely interesting, for it points up the conservative social vision of Harper and suggests something important about his courageous act to defend Beck Dozer. In many ways Harper is a very traditional Southern gentleman who takes seriously his obligation to protect women and blacks. His character is like that of Kinloch Armstrong in *Fire in the Morning*—he is a "protector." Seeing the humiliation of Tinker Taylor when as a child she had come to school wearing an outlandish homemade dress, he

had gone to her defense. He is an honorable man of the sort Senator
Upinshaw had been in the 1860s; he acts in defense of the weak
and powerless. Their need evokes and defines his courage. Although
Dozer's price and independence initially annoy him, he does finally
come to see sympathetically Dozer's situation, and to want for him
at least the full voting rights of an American citizen.

Duncan only partially glimpses what Marcia Mae wants, however,
perhaps because she herself only incompletely imagines a preferable
destiny to that of her mother and sister. Harper understood that
"she had left him because he would not run away with her and be
free from the evil she saw in her family and in the whole South."
He understood that she saw "something different from what he saw,
and had tried in vain to show it to him." The events of the novel
define the corrosive evil of the South as stemming from racism, and
Harper does eventually apprehend this evil. What Marcia Mae sees
and runs away from, however, has more to do with sexual than
racial roles. She rejects the passivity and acquiescence of Southern
ladyhood, though except for the "secretary dream," neither she nor
any other character envisions any other alternative for a woman.

In one of his most reflective moments Harper thinks, "He did
not believe that the Hunts were worse than anybody else, or that
you escaped from anything when you left Lacey and the South"
(183). This is the wisdom that tragedy teaches, but it somehow
stops short of comprehending the position of the Southern lady. As
Anne Goodwyn Jones has argued in *Tomorrow Is Another Day,* the
image of the lady, particularly the image of the "aristocratic lady,"
"receives a stronger emphasis in the South than elsewhere."[12] Cissy
and Marcia Mae Hunt, the reigning princesses of Lacey, are placed
on a pedestal more distanced from the field of Harper's public action
than is Dozer's trough of oppression. Marcia Mae's acts at the end
of the novel seem therefore frivolous and inconsequential. She tries
to warn Duncan of the approaching mob from Lacey, and in doing
so plainly aggravates the speed and confusion leading to the car
wreck. She caustically exposes Kerney Woolbright's chicanery, but
she does nothing to oppose his threat to the community. For Marcia
Mae Hunt alone of all the characters in *The Voice at the Back Door,*
there is no future in Lacey.

By contrast, the family—like the tradition at large—serves all
the other characters as a source not only of danger but of sustaining
love. Beck Dozer looks forward to life with Lucy and his newly

acknowledged son W. B., whose self-assertion at the end of the novel represents renewal and progress for the Dozers. Leaving her husband for the man who fathered her child, Bella Tallant makes way for a union left implicit at the conclusion—Jimmy Tallant may at last find the happiness so long eluding him in the person of widow Tinker Harper, his beloved since childhood. Everyone is paired up, even Woolbright and Cissy Hunt, with the exception of Marcia Mae. She may be the "last lady," anticipating Walker Percy's *The Last Gentleman,* for she can find neither a satisfying niche outside the tradition she has grown up in, nor—like the lost hound—can she forget.

Race, Moment, Milieu

In her review of the novel for the *Yale Review* Dorothy Van Ghent praised Elizabeth Spencer's creation of the "essential illusion, the illusion of life lived, of a process wrought in the synapses and felt in the pulses," and noted that the book embodies Taine's famous dictum about the nature of literature.[13] Indeed, *The Voice at the Back Door* flows from Spencer's deepest understanding of the "race, moment and milieu" that formed the American South in the mid–twentieth century, and in shaping her narrative reflecting the culture she gives her readers not only a richly detailed portrait of the South but, indirectly, an insight into how she—artist, white Southerner, female—viewed that society in the 1950s.

One cannot fail to notice, for example, that the circumstance of Marcia Mae Hunt at the conclusion of the novel resembles Spencer's own in 1955 when she returned from Italy to Mississippi to find that she "didn't belong there any more." The book poignantly reflects Spencer's dismay over the worsening tensions dividing the society in the 1950s, but it does not advance preachments or analyses of caste and class in the South. Rather, Spencer stages a full-scale local scene and imagines dramatically the background, motives, memories, ambitions, and regrets of her cast of characters. In writing the novel, she evinces an admirable "negative capability," which allows her to enter sympathetically the widely varying roles she depicts. In fact, as she said to Charles Bunting, she was not interested in generalizing about the South, but in making it specific. Further, she added, her writing the book "was partially motivated by desire to straighten my own thinking out. I'd been brought up in a very

traditional Southern atmosphere, though many people within that
traditional pattern were at variance with each other privately among
themselves and within their own most private conversations, but if
an outsider came, they would probably never express these things
in the sense they would privately."[14] Spencer's observation bears out
the comment of John Dollard in his 1957 preface to his 1937 classic,
Caste and Class in a Southern Town: "The significant, the truly ex-
planatory, data on the South is hidden behind great sets of defensive
habits. Much of the relevant material can appear only in intimate
relations where fear is reduced. The relation of friendship is such a
one; the psychoanalytic relation, another. Where friendships must
be formed or patients acquired in order to sample adequately, the
difficulties are grave indeed."[15]

With an insider's firsthand knowledge of the society, Spencer was
admirably situated to write *Voice at the Back Door,* which took its
title, according to Spencer, from the practice of Negroes who, when
in difficulty, came to the white's back door and called out, then
waited silently. As Tinker Harper thinks in the novel, "It is part
of the consciousness of a Southern household that a Negro is calling
at the back door in the night" (83). The title refers as well to the
voice of conscience that unrelentingly hails the Southern segrega-
tionist tradition. In confronting "moment and milieu," Spencer
sought to come to grips with the human racial identity, to fathom
what was intrinsically human, whatever the color of one's skin. She
explained what the process of creating the novel meant for her: "A
story is a process of discovery to the writer as well as to the reader,
and you go along with your story and you wind up different yourself,
I often feel, from what you started out, and I think the book did
that for me personally."[16]

Spencer's pursuit of her subject of racial relations rarely takes a
discursive or didactic turn, however. Rather, she employs a great
many different novelistic devices and shows a sophisticated technical
control of their uses. The novel has a nearly seamless plot, vivid
imagery and characterizing detail, credible dialogue, and, notably,
a variety of tonal shifts that give the narrative subtlety and resonance.
Her handling of point of view, which determines these tonal shifts,
warrants the close attention of one wishing to understand her narrative method.

The novel is narrated in the omniscient third person by one who
occasionally, in the traditional manner, interprets thoughts and

actions as well as reports scenic details. The concluding paragraphs of chapter one illustrate clearly both of these functions of the narrator in the account of Travis Brevard's thoughts as he drives into Lacey and in the description of his overt, exterior actions as he walks into Harper's store. Even more frequent in the novel than this traditional omniscience, however, is narration that takes the form of a filter consciousness, in which the third-person exposition is delivered through the dramatized point of view and language of a character. For example, Spencer portrays Marcia Mae's mother, Nan Hunt, in the third person, but in prose that reflects the character's own voice:

She felt that she had failed Marcia Mae by not finding some way to impart a knowledge she herself obviously possessed in quantity, as witness the darling dazzling time she had had as a girl, the foresight she had shown in selecting a man who would amount to something, to say nothing of how wisely she had weighed her assets when she had made her choice. (36–37)

Similarly, the thoughts of Cissy Hunt as she returns from an evening with beau Kerney Woolbright are described in language that subtly reflects Cissy's dialogue just preceding: "She could go on like this for hours, without even thinking about it. She thought it was disgusting, but it pleased him immensely. And he was supposed to be so smart, too. She could never figure it out" (45). Kerney Woolbright's tendency to rhetorical flourish and romantic aggrandizement is exposed more clearly through interior narration than in either his dialogue or actions. Seeing Nan Hunt, he thinks: "The hand on his sleeve, not small, more strong than weak, was still of an indescribable fragility, and the whole woman like a flower nurtured to that perfect bloom which, inexchangeable for any other, is flawed only by its surroundings: it is a trifle too heavy for its stem, and what climate yields its proper airs?" (199). The result of the method is a heightening of the characterization and thus of the psychological realism of the novel. Employing the limited omniscient point of view of many different characters, Spencer shows—rather than tells—her vivid story.

As in her earlier novels, Spencer also fleshes out the realistic detail of *The Voice at the Back Door* with numerous flashbacks, the most significant being the story of Robinson Dozer. She includes many shorter vignettes, too, such as the story of Duncan Harper's father and his eccentric Uncle Phillip. Smoothly, encapsulating memory within memory, Spencer shows Harper remembering his father, who is briefly sketched as he remembers the arrival in Lacey of Jason Hunt years earlier: ". . . back in the old days Hunts used to come to town on Saturday in a wagon, wearing shoes for the first time that week. But Jason had been a smart one: he had set out to marry a Standsbury, and he had done it" (185).

Another element of the "race, moment, and milieu" that Spencer deliberately evokes in the novel is the contemporaneous literary milieu. Duncan Harper reads books, a fact that goes far to explain why he differs so from his townsmen. Idealism, based partly on what they have read, draws Woolbright and Harper together at the outset. When they are confronted with the news that Beck Dozer may be threatened with a lynching, Harper tells his friend that he's never seen a lynching, to which Woolbright replies: "I never did either. . . . All I know is what I read in William Faulkner" (93). David G. Pugh detects several possible implicit acknowledgments of Faulkner's presence in the novel in such details as Jason's name ("there may be some shrewd overtones of the hardware store in Faulkner's *The Sound and the Fury*"),[17] but what is even more shrewd about Spencer's technique here is her development in her characters of a deliberate awareness of Faulkner and other Southern writers. She co-opts the Faulkner presence by dramatizing it as a force within the novel itself. As Van Ghent notes in her review, "Faulkner is already a part of what the characters in this novel know, and their own moment is different."[18]

The "moment" for the central male characters of this novel is the South of the 1950s, a place of extraordinary conflict and tension but finally their home, the place where they will test their manhood and find their accommodation between self and society. With the exception of Marcia Mae Hunt, the female characters, too, work out their destiny in Lacey, which chiefly means for them finding their place in family and community. Their identities are adjunct to their husbands', and their moral testing comes in their choice of a marital partner. Marcia Mae stands out as the important exception; for her, Lacey is no longer a potential home, and marriage is not her destiny. Like Elinor Dudley Gerrard, who figures in both of Spencer's earlier novels, Marcia Mae Hunt does not find a satisfying identify or fulfillment in Mississippi. The failures of both characters are muted, however, because they occupy the periphery of the central action. Rather, it is a young man's struggle for integrity that forms the dramatic focus of all three Mississippi novels. In her next major works of fiction, however, Spencer would turn her attention to a woman's search for wholeness, for integrity. In these books she portrays heroines whose most formidable adversaries are psychological, not societal, and whose victories depend upon the assertion, rather than the bridling, of the independent self.

Chapter Five
Italian Departure

In 1960 Elizabeth Spencer published her fourth novel, *The Light in the Piazza,* to widespread popular and critical attention. The book marks a significant departure from her earlier novels, all of which are centered upon male protagonists whose stories take place in Mississippi. Kinloch Armstrong and Amos Dudley contend with a sense of private destiny that overshadows relations with wives and others drawn into their quest. They struggle to fulfill the identities they envision for themselves, and in doing so they come to realize the sacrifice of intimacy with others that their egoism demands. The classic theme of the humanizing of the hero is given a broader context in the character of Duncan Harper, a man caught in a web of racial tensions and conflicting values in a small Mississippi town. Beginning with Margaret Johnson of *The Light in the Piazza,* however, and continuing with a variety of characters in succeeding novels and stories, Spencer has created a diverse group of female protagonists who move in a more problematic and complicated world than that of her earlier fiction. Whereas the culmination of her heroes' journeys is the recognition that one must learn to live with conflicting visions of life and acquiesce to uncertainty, it is precisely the ambiguous self that marks the starting point for the heroines.

Finding a New Vision

In talking about the period between the writing of *The Voice at the Back Door* and *The Light in the Piazza,* Spencer has discussed the difficulty of making the transition from her early Southern works to the later works with international settings.

What am I doing in a larger sense? I think I never questioned this . . . until the whole first phase of my work was . . . over with, the three Southern novels and the group of Southern stories about Southern themes. But then I began to see myself, because of having married an Englishman and living outside the South, as being no longer part of the Southern

66

locale in a strictly realistic way and having to find my place in a world that was geographically bigger than that and was different from that. So I began to work out both stories and situations that would illuminate that larger world and would help me find my place in it. That's why it was so difficult at first.[1]

Finding a controlling vision, a perspective on this larger world, was the necessity facing Spencer—the essential next step if she were to continue to write. The vision did not come easily, as she explains: "Everything I began went concentric. It wobbled. I couldn't find the proper center." And then the stories did start to come, stories about women who in various ways and settings seek and find a controlling vision for their lives. The fiction and the creator fed upon and nourished each other. "I think the personal result of all these later books and stories I've done," Spencer observes, "has been that I feel much more secure in being able to move and live, actually find life. . . ."[2]

When Spencer discussed her literary career with Broadwell and Hoag in 1980, eight years after the Bunting interview, she described a pattern of characterization extending from Margaret Johnson of *The Light in the Piazza* to Julia Garrett of the 1972 novel *The Snare*.

Over the years, as I wrote about women characters—primarily from Margaret Johnson on—I searched for women who could sustain a weight of experience, both intellectual and emotional. I think that often the women characters I found did not do this. For example, Margaret Johnson's triumph was . . . a fantasy that could explode five minutes after the book was over. Then Martha Ingram [*Knights and Dragons*] . . . had a weakness in her nature that kept her from throwing off her obsession. And Catherine in *No Place for an Angel* had to retreat almost out of life in order to sustain herself. But when I finally discovered Julia, I found in her a person who could take it and survive.[3]

The intellectual and emotional experience Spencer portrays in a number of these characters is a classic female bind frequently discussed in recent years, the difficulty for a woman of reconciling her human need for a separate identity with a societal definition of *feminine* in which sacrifice of the self for family and others is required.

The conflicts that Spencer's heroines experience between inner need and social reality are not, however, exclusively female territory. These characters express the universal modern experience of the self torn between a private, self-conscious inner life and a compromised outer life that demands the forfeiture of consciousness and separateness—the preeminent theme of twentieth-century literature. As Josephine Hendin discusses in her study of American fiction since 1945, the "sense of vulnerability distinctive to women in nineteenth-century novels is almost universally shared by current male heroes."[4] It is, nonetheless, the experience of women, and particularly women who are caught between two cultures, that Spencer paradigmatically employs to depict contemporary alienation.

Like ladies imprisoned in towers, Spencer's heroines seem "enclosed" women, and indeed the words *closed, enclosed,* and *confined* often appear in the texts. In the case of Martha Ingram, or Nancy Lewis in the story "Ship Island: The Story of a Mermaid," lonely isolation initially results from the circumscribed role available to a woman in society. Her withdrawal is mainly reactive, an emotional numbing that seems the only response possible to an expectation that she exist solely to attract, learn from, or take care of another. Similarly, Margaret Johnson's self-enclosure comes partly as a retreat from her husband, Noel, as Catherine Sasser's withdrawal comes as an escape from her husband. But, ultimately, the stronger motive for the action of these women, especially the spiritual and psychological journey of Julia Garrett, is the discovery and assertion of the self.

As Spencer's male hero's quest seems to be the recognition of the other, the challenge for the female protagonist is the acknowledgment and acceptance of her separate self. Whatever her circumstances of ladyhood, whether enthroned upon a pedestal or imprisoned by fears and obsessions, the heroine moves from passive acquiescence to active choice. In pursuing selfhood she finds her freedom. In Spencer's vision, the free woman stands inevitably apart from the world—a woman enclosed, but with a difference. She has freed herself from both the easily refused demands of social convention and the more compelling demands of the beloved. For these heroines the quest that ultimately tests one's courage and integrity is not the pursuit of self-denial, but of self-possession. One of the earliest examples is the protagonist of Spencer's 1960s novella *The Light in the Piazza*.

Triumph in the Piazza

The Light in the Piazza is the story of a woman's fulfillment of a dream. Margaret Johnson's dream is wholly conventional, maternal:

that her daughter Clara, who suffered a childhood accident leaving her with the mind of a ten-year old, should have a normal life. For years, however, the dream has put her in conflict with her husband. Ever a pragmatic American, Noel Johnson has long accepted the verdict of the doctors that Clara will mentally remain a child. Margaret does not accept the diagnosis and, as her only acts of wifely disobedience, has through the years continued to try "experiments" to ease Clara into life's mainstream. Her repeated failures have almost scotched the dream, but one brilliant summer in Italy resurrects it. "Nobody with a dream should come to Italy," Margaret thinks. "No matter how dead and buried the dream is thought to be, in Italy it will rise and walk again."[5]

Many reviewers noted that the novel takes its place in a time-honored subgenre of Anglo-American fiction—the traveler in Italy. "Whether it is carried on by a robust poet like Robert Browning, a chilblained London schoolmistress or an American Puritan," wrote Isa Kapp, "the love affair between the hopeful Anglo-Saxon imagination and the physical beauty of Italy never ends."[6] Granville Hicks, like most other reviewers, including Mark Schorer on the book's dust jacket, commented on aspects of the novel that recall Henry James's international novels, though Hicks concluded that "the spirit of the book is perhaps closer to E. M. Forster" than to James.[7] Spencer has spoken of her admiration for Forster's fiction, dating from her Nashville days,[8] and she has acknowledged the readiness with which critics have applied the Jamesian comparison, but from her account, she was not "particularly conscious of Henry James" when she wrote the novel. "In fact," she said, "to me that story was more the sort of thing Boccaccio might have done in *The Decameron*, a little tall tale to satirize Florence. *The Light in the Piazza* is really a comedy."[9]

In fact, the novel's central movement traces the development of a romance and of Margaret's heroic assertion of her old dream for Clara. When Clara attracts the attention of an eligible young Italian, Margaret is at first annoyed. As Clara and Fabrizio Naccarelli grow increasingly attached to each other, she begins to allow herself a bit of idle fantasy. But as the courtship progresses, Margaret suddenly becomes frightened of the consequences, fearful of impending decisions that will inevitably be demanded by Fabrizio and his family, fearful most of all of her collaboration in a courtship that will draw the wrath of her husband. Hurriedly she and Clara leave Florence for Rome. After some weeks of anguish for Clara, who misses Fabrizio and begs to make the promised return to Florence, Margaret makes the fateful decision to return.

In the novels of James the marriage game, played out by Americans with Italians in Italy, tests every moral and social fiber of the protagonists; no less so in *The Light in the Piazza*. Like James's heroines, Margaret is hopeful (but not sure) that she is right in her judgment of people, but unlike her fictional predecessors her action is rather more decisive than evasive. Armed only with courage to act, she puts obedient ladyhood behind her and becomes a woman. "What is it, to reach a decision? Is it like walking down a long Florentine street where, at the very end, a dim shape is waiting until you get there. When Mrs. Johnson finally reached this street and saw what was ahead, she moved steadily forward to see it at long last up close. What was it? Well, nothing monstrous, it seemed; but human, with a face much like her own, that of a woman who loved her daughter and longed for her happiness" (86).

The "double" whom Margaret encounters metaphorically on the streets of Florence presents an interesting reversal of a similar encounter in Henry James's "The Jolly Corner." Whereas James's Spencer Brydon, a man who has spent nearly a lifetime in Europe, returns to the United States to try to discover what he might have become if he had stayed in New York, Margaret Johnson discovers her heretofore unrealized self in Italy. The "other face" for Margaret, as for Brydon, is one of willful assertiveness, but the face she glimpses takes a loving, wholly human form, not monstrous like the shape Brydon apprehends. The egoism manifest in Margaret's Florentine double complements the self-sacrificing side of her maternal nature.

Many narrative and descriptive details in the novel express the risk and heroism represented by Margaret's decision to promote the marriage of Clara and Fabrizio. In the opening episodes, light imagery, like a spotlight focusing upon the Johnsons and the Naccarellis in the piazza, suggests an arena for testing. Nearby Cellini's Perseus triumphantly holds aloft the Medusa's head. On the occasion when Margaret meets Signor Naccarelli, Fabrizio's father, they witness a holiday ceremony, complete with medieval cannons firing. Suddenly, in a burst of light almost obscured by the sun—like the central image of *Fire in the Morning*—a man falls. Not until the conclusion do Margaret and the reader discover the outcome of the accident. "He died," Signor Naccarelli replies to Margaret's inquiry, and at last one senses through the symbolism the full extent of risk in stumbling into Italian rituals and ceremonies. From the beginning the marriage game had been for keeps, however romantic or comic its progression, and the stakes were Margaret's life—her daughter, her husband, and her pride. "She had played single-handed and unadvised a tricky game in a foreign country, and she had managed to realize from it the dearest wish of her heart" (107).

The action of the novel is rich in irony and allusion, not the least of which is the fact that Margaret's marriage plot, a strategy as old as the novel for exchanging a woman's freedom for security, actually exchanges mother and daughter's security for their freedom. Margaret finds her solitary power and uses it, and Clara is freed from hopeless dependence. It is supremely ironic—and nearly comic— that from all the evidence that Margaret can gather, the wifehood that awaits Clara is perfectly suited to a ten-year-old's mentality. The role of the Naccarelli women follows extremely traditional lines. Above all, the bride should be sheltered and innocent. Doubtless Clara Johnson is the last twenty-six-year-old girl to visit Italy with her "innocence" unquestionably intact. Innocence had begun to slip even in Daisy Miller's nineteenth-century Rome. As an Italian wife, Clara will remain in the home, pleasing and obedient to her husband. Her principal function will be motherhood, and with a well-to-do family like the Naccarellis to provide nurses and servants, and a mother-in-law whose arms ache to hold a baby, Clara's good physical and genetic health equips her perfectly to life happily ever afterward.

From what Margaret sees, Clara will be pampered and adored by a family clan that requires nothing beyond cheerfulness, love, and her wholehearted acceptance of their way of life. Least among Margaret's fears is that Clara will be unable to measure up to the Naccarellis' expectations. In fact, much earlier, at the point at which she decides to return to Florence and take up her plan, Margaret observes that a "warm, classic dignity" has come to Clara, that "no matter whether she could do long division or not, she was a woman" (59).

The daughter will never be a woman in her mother's mold, however. In accomplishing Clara's chance for womanhood, Margaret engages in intricate calculation and artifice far beyond the ken of a ten-year-old mentality. Taking the role that traditionally would have been played by her businessman husband, Margaret represents the family in the marriage negotiations with Signor Naccarelli. With wit and courage she plays the "tricky game," and though she is bested in the dowry bargaining, she wins the match for Clara. Her weapons are not maternal feelings or purity of heart, but quite the opposite. She carries the day because she devises a shrewd strategy and takes bold action. Indeed, when she returns to Florence, having set her mind upon the marriage, she *invades* the city—"whether Florence knew it or not" (64). Margaret intuits that her risk will pay off, not only in a better life for Clara but a chance for renewal of her own marriage. She thinks that after Noel gets beyond shock and anger at his daughter's marriage, he will "grow quiet at last, and in the quiet, even Margaret Johnson had not yet dared to imagine what sort of life, what degree of delight in it, they might not be able to discover (rediscover?) together" (109). In the end Margaret is confident that she has done "the right thing." Although the ethical matter of her decision is left ambiguous in the novel, the courage of her action is unmistakable. As Spencer herself has said of her: "She liberated herself with her decision to push through that marriage. This gesture shows that Margaret Johnson will not be dominated, not by her husband, her doctor, her culture—or even by honesty."[10]

Reviewing the novel in the *New York Times Book Review*, Elizabeth Janeway liked everything about the book but its ending. Specifically, she objected not to the event of Clara and Farbrizio's marriage, which she found "entirely likely," but to "the emotional tone of the event. For everything in the story seems to point to this being a *happy* ending. This is where the uneasiness sets in." Janeway faults Spencer for not qualifying the comedy of the ending, the tone of the happiness, which Janeway highly suspects belongs to fairy tales but not to realistic stories of a retarded girl's marriage to a quite normal Italian. "Why," she asks, "does no bell toll for a moment in the background, no magpie fly the wrong way across the road, to hint that life never freezes into simplicity and that 'a happy ending' is only the beginning of something else?"[11]

There are, of course, many intimations of just such sinister realities lurking beneath the brightly lit surface of Florence. They are there for the reader to see, even though Margaret Johnson largely does not see them, either because she cannot or will not. Janeway's commentary seems to miss the irony implicit in Margaret's point of view, the limited omniscient controlling point of view through which the action is filtered. With only a few slight exceptions in the narration, *The Light in the Piazza* is Margaret Johnson's story, and what the reader views directly is seen through her eyes. She is a dramatized—and hence to some extent an unreliable—narrator, but her lapses clearly are not Spencer's. Indeed, Spencer furnishes numerous details that are just the sort of bell-and-bird clues that Janeway mentions, by which the reader is given to understand that malevolence can threaten the romantic interlude at any moment. The cannon fire that accidentally kills the onlooker is a vivid example, reminiscent of Henry James's ironies, of a narrative detail that reveals more to the reader than it does to Margaret Johnson. There are other signs of a threatening world lurking only slightly beyond Clara and Fabrizio's idyll. A cruelly frightening and exploitative carriage driver and a bullying Signor Naccarelli both represent other aspects of the Latin nature than the charming boyishness of Fabrizio and the motherly nurturance of Signora Naccarelli.

Margaret's is a willed optimism that almost certainly is shortsighted. Her "reading" of her husband's thoughts and actions (with a transoceanic extrasensory perception) and her inferences about Signor Naccarelli's mind at work are reasonable and convincing, but they are clearly the character's, not Spencer's, interpretations. We watch Margaret's crafty and shrewd approach to the marriage of her daughter, but we see a woman whose heart, more than her head, predominates in the shaping of her dream for Clara. In the early days of the courtship, before she decides to pursue the marriage plan, she seeks the advice of a Presbyterian minister, to whom she tells a half-true story about the problems that bother her in contemplating the possible marriage. His dour reply, "I urge ye both to make very careful use of your brains" (49), dints neither Clara's infirmity nor Margaret's hopefulness for her daughter's future.

Symbolically, Spencer presses the revelation that much of Margaret Johnson's seeing goes no further than surfaces. Perhaps she senses a bit uneasily that sinister depths do exist, but she refuses to let such doubt deter her from her pursuit of Clara's happiness. In the closing scene, however, even Margaret senses the peril that the future may hold. Cellini's famous statue of Perseus, holding aloft the Medusa's head, prominently occupies the piazza setting in both the opening and closing scenes of the novel. Perseus, the model of heroic triumph, reflects Margaret's own heroic undertaking, but the Medusa, no less a model of victimization and defeat, represents the undeniable other side of the hero's victory. One is reminded here of Eudora Welty's use of the Perseus-Medusa figures at the

conclusion of *The Golden Apples,* for Margaret Johnson, like Virgie
Rainey, senses the implicit presence of defeat in the image of triumph.
Margaret's confident assertion to Signor Naccarelli that she has done
"the right thing" is contradicted by a painful memory that suddenly
comes to her. She remembers the man struck by the cannon, and
his futile efforts to rise. His vulnerability and mortality are unsettling for Margaret, but the novel ends with her happy moment
intact. Nothing about the final scene suggests, though, that the
future will neatly and simplistically fulfill Margaret's happy-ever-
afterward dream for Clara.

Of all the illusory surfaces in the novel, no detail is more problematic than the light that bathes the Italian city. One would
suppose that, in such brilliance, seeing might easily be assured. But
the sunlight can mask, as well as reveal, as Margaret recognizes
with the cannon's blast. The most overtly duplicitous act in the
novel, which comes not at an Italian's but at Margaret's hand,
involves Clara, whose name means clarity and brightness. Whereas
all other appearances may be illusions, as Margaret vaguely knows
and acknowledges, the appearance of a beautiful, blond, *normal* Clara
is sadly, surely false. About this illusion, neither Margaret nor the
reader requires subtle clues and inferences. Through such direct and
oblique details, Spencer leaves little doubt that "triumph" and "light"
may as well turn out to be Margaret's fantasy as her truth.

The Composition and
Reception of the Novel

In discussing the ending of the novel Spencer has said she concluded the story without knowing whether "Clara's marriage will
last." She went on, "what happened is that I had to drop the story
when I did because it had reached a point of absolute balance. . . .
So how long Margaret Johnson's triumph lasted, I don't know."[12]
Several times Spencer has talked of the relationship of *The Light in
the Piazza* to sculpture, representing as it does an art object toward
which a viewer can take many different perspectives. "You can walk
around *The Light in the Piazza;* you can look at it from this angle,
from that angle, and it never completely gives up its final answer;
you know, 'Was she right; was she wrong?' You get all this sort of
effect without ever really getting an answer, but it gives off a certain
solidity just the same."[13] At the conclusion of the novel the reader

is like a viewer who has encircled a piece of sculpture. Spencer's framing is precise, and the reader returns at the end of the story to the piazza, to the German tourists' trying to catch an image with their cameras, to the statue of Perseus, and, over everything, the light. Paralleling Margaret's ethical problem within the story is the reader's problem of how best to see and understand the world Spencer shows us through Margaret's eyes. The effort to see—for Margaret and the reader—reveals as much of nuance and shadow as of "final answer" and light. Spencer's strategic closure at the moment when Margaret realizes her dream completes a comedy, as the author herself has said, but it is a comedy rich in suggestiveness about the world that impinges upon this Italian romance.

On several different occasions Spencer has talked of the original central impressions that gave rise to *The Light in the Piazza*. In a conversation reported by Hilton Anderson she spoke of having with her husband once seen a woman with a daughter, who "while sweet and attractive, seemed retarded. The girl struck up and enjoyed, nonetheless, a flirtation with an Italian waiter." Her husband is said to have remarked that, "as far as Italy was concerned, there need be no check to the romance." Anderson also mentions Spencer's recollection that at another time she watched a young woman run across the piazza, an incident that furnished the "germ of the book."[14] Ten years later, discussing her use of myths and fairy tales, she speaks of using tales sometimes as framing devices. "In *The Light in the Piazza*," she says, "the story sprang out of the tale of the princess with the harelip and the prince who fell in love with her. Love being blind, he could not see her defect."[15] Spencer also describes to Josephine Haley one other impression that she drew upon in creating her story. "The mother in *The Light in the Piazza*—I know I've seen her somewhere before. I can see her in my mind's eye in navy blue with that kind of short blond hair that women have when they get rinses, walking off down the street. I can't place that woman, but I can see every detail about her. It was out of that impression that the whole character developed. I'm a great believer in central impressions. You have to trust that—everything develops from that."[16]

Spencer's direction toward comedy may be partly explained by these germinating impressions and by her initial intention to write a short story "as a sort of an amusement in six weeks." At the urging of a friend, she sent the early draft to the *New Yorker,* which turned it down. Then, at the friend's further urging, she revised it and sent it again to the *New Yorker,* which published it on 18 June 1960. "Then came the movie contracts and the book clubs. So the book was really a financial success."[17] The irony of having spent only a month or so on a piece that had enormous success, that has come to be the work for which she is best known, has been noted by Spencer. Still, she says, "I try to be generous. . . . I'm glad [readers] at least have read that."[18]

In addition to winning a $10,000 McGraw-Hill Fiction Award and a sizable movie contract with M-G-M,[19] *The Light in the Piazza* received excellent reviews from book critics. Orville Prescott, who had praised Spencer's earlier work, wrote in the *New York Times* that "this is one of the four or five best novels of 1960."[20] In the *New Republic* Susan M. Black found it "at once the shortest and the best new novel I have read this year."[21] Many critics, in fact, approvingly noted the book's brevity. "A lesser novelist could have turned this plot into an agonizingly long chronicle of human tragedy," wrote Shirley Spieckerman in the *New Mexico Quarterly,* and Phoebe Adams in the *Atlantic Monthly* admired Spencer's "wily construction" and "flawlessly precise choice of words," by which she had "compressed a story that most novelists would make the occasion of a three-decked monstrosity."[22] The *Time* reviewer liked the ending, finding it "delicately contrived and impeccably honest."[23] Max Cosman in *Commonweal* praised "the book's control of sentiment. There is never a slopping over into sentimentality."[24] Just this control, however, led Virgilia Peterson to a different conclusion: "Out of what in real life could only have been a macabre situation, Miss Spencer has spun a fiction too worldly, too shiny, too neat, to touch the heart."[25] Granville Hicks and Isa Kapp, mentioned earlier, both praised the novel; indeed, with the exception of some of the eastern literary journals the book drew strongly approving reviews from all quarters.[26]

The Light in the Piazza was Spencer's first published work set outside the South. By her own account, it represented an important change for her, a widening of horizon. In an interview with John Griffin Jones she says that the writing of the book, as well as its reception by the critics, convinced her that she should " 'take a wider scope on things.' . . . So then I went on and did things that challenged me in a new way. . . . The outer world seemed to interest me more. . . . It seemed to give me a bigger horizon."[27]

Although she does not mention it in the interview, another significant change marked by *The Light in the Piazza* was Spencer's turn to female protagonists. It seems likely that their lives, like the world that lay beyond Mississippi, offered her "a wider scope on things."

Chapter Six
Two Women Adrift

After the publication of *The Light in the Piazza* Spencer wrote a series of stories and novels in the 1960s and 1970s in which she portrays characters considerably more vulnerable than Margaret Johnson, women whose efforts to establish a self and achieve a measure of freedom are often desperate and convoluted. The protagonists of the extended short story "Ship Island" and the novella *Knights and Dragons* win victories more muted than Johnson's, but then, as women, they undertake perhaps a more ambitious challenge than hers—action in behalf of the self. These women, like the later heroines of *No Place for an Angel* and *The Snare,* frequently exist in a kind of limbo, expressing through their fictional lives what Rachel M. Brownstein in *Becoming a Heroine* has called a pattern of "thinking simultaneously about what it is to be a woman and how to choose what and who and how to be." In her discussion of the portrayal of women in novels since the eighteenth century, Brownstein notes the centrality of questions about whether "intimacy and identity can be achieved at once, and whether they are mutually exclusive, entirely desirable, and, indeed, other than imaginary." Like the classic novelists Brownstein studies, Elizabeth Spencer "explores the connections between the inner self and its outward manifestations— between the personal and the social, the private and the public— by focusing on a woman complexly connected to others, who must depend, to distinguish herself, on the gender that delimits her life."[1]

One of Spencer's earliest portraits of a heroine adrift, one who tries to find a mooring without sacrificing her individuality, is Nancy Lewis in "Ship Island: The Story of a Mermaid." Originally published in the *New Yorker* in 1964, the story contributes the title to the collection *Ship Island and Other Stories* (1968) and appears in *The Stories of Elizabeth Spencer* (1981). Spencer has often expressed her fondness for the story. She told Charles Bunting, "For some reason, that story stays with me, I don't know why,"[2] and she explained in more detail to J. G. Jones, "That was a very significant story for me. I think it's about my favorite of my stories. But it started a new theme in my work. I don't quite know how to put it, but it was the same thing in *The Snare*. . . . It's that women feel themselves very often imprisoned by what people expect of them. . . . Some people mount rebellion: they are not going to put up with it. This has come to the surface in many aspects of my later work. That story was what started it. I just thought it had a compelling feeling. I felt it was very sensual and very right, and I like it a lot."[3]

A Mermaid

In "Ship Island," Nancy Lewis, a young woman who has spent two years in a "cow college in Arkansas," has recently moved with her family to the Mississippi Gulf Coast. Although she quickly meets and begins to date a local boy who introduces her to his university crowd of friends, Nancy feels alien and threatened. Shortly after moving, Nancy began the summer with the intention of studying French, but soon she "could no longer find herself in relation to the girl who had sought out such a good place to study, had sharpened the pencils and opened the book and sat down to bend over it."[4] What happens is that Nancy loses her grip on the "perfect girl" dream of success as the task of pleasing others and denying herself finally exhausts her. Leading to her break with the "normal" world, when she impulsively joins two strange men for a trip to New Orleans, is a series of unsettling revelations. She discovers that, of all the people around her, no one knows her. Only the young neighbor, Bernard Nattier, a little boy she fights with rocks and oyster shells, finally reaches her with an impulsive expression of love. Her parents, her boyfriend Rob, everyone else, sees only the surface—blue eyes and pale, untanned skin.

On the beach one day Nancy is shocked by a blistering rain, but her report is dismissed by her mother, who "never heard of such a thing." Similarly, her alcoholic father signals his disdain with the display of a grinning china donkey bearing the message, "If you really want to look like me—Just keep right on talking." By all accounts Rob Acklen should be the perfect catch for a girl like Nancy, but "he, with his Phi Beta Kappa key and his good level head and his wonderful prospects, found everything she told about herself cute, funny, absurd" (*St,* 91). An invitation to a party at Rob's friends brings the following exchange, in which Rob, despite a show of understanding, patronizingly ignores her.

"What did you say?" he asked her.
"Nothing."
"You just don't want to go?"
"No, I don't much want to go."
"Well, then, we won't stay long." (*St*, 96)

Rob, seemingly immune to the mosquitoes that assault Nancy, likes to make love on Ship Island or some bayou, and his snobbish friends seem to her so many human mosquitoes. "They'll sting me till I crumple up and die, she thought" (*St*, 100). Like a forsaken mermaid caught in a human snare, Nancy escapes Rob's party at the Fishnet nightclub and retreats to the bar. Finding there a man she recognizes from her morning on the beach when the hot rain fell, she strikes up a conversation. "What's your name?" he asks. " 'Nothing,' she said by accident." The inadvertent reply expresses Nancy's desperation. Bolstered by finding someone who verifies her strange experience of the stinging rain ("he positively seemed to Nancy to be her own identity"), she goes with him and his friend when, in a childlike game, they propose to take her wherever in the world she wants to go. New Orleans's image of exotic strangeness has long appealed to her, perhaps because it seems to her a more companionable home for her own strangeness, and so it is to New Orleans that they drive in a yellow Cadillac. There Nancy finds her exotic element, which turns out to have its dangers, too. In the French Quarter the two men quarrel, and the friend Dennis takes Nancy as spoils. "What he had to say to her was nothing she hadn't heard before, nothing she hadn't already been given more or less to understand from mosquitoes, people, life-in-general, and the rain out of the sky. It was just that he said it in a final sort of way—that was all" (*St*, 109).

If Nancy harbored romantic fantasies, she returns home without them, with big bruises on her face and body to show for her adventure. What is interesting about the conclusion of the story, however, is her response to Rob's questioning of her motive for running away. She doesn't refute his claims that he has liked her, "tried his best" to be nice to her, but neither does she recant her rejection of all the numbing niceness. " 'I guess it's just the way I am,' Nancy murmured. 'I just run off sometimes.' "

Spencer draws upon the familiar mythic figure of the mermaid to expose Nancy's radical sense of loneliness and differentness from the "human" world she inhabits. In fact, Spencer has said she read all she could find "about mermaids—about their affinity for sailors, their breathing under water, their unhappiness when on land, all of that." She has noted that she quite deliberately "worked those ideas into the fabric" of the story.[5] She accomplishes the weaving together of allusion and realistic detail through a filtered, third-person narration. Through the heightened consciousness of Nancy, Spencer traces the young woman's growing anxiety and desperation until the moment when Rob confronts her. Then, she signals Nancy's mental confusion and panic in a surrealistic collage of images, yoked together in a long rhythmical sentence:

Her father at last successfully reached the donkey, but he fell in the middle of the rug, while Nancy, on the stair landing, smelling seaweed, asked herself how a murderous child with swollen jaws happened to mention love, if love is not a fever, and the storm-driven sea struck the open reef and went roaring skyward, splashing a tattered gull that clutched at the blast—but if we will all go there immediately it is safe in the Dupré house, because they have this holy candle. There are hidden bone-cold lairs no one knows of, in rock beneath the sea. She shook her bone-white hair. (*St*, 110)

Imagistically, Nancy leaves her human form and deserts the malevolent world of land and people. "Her voice faded in a deepening glimmer where the human breath is snatched clean away and there are only bubbles, iridescent and pure" (*St*, 110).

Spencer has herself discussed the symbolism of the mermaid in some detail. She explained to Charles Bunting that Nancy exists both as an "ordinary pretty little girl" and as a mythic creature. She mentions several details in the story that point up the extraordinariness of event and character, specifically the scalding rain and Nancy's ability to sleep in water. "Whenever she gets on land, in land situations," says Spencer, "people seem to be insulting her and treating her as an inferior. . . . She feels that she can swim around these people and look in the windows of their houses without being a part of the world they inhabit. On land all kind of bad things happen to her. . . . But when she's in a water situation, she comes into her own." Spencer concludes the critique by noting the intensity of the symbol at the conclusion—"it's as if she dove away" from her boyfriend and found her refuge, her identity, in the sea.[6]

In this story, composed in 1963,[7] Elizabeth Spencer has created
in the compelling image of the half-human mermaid a metaphor of
the female condition that is explored in great richness and depth
by Dorothy Dinnerstein in *The Mermaid and the Minotaur: Sexual
Arrangement and Human Malaise* (1976). Dinnerstein argues that "the
division of responsibility, opportunity, and privilege that prevails
between male and female humans, and the patterns of psychological
interdependence that are implicit in this division" have produced a
"human malaise." We cast men and women into half-human roles,
she writes, perhaps best understood through the imagery of the
mermaid and the minotaur. (Our tendency to adopt such images is
fed by psychological patterns stemming from the female's exclusive
responsibility for child rearing, Dinnerstein maintains.) She characterizes the two controlling images as follows: "The treacherous
mermaid, seductive and impenetrable female representative of the
dark and magic underwater world from which our life comes and
in which we cannot live, lures voyagers to their doom. The fearsome
minotaur, gigantic and eternally infantile offspring of a mother's
unnatural lust, male representative of mindless, greedy power, in-
satiably devours live human flesh."[8]

Although Dinnerstein's mermaid is no gloss of Spencer's Nancy
Lewis, there are some instructive points of similarity between them.
For all her youth and passion and curiosity, Nancy seems to herself
"like a person who wasn't a person—another order of creature passing among or even through them" (*St,* 105). She tries to overcome
her alienation by joining Rob's circle, and by making love, but she
still feels like a fish out of water. To Rob, she callously destroys
their summer romance. When he confronts her with frustration and
displeasure she thinks, "He's coming down deeper and deeper, but
one thing is certain—if he gets down as far as I am, he'll drown"
(*St,* 109). Nancy's answer to her dilemma, however, is like that of
many of Spencer's later heroines. She does not deny her condition,
but chooses to live out her life, wide-eyed and free. Better to live
one's painful condition in harm's way than to relinquish one's identity.

In Jones's 1981 interview of Spencer she speaks of coming to feel
at the time she was writing "Ship Island" an affinity for "waif-like
women that were free. They have no particular ties, or no ties that
are worth holding them, and so they become subject to all kinds
of encounters, influences, choices out in the world. You know,
they've got to find a foothold, they've got to find something to

hold to" (*St,* 122). At the end of "Ship Island" Nancy Lewis has not found the "something to hold to," other than her lonely, separate self. And in Spencer's next work, *Knights and Dragons,* protagonist Martha Ingram too finds only herself at the end of her struggle, though, to be sure, a changed, cleansed, simplified self from the woman who opens the story.

Escape from Knights and Dragons

The novella *Knights and Dragons* was first published in *Redbook,* July 1965, though Laura Barge notes that the magazine editors so revised the story that, according to Spencer, it seemed "hardly recognizable."[9] The work, begun as a short story, was intended originally to appear in a collection of stories. Spencer has said that she was "very tentative" about its publication as a novel, but that her publishers wanted to bring it out separately.[10] The book was published by McGraw-Hill in 1965. When Spencer collected her stories for the 1981 *The Stories of Elizabeth Spencer,* she included *Knights and Dragons,* though not *The Light in the Piazza.*

As in the earlier novella, there are features of theme and technique in *Knights and Dragons* that recall the fiction of Henry James. Tissues of emotional haziness and layers of introspection and perception are evoked in this interior story of a woman imprisoned by fear and guilt. The brilliant Italian setting reflects the poles of experience pulling at the protagonist Martha Ingram. Here as elsewhere throughout her fiction, Spencer is particularly skilled in her evocative and metaphoric depictions of settings. The throbbing, sunlit landscape embodies the energy—sexual and psychological—that propels the characters, and the shadowy, labyrinthine Italian walkways mirror the masks and complexities that exhaust their energies.

Initially, Martha Ingram has come to Italy to escape the psychological tyranny of her husband, Gordon, a mysterious figure who appears in the novel only through the recollections, dreams, half-perceptions, and vague reports of Martha and a number of other characters. Gordon Ingram is an American scholar, a philosopher beloved of his friends, and a mentor to Martha during the ten years of their marriage. Now divorced, Martha is afflicted with the guilty feeling that she has somehow betrayed him, that in refusing to live her life for him she is destroying him. More powerful than the guilt, however, is her fear that ultimately she will not be able to resist his menacing power.

Spencer's evocation of Gordon is strikingly like that of Dinnerstein's definition of the minotaur, and indeed he is depicted in
imagery as the dragon who threatens Martha. She fears that he will
"rise up out of the ground and snap at her," and imagines that she
can hear him across the ocean "rumbling and growling, breathing
out complaining letters and worried messengers" (*St,* 129). George
Hartwell, her employer at the U.S. cultural office further verifies
the image of Gordon, seeing in a photograph of him a "huge figure,"
with "gross hands," "shaggy head, and big, awkwardly tilted feet"
(*St,* 129). Imagining the former husband as a dragon makes Martha
even more fascinating to George, who is attracted by her vulnerability and the flattering prospect that he may rescue her from all
that threatens her. To him, she is "sequestered" in an apartment
that is reached by "devious stairways, corridors."

Martha does not regard herself as some mythic or medieval lady,
however, but rather as "someone, not unusual, who had, with the
total and deep sincerity of youth, made a mistake; now, the mistake
paid for, agonizingly paid for, the only question was of finding a
workable compromise with life" (*St,* 143). The novel opens to a
breaking of Martha's emotional stalemate with the arrival of a group
of Americans on cultural exchange. Among these are the young
couple Rita and Jim Wilbourne, an economist who eventually does
play, in an ironic way, the knight's role in the release of Martha
from her past. There are also the Cogginses—Richard, who has
come to lecture the Italians on Italian opera, and amazingly wins
their admiration and affection during his stay; his wife, Dorothy;
and his daughter, Jean, a kind of cross between *The Light in the
Piazza*'s Clara Johnson and Nabokov's Lolita, who attracts Italians
and Jim Wilbourne alike.

To Jim, Martha seems aloof, distracted—"enclosed," he says. He
upsets her carefully wrought equilibrium with a story about her
former husband's having been in an accident, a story that proves to
be false but fateful. It lures Martha into imagining Gordon Ingram's
destruction and, thereby, into imagining the possibility of ridding
her life of his influence. Risking hurt, even madness, she reaches
out to Jim, taking him as lover, using the sexual energy, as well
as the imaginative energy aroused by the story of Gordon's accident,
to effect her "workable compromise with life."

The erstwhile knight, George Hartwell, recognizes Martha's
growing sense of selfhood, and thus his own lost chance to "rescue"

her. In a fit of nostalgic remembrance he thinks of his "long lost Missouri days," when women living in shady white houses had spirits "clear to transparency," serving as they did some "trembling cross old father or invalid brother or failure of a husband or marvellously distorted and deeply loved child," always moving with "the sureness of angels." Increasingly, Martha no longer fits George's idealized vision of womanhood—a kind of angel in the house—and it suddenly comes to him in his daydreams that "Martha Ingram did not, any longer, exist" (*St,* 168). Spencer's characterization of Hartwell, like that of Martha and to some degree all the other characters, bears out her view that Americans abroad, particularly those she observed during her years in Italy, were obsessed with "things back home." Intensely preoccupied with "what's been left behind," she says, they "become neurotic about these issues because they could not do anything about them. There was no theatre for action except in the mind, and in the mind things get distorted."[11]

In the course of *Knights and Dragons* Spencer shows Martha to be a woman neurotically obsessed with the past, who comes finally to recognize the danger of trying to live a life defined by old tales and images of "ladies," "knights," and "dragons." For example, she acknowledges the coercion implicit in the good-hearted Hartwells' protectiveness: "love of the innocent, protective sort which George and Grace Hartwell offered her and which she had in the past found so necessary and comforting seemed to her now somewhat like a risk, certainly an embarrassment, almost a sort of doom" (*St,* 181). She also comes to see that the romantic escape with a dashing, willful knight is a delusion. The waning of Jim Wilbourne's knighthood is poignantly foreshadowed in a story Martha tells him on a weekend trip they take together to the seaside. She remembers hearing once of an Italian farmer who dug up a statue of Aphrodite and, unable to decide finally what to do with it, simply reburied the love goddess. Jim is no less perplexed than the Italian farmer by all the unanswerable questions looming in his life and, ill suited to Italian weather, coughs a reply to Martha. In many ways Jim Wilbourne fears the complex, unpredictable life that Martha represents as much as Henry James's Winterbourne fears Daisy Miller. Jim longs for hearth, home, his nurturing wife. Martha, who has spent ten years as girl-wife-protégée of Gordon, clearly is uninterested in spending her middle age as mother-wife-nurturer of anyone, save herself. In contrast to Jim, she comes to feel at home in Italy, with its energy, elegance, and toughness—its self-sufficiency.

By the end of the novel Spencer has exposed vividly the illusion of knights and dragons: they depend for their lives on some lady's dependency and fear. For Martha, the price of intimacy is too great; she withdraws to a new enclosure of her own making. At work, the reports she writes for George Hartwell reflect her completeness; they are "smooth and crisp, brilliant, unblemished. . . . There was nothing to add, nothing to take away." To George, her new state is "sinister." It reminds one, in fact, of the life Marcia Mae Hunt dreamed of in *The Voice at the Back Door,* the wish to be "anybody's secretary," to go to work in a gray suit and white blouse to a soundproof, air-conditioned office in a skyscraper. Both Marcia Mae and Martha long to distance themselves from draining emotional involvements, and indeed Martha Ingram succeeds in doing so, though certainly not without cost. Only when she no longer cares "very deeply about anything," does "the emotional target she had once plainly furnished" disappear (*St,* 217).

The final break in her long involvement with Gordon, for example, brings her almost as much pain as ease. The moment comes at the same time Jim Wilbourne is leaving her apartment for the last time, in a scene that fulfills a premonition Martha has long had—an image, a vision, of the three of them, Gordon, Jim, and herself, inextricably linked together. She intuits that Jim's physical presence and Gordon's haunting presence are necessarily linked. The novella is narrated from an omniscient point of view, and the climactic scene occurs twice in the story, first, near the end of part five, in which Jim's view is given, then in the concluding part six, in which we see Martha's view. Gordon's young nephew comes to visit Martha, but Jim intercepts him on the stairs outside the apartment and tells the young man that Martha has left the city. He rationalizes to himself that Martha would not want to be bothered by a relative of Gordon's. His motive is more selfish than benevolent, however, for it seems his real desire is to "liberate" Martha so that he can become the new possessor. In the later section, in which we see Martha's reaction, it is clear that she did very much want to see the young man, that she remembers him fondly from the past. He was, in fact, as Spencer has discussed herself, "the one positive element that Martha remembers from back home; and she wants to make contact with that element."[12] When she sees through the window what has happened—the nephew leaving in one direction, Jim, having met Jean Coggins, leaving with her in another direction—Martha runs to catch the young man, but is too late. The moment is the turning point, when present and past both seem to slip away from her, draining her of what is beloved as well as what is destructive and demonic. Martha "felt her life tear almost audibly, like ripping silk" (*St,* 216).

What Martha experiences, nonetheless, is a freeing from old complexities, a shedding of old obligations of feeling. Her twisted former self is like an intricate structure "no longer habitable." She may not thunder her "No," but her rejection of others' definitions of what she should do/feel/want/be is no less certain because of her stillness and quietude. Freed of her interior prison, she gains her niche in the world. "She more and more arranged to do things alone, a curious tendency, for loneliness once had been a torment, whereas now she regarded almost everything her eyes fell on with an equal sense of companionship; her compatibility was with the world" (*St,* 217). Doubtless Martha Ingram might have found a more satisfying life in a world where men were something other than knights and dragons—or minotaurs. One imagines companionship and intimacy to be more desirable than loneliness. But on the terms that are available to her in the world she encounters, she opts for the freed self. In the end, Martha resembles a survivor of Stephen Crane's *The Red Badge of Courage* or "The Open Boat": "She was of those whom life had held a captive and in freeing herself she had met dissolution, and was a friend now to any landscape, a companion to cloud and sky" (*St,* 218).

A "Symbolic Poem" about Life

Knights and Dragons was very widely reviewed and, with a few notable exceptions, such as Granville Hicks's praise,[13] was panned by the critics. Even those who clearly wanted to like the book, like Orville Prescott, who had written admiringly of *The Voice at the Back Door* and *The Light in the Piazza,* complained that it lacked "flesh and blood, ideas and emotions."[14] Some critics so much admired the craftmanship of the prose that they were willing to grant a necessity to the story, which they, like Prescott, found attenuated and lifeless. Rosemary E. Jones wrote in *Commonweal,* "The static quality of her heroine's responses may cause some impatience. But it is doubtless necessary to her intent, as is the oblique manner of her expression and humorless examination of nuances of feeling." Jones concludes that the novella "is a fine female mixture of poetry, psychology and even allegory."[15] Arthur Mizener, in a review for the *New York Times Book Review,* wrote a page-long critique that began: " 'Knights and Dragons' is a beautiful book, possibly a too beautiful book." He praises the craftmanship but confesses to puzzlement about "what Miss Spencer thinks matters" in the portrayal of Martha Ingram. He calls it "a curious book, at once distinguished and deliberately deprived. Its vision is of a life conceived on the largest scale and realized in the ordinary everyday world, and what it presents is not an image of everyday life at all but a symbolic poem about it—the love song of Martha Ingram, an exquisitely made lyric."[16]

It is precisely Spencer's lyricism in *Knights and Dragons* that elicits vehement reproof from Stanley Kauffmann in a lengthy review for the *New Republic*. Calling it "a novel of sensibility, much as defined by the Mother Eve of the school, Virginia Woolf," he goes on to castigate the style as "a later phase of romanticism," an "egotism passing as an honesty." He claims, however, that "we now feel the internal world to be too subtle to be left to imagism, to be encompassed by a series of lyric sweeps," and he finds *Knights and Dragons* old-fashioned: "It is the enlarging of our cultural arteries, not their hardening, that seems to have aged the novel of sensibility." He cites several passages that exemplify the lyricism that he objects to and concludes that, although the lyric style may have "filled a need in the literary—one may say psychological—spectrum" for two generations, "now it seems, in several senses, self-limiting."[17]

Kauffmann's objection to lyricism in fiction is, of course, an old-fashioned complaint. The points he makes are essentially the same ones raised by critics who objected to the lyrical Woolf and to, say, the lyrical Eudora Welty. The action is interior; the external plot is attenuated; states of feeling are rendered indirectly, often in figures of speech. It seems to go without saying, though, that these attributes of lyrical fiction do not in themselves produce inferior or superior fiction. They are literary devices, strategies for telling a story, and they work or not, depending upon the writer's skill and vision, to reveal human experience in expressive, affecting ways.

The limitations of *Knights and Dragons* seem not to be not so much a function of the style as of the central character. Martha's problem at the beginning of the story is that she has no sense of herself. The fact that the controlling presence that oppresses her, the haunting memory of Gordon, is a *memory*, not a direct adversary in the novel, further constrains the possibilities for direct conflict and for character revelation through action. Furthermore, the other characters who do appear in the novel are not very powerful or attractive people. No one really holds enough power to win Martha's attention from the obsession with Gordon; they are like figures in a shadow play to Martha and to the reader. If one does not find Martha's problem convincing, her state of mind compelling, then nothing much works in this book. What Martha confronts is her existence as a *reflection* of the men around her. She tells Jim at one point, "I live in a mirror, at the bottom of a mirror somewhere" (*St,* 192). As Virginia Woolf and Simone de Beauvoir have suggested, the mirror-image existence is in many ways a distinctly female existence in Western culture. In *Knights and Dragons,* through an oblique but richly suggestive, lyrical style, Elizabeth Spencer shows us what life is like, as lived inside a mirror. And in this portrayal of Martha's quest to find some more satisfying life for herself, Spencer tightly controls, even understates, the emotion in the book. This muting of feeling adds further to the distanced, allegorical effect of the narration.

The author herself has said that the novella "is to some extent an allegory." She adds, "The characters represent elements in a psychic struggle; oh, not all of them and not at every point, but in general that's true. The story becomes a study in evil influences over one woman." Spencer has also voiced doubts about whether her technique produced a book that was "overly poetic." What she tried to do in the book, she says, was "create a lot of physical details, to overlay the psychic images onto the literal progress of the story." She acknowledges that the "critics didn't seem to think [she] succeeded."[18] In a later interview, in fact, she spoke of the novella as having cost her dearly in literary reputation.[19]

Spencer has discussed not only her narrative intentions in *Knights and Dragons,* but also the locus of the story in her personal experience. "Martha Ingram was a demon-haunted person, and I wrote this story at the time of great personal inner tension, which may have come out in some of the characters." In fact, the dreams and memories that haunt both Martha Ingram and Catherine Sasser in *No Place for an Angel,* the novel that Spencer would next write, resemble Spencer's own struggles during the period of their composition. She told Charles Bunting in 1972, "I admit that as a person, without going very much into things that are really important just to me, certain dreams and memories and replays of things did haunt and upset me for a long time and were destructive to me personally. I think that just in the last couple of years that's changed, so that I suddenly find that dreams and memories have become life-giving again."[20]

Unquestionably, Spencer's fiction since the early 1960s has turned inward to explore the inner drama of characters, mainly women, who struggle to find a "workable compromise" between the self and the outside world. In the two novels following "Ship Island" and *Knights and Dragons* Spencer creates in Catherine Sasser and Julia Garrett two women who move further than her earlier heroines in achieving such a compromise. She tells their stories by utilizing the full range of her style, including not only the vigorous realism of the early novels but a steadily developing lyrical impulse.

Chapter Seven

Angels in a Gray World

In 1967 Elizabeth Spencer published her sixth novel, *No Place for an Angel,* to mixed reviews. Once again, Granville Hicks in the *Saturday Review* proved to be one of her strongest supporters in his outspoken admiration for the new book. He praised the "strong, solid story about real people in a real world" and pronounced the novel better than any previous work Spencer had done. "What is bewildering and bewitching about the novel," he wrote, "is that Miss Spencer shows us the way we live now without needing to employ the documentation to be found in Dreiser's works and John O'Hara's." Remarking "the artistry of her flexible, light, almost casual style," the "magnificent" figurative language, and a tone that "ranges easily from the calmly factual to the beautifully evocative," he concluded that she had never written more adroitly.[1]

The elements of the novel praised by Hicks are the same elements other critics faulted. The clash of literary opinion among reviewers is common enough, of course, but Spencer has seemed to elicit more than the usual instances of critical stalemate. For example, Carlos Baker in the *New York Times Book Review* shared in part Hicks's view of Spencer's achievement, calling the book a "wise and intricate" novel. But despite his ostensible praise of the author's style ("as a stylist, Miss Spencer is one of the best we have"), he pointedly disliked the casual shifting about of time sequences, as well as other evidences of lyricism that he, like Stanley Kauffmann writing about *Knights and Dragons,* associated with the later novels of Virginia Woolf.[2] Similarly, Walter Sullivan in the *Sewanee Review* began his review of *No Place for an Angel* by referring to Spencer as "one of the best novelists writing today, and certainly one of the most underrated." He wrote that "the sense of life, the human pulse, beats through every scene and sequence." After briefly considering some particulars of character and theme, however, he remarks—somewhat reprovingly and regretfully, it seems—that Spencer "eschews action in favor of introspection; she pursues the heart and the

91

mind rather than the glands in a fashion that can only be called Jamesian."[3]

Whether Woolfian or Jamesian, the introspective novel clearly draws mixed reactions from readers. But to Spencer herself, writing the novel in the 1960s, the psychological or introspective approach was necessary to the realistic portrayal of contemporary men and women. Speaking to Charles Bunting of the shifts back and forth in time in *No Place for an Angel,* she said that in trying to understand why some person or character could not emotionally move forward, she often discovered that something from the past—or the periphery of experience—hindered the forward motion. "It's generally an interference from the past because many modern people are introspective. We don't live in an action world. (Pointing to her head.) We live a lot up here, so this mental action of our lives is like . . . static from an interference. . . ."[4]

"Angels Don't Belong in America"

Set in the gray world of the 1950s, *No Place for an Angel* depicts a broad canvas of characters and settings. The story begins in the summer of 1958 with the artist Barry Day and his friends, the Waddells—Irene and her businessman husband, Charles. Their relationship with one another and with Catherine and Jerry Sasser, a Texas attorney turned Washington, D.C., political operative, unfolds through a complex narrative, involving abrupt shifts of scene (from Washington to Florida to Dallas to Sicily to Rome to Massachusetts, and elsewhere) and of chronology (flashbacks within flashbacks zigzagging from 1958 back to the early days of the century and forward to the New Frontier of the 1960s). All the characters confront in one way or another the threatened, demoralized world of the postwar era. The peril of the atomic bomb, as well as the affluence and cynicism brought on by the war, has exacerbated the typical and perennial pressures men and women have struggled with in an effort to make some meaning, some sense, of their lives.

The Waddells respond to the good-bad times in a very traditional way, traditional particularly for Americans, Spencer suggests. They do not seek transcendence of the corrupted world, nor acknowledge any angelic intermediary that might relieve them of responsibility for it. Rather, they strike a peaceful coexistence by tailoring their desires and ideals to what one can reasonably expect in such a world:

pleasures of the flesh (food, sex, flashy apartments, amusing friends, exotic travel) and satisfaction of one's longing for immortality through handsome, successful children (twin sons who are "Greek perfection"). Barry Day, who dreams for years of being a sculptor and goes to Italy to try to realize his dream in sculpting an angel, likewise wearies at last of complexities and conflicts. He returns to the United States, and in the end he meets a young woman at Macy's, marries her, and commences an invisible American life.

The most radical accommodation to the tainted world is that of Jerry Sasser, who after the war comes home irrevocably changed from the hopeful, eager young man he had been. Catherine fantasizes that somehow an impostor must have changed places with Jerry—a whimsical view shared by her sister Priscilla—for no other explanation quite solves the puzzle of his acquiescence to evil. At the end of the novel the reader sees a middle-aged man who is barely holding himself together. Whether his childhood with a religiously fanatical father, his war experiences, or his disillusionment with government has caused him to reject the possibility of goodness, one is uncertain. What is clear is that Jerry's terror and rejection of life are absolutely antithetical to Catherine's outlook.

Catherine Sasser, the central figure in the main cast of five, is a woman who makes an arduous journey from the innocence of a protected, happy childhood in a little Texas town and the hopeful naïveté of a young bride-mother, to a disillusioning break with her husband. In the end she comes to make a modest but satisfying existence for herself "in a small Massachusetts town strong enough and old enough to envelop her."[5] Throughout her life Catherine holds to a vision of generosity and goodness, an ideal of spiritual transcendence that raises life above the material world, that is, Jerry's world of value-given-for-value-gotten. Through flashbacks we see her struggle to reconcile her desire for wholeness, for living what she believes, with Jerry's unrelenting pragmatism. He shapes his beliefs and actions to whatever "image" is called for; he is unfaithful; he lies and defrauds; he is, as Catherine finally admits, a man who feels no power of human sympathy.

The consequence for Catherine of a life with Jerry Sasser is madness. Like some premonition of Martha Mitchell in the latter Nixon days, Catherine has "truth serum phases," in which she speaks the unvarnished truth to the people around her—in one instance, at a political gathering for Jerry's employer, a U.S. senator from Texas.

Jerry takes her to Denver for psychological treatment, but as readily takes her out when political images must be served. Catherine's rejection of an irrational, purposeless world is, of course, a sure indication of her sanity. Even Jerry acknowledges that "if life were made up of one percent decencies, one percent of decent attitudes and right answers and good generous things to know, Catherine would never fail to understand it. It was when even that one percent was gone and not to be found that she went crazy—or crazy was what the psychiatrists were trying to say by calling it a lot of other names" (282).

It is highly ironic that such a modest expectation of decency should be viewed as "angelic." Catherine is certainly no angel, at least according to the ancient tradition of the Christian church, and Spencer goes to pains to show that neither is Catherine a saint or goddess. But by contrast to the others, she is the lone exception who, Antigone-like, refuses to live under the new dispensation. "She would literally go mad rather than give up her unity" (277). Thus she divorces Jerry and renounces his world of "power." Though "angels don't belong in America," as Irene Waddell tells Barry Day on the first page of the novel, Catherine searches for some meaningful order in life, some kind of relation between the individual and a transcendent principle of living. She finds a spot that does recall a time when the spiritual life at least kept pace with the material— the Puritan beginning of the republic. Visited by Jerry at the end of the novel, "she was lying in a glider in late summer on the side porch of her New England house, sun on her face, hair catching the sun, freckles, no make-up, broken nails from gardening, reading in a grey wool skirt and white blouse" (303–4). Interestingly, the ordered routine of her life and, specifically, the simple gray skirt and white blouse resemble the image that Marcia Mae Hunt describes in *The Voice at the Back Door* as that of the life she longs for.

Catherine's life in New England includes her crippled son Latham, who lives nearby, pursuing his love of nature as a biologist, and even the memory of her life with Jerry, for she cannot expunge the lines of attachment, pity, and love that link her to him. In fact, a kind of Wordsworthian attachment of "a thousand threads of interest and mutual sympathy, generosity, even emotion" unites her to the town and the spot of land she has chosen. Nonetheless, Catherine is essentially alone. Like Martha Ingram in *Knights and Dragons,* she accepts separateness as a condition necessary for integrity, for wholeness. No angel, she lives with her human limitations—but on her own terms. She insists upon decency and sympathy in life, even if her insistence means living with lonely hope and suffering.

The Design of the Novel

Spencer has described on several different occasions the central impression that first prompted her to imagine a cast of five characters who shuttle rootlessly about the Western world. "I was driving to the airport one day when I saw a huge jet rising slowly into the sky. It was a striking image, and it stayed with me. In fact, I found myself wondering who was on that plane and where it was going. Soon after that I had a dream about some national politicians arriving in Texas. There was a man sitting in a car, quarreling with his wife, having his neck stung by a bee." As Spencer began to write the scene of the big airliner's departure from Washington, which occurs on page 66 of the novel, she found herself, she says, thinking of related characters and story lines, with the result that she was soon working on "a kind of panoramic novel" she had never before undertaken. "I ended up with an episodic book based on the crossings of many people's paths."[6]

During the years she was working on the book, 1961–1967, Spencer followed her inclination to compose the book in episodes, as the various characters came to occupy her thoughts. She told Josephine Haley that she felt the characters "very deeply," and that she wrote about a character when he or she came to "stick" in her mind. "Some days it would be Irene—she was so real to me that sometimes I felt I had a luncheon date with her. Then Catherine would stay with me, with all of her problems that were caused by the kind of life that those around her were projecting on her. These different characters would recede like chords of music, with different characters taking the spotlight at different times."[7]

Spencer has so designed the novel that no single character focuses and unifies the narrative. Rather, at the center of her design is an idea—the strength and power that marked the United States during the postwar years, a monied and technological power that is symbolized by the sleek jet airplane that carries Jerry Sasser, the politician's aide, to Texas. Hovering over the skies of America is no angel, but a "long-nosed magnificent jet, rising silver in the cloudless summer blue," which seems "to quiver itself with what it communicated—the delight and pride of power" (66). The characters Spencer assembles react variously, representing a kind of spectrum of society, to the pride of power, to the idea of a world ruled by no god or man, but by whatever main chance at any given moment presents itself.

The world Spencer depicts is one in which American materialism and acquisitiveness reach a nadir reminiscent of Melville's nineteenth-century times. In fact, Spencer comments on the similarity, noting that Melville wrote of the "slimed" foundations of society following the Civil War, a time when idealism gave way to a "wallow of affluence" like that of the 1950s and 1960s.[8] The characters of the novel represent the variety of attitude and action that Spencer regarded as the response to power she saw in the society around her. "I began with a certain idea," she said, "and carried it out by means of the characters."[9] As an assemblage, the chief characters of *No Place for an Angel* embody the American experience during the postwar years. To understand the range of experience represented, it is instructive to look at them in some detail.

Irene Waddell dominates the first section of the novel, entitled "Blood Sports," and she speaks the closing words of the novel when she sums up the lives of Catherine and Jerry Sasser. "You both must have suffered a great deal," she says to Jerry, "wisely," in the word of the novel, though her wisdom is like that gained by a spectator at a game or a play rather than that of a fellow sufferer. Irene is a woman of fashion, a person of charming surfaces and quick feelings. She is clever and kind, but finally she has no moral or intellectual intensity. She perfectly expresses the amoral, rootless gray world that she inhabits. "I guess we've all been just about everywhere," she says near the end of the novel when Catherine mentions the trip she had once made to Denver for psychiatric treatment. The difference between the two women, of course, is that the journey to "everywhere" has in no way dinted Irene. She constantly consumes fresh experience, but since for her newness is simply fashion, which can be counted upon to change regularly, she never exhausts the world's supply of novelties that can amuse and refresh her.

Catherine's sister Priscilla mirrors a Texas reflection of Irene's materialism. When Priscilla made trips East, for example, "she could enter with Irene on long meditative sessions about modern living, together they could gain a speechless nirvana of decision about clothes, people, food and decor, a special exalted area of transfiguration which comes to women who have dealt through a lifetime with products, styles, and who is who and what you can get where" (266). Priscilla is an oil heiress, a millionaire, and Irene has the comfortable income of her executive husband, so both of the women are rarely deprived of the amusements that satisfy them. For most people of the world poverty eliminates the possibility of such a fashionable, fast-track life. And there are a few, like Catherine, for whom the purposeless, flashy life holds no wonder. But Irene lives the glossy life and likes it. She thinks, "practically everybody in the world is out of it. . . . I guess they do all right. I will always be in it. . . . I created it. It is me." What is most remarkable about Irene is that she lives her materialistic life with so few illusions about it. She does not expect, Emma Bovary fashion, to find grandeur and exhilaration, for example. In this regard she poses an anomaly to the figure she otherwise so fully illustrates, that of the modern American Daniel Boorstein described in 1961 in *The Image*—one who lives for images and pseudo-events. Unlike the stereotype delineated by Boorstein, however, Irene harbors few if any "extravagant expectations." Rather, she reminds one of a bored lady from *The Waste Land,* who looks at the dying world and decides, simply and resolutely, to turn her eyes away.

In an interior narrative at the end of part 3, "Where Paths Divide," Irene, in a rare moment of introspection, thinks of what lies ahead for her. The wild daisy on the roadside, her childhood pet, her aging mother all bespeak the mutability that for men and women eventuates in death. What perplexes Irene is that Catherine faces such defeat with stoicism and charity. She apprehends how Catherine lives, but not why: "To be good, not to be mad, to accept, live, perceive, with steadfastness and grace . . . was that all? To love, to love, to love, constantly, the very rhythm of it like a beating heart? What about it chilled her, touched her with dread?" (270–71).

Irene despairs without knowing she despairs. Indeed, her reaction to the disturbingly introspective thoughts that Catherine arouses in her verges on the satiric. She automatically lights a cigarette and quickly stubs it out. In a scenic metaphor that embodies her insistence upon a life furnished with things and emptied of feelings, she directs the maid to move a vase of flowers, "You can't put red chrysanthemums next to goldfish. Put them on the other side of the room" (271). Then, with an overtone of T. S. Eliot, Spencer describes Irene as touching her hair at the mirror, and "settling her face, her smile, toward whatever face should appear" (271).

The culminating image of Irene as a woman lacking emotional depth is foreshadowed by a series of revelations throughout the novel. The book opens during the summer of 1958, for Irene a time of bomb scares, the uninspired attempts of Barry Day to sculpt an angel, and the loss of her husband's job—all of which she registers with genial acceptance. On a vacation trip to Florida with Charles, her sons, and Day, she is shocked, for once, when on a fishing trip she watches the boat owner smash a turtle's head. Later, when she learns of the suicide of a boy they had casually met at the motel, she thinks of the turtle's death, as they head casually and thoughtlessly toward Key West. Irene's outburst at the killing of the turtle ("Blood sports are cruel. . . . I loved turtles more than I thought") is ironically unmatched by her reaction to the human world.

In the middle section of the novel, "Dangerous Journeys," all of the main characters are shown as having made journeys in the past that tested their courage and character. For Irene, it was a trip to Sicily in 1956, while she was living in Rome during years that Charles worked for the American embassy in Italy. In Charles's absence she sought the aid of an Italian intellectual, Mario Marcadante, to drive with her to Siracusa to see to the care of her seriously ailing friend, Barry Day. The episode, one of the most vividly realized in the novel, is highly visual, with the story of the passionate love affair that develops between Irene and Mario taking place in the ancient stone quarries where imprisoned Athenians had died during the Peloponnesian wars. Despite her passion and her later sorrow at the prospect of leaving Mario, Irene stays with Charles, just as he had hoped and expected her to do, counting "on her absolute materialism to conquer all" (220). A mocking quality of sentimental pretense, in fact, suffuses the episode, as Barry Day quickly senses. Irene's wearing a black raincoat for her last meeting with Mario was "the perfect thing," he thinks, the right gesture, like a piece of stage business well brought off.

Irene is spiritually and emotionally anemic. Despite her charitable rescue of Barry and her amorous love affair, she shows little capacity for sacrifice or sport. Neither blood sports nor dangerous journeys daunt Irene, for her superficial response to life rarely exposes her to risk. Perhaps she is seen most clearly by her twin sons, who tell Charles, "We've decided Mother is our little sister." The teenage boys, still children enough to have a clear-eyed vision, rejuvenate their father's waning sense of power by showing him a way to regard Irene that lets him feel her superior: "She was a venturesome child, seductible, overweight, easily impressed, comical. He almost howled with laughter. Far into the night, he lay on the tousled bed of his motel room and beat his fists into the pillow with sheer delight. When you conquered Irene, the world was yours" (258). Ultimately, the joke rebounds on Charles, whose "explosions" of delight and joy at the turn his life takes suggest an adolescent eagerness and innocence. Charles, like Irene, seems trapped in a "gee whiz" mentality, which is ironically counterpointed by their sons' intelligence and maturity.

As a character in the novel's assemblage of types of postwar, affluent Americans, Charles Waddell is a vividly drawn Midwesterner who dutifully sets about the proper American business of working, competing, and winning. Perhaps partly because he so simplistically and wholly takes up the role, he is portrayed as less complex and perceptive than Irene. In characterizing Charles, Spencer creates a slightly feckless version of Irene and Jerry Sasser, making Charles a materialist with only limited power to enjoy consumption and an arrogant executive, accustomed by the war to giving blunt commands, with no important business to direct. The opening scene of the novel establishes his churlish manner, when he taints an otherwise pleasant day by insisting that after a day in the country, the picnickers—the Waddells, their friends, the Giffords, and Barry Day—avoid the traffic into the city by stopping off to see a movie, any old-time movie, in whatever sleazy moviehouse they can turn up.

Charles is ill suited to the era of the organization man, having come to maturity in a slightly earlier, less subtle time of manly competitiveness. As Irene explains to Barry Day when Charles loses his job, "The complaint was, verbatim: He can't take his army boots off. . . . The big word is coordination" (19). The loss of the job is simply the culmination of a series of failures afflicting Charles. Several years earlier, as we learn in a flashback that does not unfold until pages 180–226, Charles has suffered the humiliation of botching an important assignment in Egypt and then of returning to Italy to find himself a cuckold. The false glitter of his life with Irene, which recalls Scott Fitzgerald's world on many occasions, is epitomized in the scene of the Waddells' leave-taking of Italy.

Belying the photographs of the "happy" couple and their sons aboard
the first-class deck of the *Leonardo da Vinci,* which appear in "the
Paris *Herald Tribune,* the Rome *Daily American* and one of the Italian
papers, along with a brief summary of Charles' career abroad" (245–
46), are Charles's shame and disappointment.

Charles Waddell is a man whose emotional development is stunted;
his spiritual anemia is even more severe than Irene's. He is described
in the novel as one who had "refused or scanted what opportunities
there had been for the big emotions to grow in, and now this green
time was gone forever; it was too late." Early on, he put aside
warmth and affection, for he found such expressions were "the American mannerism Europeans were quickest to view with contempt."
It occurs to him to wonder where the "heart" is in such a life as
his, but unwilling to risk despair, he will not pursue the thought
far. "He would not think of it" (245).

In September 1958, three months after the picnic in the country,
the Waddells and Barry Day leave New York for a vacation in
Florida, mainly to get away from the depression of the job loss in
the city. In a roundabout way the trip to Florida does rejuvenate
Charles, but the renewal comes not from any magical fountain of
youth but his discovery of the hope for immortality that is represented by his sons. First, he goes through various stages of resentful
reaction—alcohol, anger, the "new start" of trying to sell real estate
in Florida, after Irene has tired of his troubles and returned to New
York. Nothing works until, on his way home, he stops to visit the
twins at the Virginia academy they attend. As if he is seeing them
for the first time, he suddenly finds them engagingly, infectiously
alive. "A phrase here and a joke there struck him with the freshness
of light, night-long rain falling on land as dessicated as a two-year-
old corn shuck in the corner of a bar loft." Charles discovers fa-
therhood and is reborn. His spirit becomes "like a child itself,"
splashing about "with overgrown baby gurgles, the awakening to
his children like the primal contact with water in a tub" (258). He
no longer wants alcohol or feels conquered by Irene or life in general.

Unfortunately, Charles's euphoric discovery of his sons is shallow
and fantastical, a momentary phase of exhilaration that will clearly
pass. Not long after he returns to New York and to Irene, feeling
the boys' vitality having grown "into his own identity," giving him
"youth to sport in once again," he reverts to the familiar Charles
who appears on the first page of the novel. "Drunker than he had

ever been," he suggests to Irene that they go to a movie—"something old-timey" (261). Like Walker Percy's Binx Bolling, Charles finds that moviegoing is preferable to empty encounters with life, but he doesn't even seem to recognize it as the palliative it is. Except for the encounter with the sons in Virginia, which excites his childish wonderment, and his frustration at Irene's affair with Mario, which he ignores while he patiently awaits its end, he is undaunted by idea or ideal. It is no surprise that when he last appears in the novel, through Jerry Sasser's remembered encounter with the Waddells (this in the early 1960s), he has found the right image to land a job with a New York publisher and insinuate himself into the New Frontier White House. The final evidence of Charles's woeful emptiness is that, again, he doesn't even seem aware of the image he's adopted so as to take advantage of the changing scene. "His wife had picked the new manner out for him, no doubt," Jerry thinks, "and got him to wear it without his knowing he had it on" (295).

Spencer herself has said of Charles and Irene Waddell that they are "awful people who live in constant compromise." Nonetheless, they obviously interest her as characters, and she imbues them with a vividness and uniqueness that make them interesting to the reader. They are more than types of *The Organization Man, The Power Elite, The Lonely Crowd,* and so on among the numberless books describing the social character of the United States in the 1950s and 1960s. They are people whom one comes to know and wants to understand. In both characters one senses a potential for an energetic, principled life failed by a materialistic, ever pragmatic America that encourages their childishness. Spencer says that their "real tragedy is that nobody regards them as being particularly bad. . . . It takes a critical society to perceive evil; and the society that I was writing about in that book, America in the fifties and early sixties, was not critical."[10] One of Spencer's major achievements in this novel is her ability to depict the Waddells as representatives of a shallow society, to see them with an affectionate but critical eye, and engage the reader's belief in and care about them. It is the mark of an estimable talent to reveal characters so that the reader apprehends them at once empathetically and critically. In the case of the Waddells, Spencer applies her talent chiefly in the mode of irony and creates within *No Place for an Angel* a novel of manners that richly reflects one segment of American life during the postwar years.

In the figures of Catherine and Jerry Sasser, Spencer represents a more extreme and more tragic reaction to the national character of prideful power. Their story partakes of the American past, of the nineteenth-century dream of success, of fierce, obsessive religious practices, of the obedient, pedestaled purity of ladyhood, and the lonely effort of the individual to pierce the mystery of good and evil. In attending to their pain and failures one is drawn into an intricately symbolic American "romance." Spencer thus assembles at the center of her spectrum of contemporary malaise the venal materialism of the Waddells, with a focus upon manners, and at the outlying poles, the spiritual longing and terror of the Sassers, with a concomitant emphasis upon psychology and religion.

It is, of course, revealing of modernist ambiguity and complexity here that characters, author, and reader all amalgamate, almost reflexively, questions of mind and soul. In either realm, the territory is that of interior experience, which Spencer explores in this novel in a prose style that often differs markedly from that devoted to the Waddells. Particularly in the concluding section, "The Grey World," we encounter a dense narrative, in which the omniscient persona, filtered through Jerry Sasser's consciousness, reveals the desperate emptiness of his life. The section begins, "Dark and impassive as a savage, a carved, great-featured face lived constant in his mind among the ruins of his own lost glory." A kind of exaggerated, haunted prose, consisting of figurative language, flashbacks, memories recollected through a collage of images, and hallucinations or fantasies, mirrors in language and structure the breakdown of social order.

Jerry Sasser, a Texas boy who makes it to the "big time," however briefly, epitomizes the urge for power and possession that also characterizes the country. He starts out as a prototypical American hero who, resembling Amos Dudley of *This Crooked Way,* has a startling encounter with religion through the agency of his father and a glimpse of wealth and status furnished by the example of the Lathams, the main family of Merrill, Texas. Sasser's father, a professor of economics in a little school nearby, is a religious fanatic who has left his wife and daughters, bringing his son with him to live in Merrill, where he leads a nearly monastic life in service of the "Blood Union of Messiah's Brotherhood." On his seventh birthday Jerry submits to a ritualistic initiation into the Brotherhood by drinking drops of his father's blood diluted in a glass of water. He grows to manhood under the indoctrination of his father, but the effect of it all is to give him not an active faith but a disturbing, insistent sense of vacuum.

More compelling than his father's religion is the image of power illustrated by the prominence of the Lathams, whose new wealth comes from Catherine's father, a shrewd purchaser of oil leases from a neighbor down on his luck. Jerry Sasser thus draws from two deeply rooted traditions in the New World, one formed by a vision of an omnipotent God and the other by a dream of earthly wealth and glory. The tension provided by the religious strain is what is prominently missing in the life of Charles and Irene Waddell. Jerry might have had an unremarkable life, during which by marrying the wealthy Catherine and becoming a Sunday School teacher, Kiwanian, lawyer, etc., he would have so secularized and diluted his father's Blood Brotherhood as to pass for an ordinary materialist. But "the war changed everything," in the words of the novel.

As a member of an admiral's staff, Sasser comes to serve the "power elite," as described by C. Wright Mills in 1956. A public relations man, Sasser provides the words that vindicate the power of the American military establishment. He peers behind the veneer of words that describe our institutions, and what he discovers is horrible—it is the "nothing" that Conrad's heroes find when they no longer have the tranquilizing illusions of their comfortable culture to sustain them: "He discovered what everybody had been doing all the time, not just in war or over the machines, but all their lives, only did not know it. They had been shifting words around to suit themselves. . . . Once you got the key to life every door was apt to open." What Jerry Sasser comes to believe is that there is neither cause nor consequence in life. The world exists only in whatever images we care to utter. "The sea was vast and blue, the ships beautiful, the combat a blur of blank tension and mindless trial, the islands green as paradise. He cared for no one and went up quickly" (276). The disillusionment is bitter, and the only way Sasser finds to sustain himself in such a world is to submit himself to it. His situation is like that described by the trader Stein in *Lord Jim:* "A man that is born falls into a dream like a man who falls into the sea. If he tries to climb out into the air as inexperienced people endeavour to do, he drowns. . . . The way is to the destructive element submit yourself, and with the exertions of your hands and feet in the water make the deep, deep sea keep you up."[11]

Jerry's failure is that, instead of submitting his ideals and ambitions to the world, he surrenders to the world and drowns.

Sasser's radical rejection of morality on his return from the war bewilders Catherine, but it has the effect of enhancing his rise to power in Washington. His political power as a senator's aide, his sexual attractiveness to women, his own self-delight in the macho image of wheeler-dealer—all feed one another and seem tied to his careless, uncaring outlook. Life presents him with events that might have shaken a man less purged of sentiment: his son's near-fatal attack of polio, his wife's mental troubles. But it is his failure to "fix" a story in the national media injurious to the senator's "image" on civil rights that finally subjects him to crisis. For Jerry, the "dangerous journey" begins aboard the jet airplane leaving Washington for Dallas in the mid-1950s, a trip that takes him home to face his father's death, Catherine's departure, and the collapse of his political career.

Sasser does not experience the troubling disjunction between the self and the world that proves so destructive to Catherine because he forces the self so far underground that it effectively has no existence. On the surface, he seems to be an egoist caring only for himself, but the manner is misleading. In truth, he cares for no one, including himself, a stance that protects him from having to feel and confront the terror Catherine acknowledges. In the last years in which we see Jerry in the novel, he lives with a woman, Bunny Tutweiler, who bears his child, Diane, and agreeably brings a bland structure to his life. With less imagination than Irene Waddell or Catherine's sister Priscilla, Bunny is nonetheless like them in her matter-of-fact acceptance of life. With her, Sasser patches together his old charade, again wheeling and dealing in Washington, though somewhat sleazily and ingloriously. Her accidental death leaves him with the care of his daughter, and that, along with the nagging memory of Catherine, his father, and his lost glory, forces him into unaccustomed contemplation.

Jerry Sasser is a ruined hero at the end of the novel, partly because of his flawed character and partly because the modern world offers so little possibility for heroic action. The words we use to define such action have all become suspect, a disquieting truth that Hemingway's Lt. Henry learned in World War I, and that Jerry Sasser learns in World War II. His most noble quality is his honest intelligence, which is contrasted sharply with the windy intellectualizing of Millard Warner, his sister-in-law's husband, who transforms meaninglessness and amorality into a "theory of action." Jerry's phrase, "the grey world," says more with less pretension. It suggests the colorless, indistinct surfaces that pass for reality in the world of action. As a boy, Jerry dreams of entering into the action, of following his ambition and finding completion, but he gets caught in the rushing bad times that destroy him. Once again an American Adam fails to find a new world.

There is a haunting, recurring family story that Catherine first heard as a child from her aging uncles and that prefigures Jerry's experience and gives it a historical context. In the late nineteenth century a wagon train passed through the old home place of the Lathams at Sandy Gulch, where one of the wagons foundered in the sand. A boy in the party, trying to shore up the wheels with logs, slipped beneath the wagon, broke his back, and shortly died. Catherine grew up hearing the claims of many in the community that they could sometimes still hear the boy's dying words—"Mother, mother," according to some, "Mercy, mercy," according to others. Later it was reported that the boy had been an orphan, but one of the Lathams had evidence to refute the story. By the time of Catherine's childhood the story has already passed into a legend with several versions, all of which seem to gather up in the retelling much of the vaunting dream of westward expansion and the suffering that followed in its wake. Years later, when Catherine finally leaves Jerry, having decided that his unrelenting drive for power is literally killing her, she thinks, "Jerry was the boy beneath the wagons. . . . That has been true all the time" (165).

Jerry Sasser joins a long line of American heroes whose extravagant expectations lead to psychic paralysis. There is perhaps the glimmer of hope that his responsibility for his daughter will somehow pull him back into sentience, but he remains wary of connections that threaten his automatic life. To maintain his control, his balance, he submits to the world's ways. Unlike Catherine, "he accepted corruption. It was the only way to meet the terror within" (304). On Spencer's spectrum of contemporary Americans who reflect the postwar era of U.S. prominence, Jerry Sasser represents one who started out with sensitivity and intelligence, but who was seduced by a dream that offered power without purposeful direction. In the end, he has a flattened soul to show for his failure to discover any truth that transcends the self—anything worth living for.

Perhaps if Jerry Sasser had lived in a blazing world, instead of a gray one, he might have loomed as a demonic figure, but Spencer's contemporary setting provides no canvas for such sweeping power of evil. Only by the presence of Catherine are we made to feel the dangerous threat a man like Sasser poses. Catherine is a kind of barometer of morality; she reflects the pressure the American (and European) society of this period exerts on a person who actively seeks to live out a daily life according to some transcendent principle.

The chief obstacle to Catherine's living a life of nobility and integrity is the ageless difficulty of discerning truth from falsehood, illusion from reality, that is, the arduous matter of discovering what standards are worthy. In the end she overcomes the inhibitions and blindness posed by her sheltered life, but her path from western wealth back to eastern spirituality is marked by disillusionment as least as great as Jerry's and courage of a kind that no other character in the novel displays. Her "success" in the modern world is extremely modest, muted like that of Martha Ingram in *Knights and Dragons,* but it is the most hopeful example of contemporary life that Spencer shows us in the novel.

A "princess" of Merrill, Texas, Catherine as a child has several premonitions of the tragedies and confusions that belie the Lathams' smug affluence. She senses that there is a world beyond their big comfortable white house with a turret from hearing her uncles' stories of the boy killed in the wagon train and, more crucially, from the pain caused the family when her brother Edward unexpectedly leaves home one day. (He vanishes for a time, to turn up ten years later with the explanation, "I just never did like oil.") Hungry for someone who will understand and resolve her confusions, Catherine turns with youthful naïveté to Jerry Sasser, whose father's strange religion, though slightly scary, intrigues her with its suggestion of a spiritual world, and whose "understanding" of Edward's leaving seems to promise a sensitivity slightly superior to that of the other inhabitants of Merrill, Texas. Catherine marries him, eagerly expecting him to bestow upon her an identity, a direction, a purpose. "She quit school and she and Jerry got married in Merrill at the First Baptist Church, and went to live in Dallas for two years while Jerry studied law, a blissful bit of canoe-drifting toward the war" (82). Spencer's prose style in the section describing the youth of Catherine and Jerry is wittily ironic, as befits the satiric exposure of their innocent sentimentality.

When her husband returns from the war, Catherine's dollhouse life deteriorates. For a while she attempts to play her part in the tableau of "making a good impression," "presenting an image," but Jerry's infidelities, political chicanery, and puzzlingly unfeeling response to their son Latham finally wear her down. During the years that Catherine is caught in the limbo of indecision about what kind of man Jerry really is, she verges upon madness. The turning point for her comes during the journey they make to Texas in the middle 1950s. All her former confusions are heightened on the journey, and ambiguous actions suggest the impossibility of one's ever separating illusion from reality. For example, she "knows," but knows only uncertainly, that Jerry is planning an assignation with the stewardess on the plane. She knows her place as a wife is to be with Jerry at his father's funeral, but when she tries to join him she is turned away by the Brotherhood. The ambiguities that Catherine struggles to resolve are extended in the novel by Spencer's giving conflicting information from the views of several characters without providing any authorial resolution. For example, Priscilla looks at Jerry and Catherine sitting in a car outside her house and sees Jerry slap her. Jerry's explanation that he's struck a bee is borne out by Catherine's report and Millard's evidence of a dead bee, but Priscilla's report that she saw a blow angrily struck is never really undermined or refuted.

Catherine's confusion and fatigue culminate in her seeking retreat at the old family farmhouse. Here two contrasting visions crystallize the alternatives that lie before her. On a walk to Sandy Gulch, where the wagons used to cross, she has a vision of her beloved Uncle Dick, an image of goodness that has "nothing to do with ambition, with power, with blood" (160). It is an ecstatic vision of serenity and kindliness, but the effect even here, in what might have been the novel's most compelling example of a transcendent life, is finally ironic. Catherine's vision of a better life is a nostalgic glimpse of an unrecoverable past, a past that probably never existed. "She had her moment's paradise and knew the streets of heaven to be plain and shady, where the horses stood quietly and dogs lay waiting for their masters, who were greeting old friends and understood each other" (161). Her wistful, nostalgic image is nevertheless more vital than the alternative, the spectacle of Jerry's moral degradation figured in a Hollywood-like mobster scene, complete with "a long black car with Dallas license plates, chauffeur-driven, carrying strange men." The ominous appearance of the men, a frightening shotgun blast (which Jerry later implies was her own mad doing), and the specter of her destruction convince her to leave her husband and quit Texas. "She seemed to herself like setting out on a journey to an ocean she wasn't even sure was there" (165).

Subsequently, Catherine does make an independent life for herself, a sort of Waldenesque life in which she tries to join garden solitude with some sustaining human relations. Spencer portrays Catherine's refusal to continue as the passive victim of the gray world sympathetically, but she maintains an edge of irony that partially undercuts the character's moral stance. Catherine is unquestionably the most admirable among the five main characters, but like Jerry she cannot get beyond the lackluster world that furnishes her imagination. Even in Catherine's anguished recoil from such a world, there is ultimately no relief from the "slimed foundations."

The fifth of the central characters, Barry Day, strikes out from his Arkansas boyhood with the most exuberant ambition of them all, but at the conclusion he has settled for the most conventional life. He dreams of being an artist, and he flees home and wife, changes his name, and travels to Italy. The sculpture of an angel is to be his crowning achievement, but in his haste to leave Italy after an unpleasant exchange with officials over an automobile, he leaves the angel unfinished in Italy, to be rescued and sent to him in New York by Catherine. Barry Day's too-easy sensitivity, really a self-deluding sentimentality, Spencer exposes with an affectionate, but continual irony. For example, he worries over the bomb scares, then worries that he worries, and mourns the prospective loss of beloved things: "When he really got going, trees on a corner caused him a stab of pain, just by standing there, as did cats sleeping precise in their habits on sunny window sills, children playing in a poor street, a girl with a pony-tail flying out for milk or bread. The list was infinite, and he had to stop for it. He stopped it by thinking about the angel" (16).

Barry Day's wish to be an artist is finally realized not in the creation of a sculpture but in the marriage to a woman whose "quiet look" assures him he is a "great artist." The brush with death far behind him in Italy, he is "like a brave little boat which had got out too far and had turned back toward shore at last" (265). Spencer's ironic persona does not spare Day, but through Catherine the author provides a gentler, more uncritical view of him. "He's complex,"

Catherine insists to Irene in one of their last meetings in the novel, and then swears to herself that she won't "summarize" him. At the end of the long second section, "Dangerous Journeys," Day does indeed reveal a capacity for sensitive perception and warmheartedness that partially offsets his callow enthusiasms and lack of discriminating intelligence. In fact, one finds in the last two paragraphs of this section an instructive illustration of the ironic mode of the novel, in which Spencer portrays the characters realistically and largely sympathetically, but in such a way as to remind the reader continually of their romantic pretensions and human limits.

This scene takes place in New York, shortly after Barry Day has received the sculpture of the angel that Catherine arranged to be shipped from Italy. "When he saw what she had done, the whole earth seemed renewed. . . . He heaped her with praise and tenderness; he all but left the earth altogether behind, rushing in on her before lunch one day at the Plaza to beg her to marry him." The narrative voice here describes Day's eager boyishness in a tone of amused acceptance. In the next sentence Day's manner is exposed to slight ridicule by means of a humorous figure of speech and a flat, terse summary of events: "When he came to earth with a crash, like a homemade airplane in a cotton patch, he limped for a long time, licked sores, lost his job and drank too much." In the concluding sentence of the paragraph Spencer views Day—as she typically does the other central characters—with something of Thomas Hardy's commiserating eye, seeing their efforts to withstand life's assaults as doomed but endearing. "Through it all he was returning in spirit to his own personal defeat, which was always there waiting for him, like a plain but faithful wife whom through the years, since he couldn't get rid of her, he had to learn to love" (248).

Meeting for the first time as lovers, Day "ruefully realizes" that Catherine comes to him only in fleeing her husband; he sees "the extent of her much-talked-about darkness"; he sees, in fact, "at close range, Catherine's madness," which he perceptively describes as "a heavy eclipsing shadow which she was powerless to lift." His knowing appraisal of the Waddells' character seems almost identical to that of the authorial persona: "Irene seemed to him coarse and at times almost evil, and the whole Waddell world a sort of underscoring of a lurking corruption that he could sense everywhere." In short, Barry Day just misses being a wise fool. He understands the weakness and foibles of the people around him, but he never quite reaches an understanding of the tragicomedy of the human condition. "The bomb threat came and went, but the other, nameless thing was worse, subtler, more profound and powerful, and it did not show any sign at all of going. He longed for the angel, but when he risked saying this to Irene, she treated his confidence summarily. Angels never crossed the ocean. Well, this was true; how could he answer it?" (249).

Unlike the author, Barry Day has little sense of the irony of his predicament, though he understands its pain and confusion. In a different way, chiefly in their eschewing heroic aspirations and holding to a spiritless consumerism of life, the Waddells likewise are subjects, not agents, of irony. And Catherine Sasser specifically rejects the double (duplicitous) vision that informs irony, refusing to immerse herself in the gray world, where there are no absolutes, no clear definitions of evil or goodness. We take seriously her insistence on some minimal nobility and decency in life, though we also know that her seriousness is tinged with madness. By contrast, Jerry Sasser, whom Spencer places at the center of the concluding section of the novel, comprehends and accepts the human condition as inescapably ironic. But through this character Spencer ultimately dramatizes the limits of the ironic vision. Like a self-reflecting critique of the ironical authorial voice that describes the Waddells and Barry Day, the depiction of Jerry Sasser shows the ironist as a poseur, one perhaps intellectually brave, but emotionally a coward.

In *Anatomy of Criticism* Northrop Frye discusses as part of his theory of myths a phase of literary irony that we can recognize as the mode Spencer employs in *No Place for an Angel*. "It stresses the humanity of its heroes, minimizes the sense of ritual inevitability in tragedy, supplies social and psychological explanations for catastrophe, and makes as much as possible of human misery seem, in Thoreau's phrase, 'superfluous and evitable.' This is the phase of most sincere, explicit realism."[12] In *No Place for an Angel,* a rich, problematic, realistic novel, Spencer re-creates the social and psychological tensions that bemuse contemporary society. She shows how readily our national pride in intellect and power leads to disillusionment, which we sustain with an ironic, contemptuous view of life. Unfortunately, the ironic temper catches us in an imprisoning circularity. In Spencer's novel the promise of a transcendence to break the deadening circle of the intellect in self-contemplation is finally rather tenuous. There are only the fanatic belief of the Messiah's Blood Brotherhood and the gentle faith in human goodness of Catherine Sasser. Even so, the novel suggests that other, spiritually vacuous alternatives to life are more desperate and doomed.

Chapter Eight
The Life Snare

The central figures of "Ship Island," *Knights and Dragons,* and *No Place for an Angel* all illustrate to some degree Josephine Hendin's comment that the contemporary heroine's desire to change her life is "reactive, caused by disillusionment rather than conviction or ideology."[1] The protagonists in these three works start out at least with the conventional expectation of finding meaning for their lives through relationships with men. Inevitably, they find such relationships to be oppressively defining, indeed threatening to their maintaining any separate identity. Julia Garrett, the central figure in Elizabeth Spencer's seventh novel, *The Snare* (1972), presents a somewhat different case.

From the time when she comes as a child to live in New Orleans with her mother's sister Isabel and Isabel's husband, Maurice Devigny, Julia grows up knowing that life holds more than a comfortable, airy innocence. Seeking a vital life, something other than the genteel world of Garden District society, she rejects marriage to a wealthy Mississippian, Martin Parham, because she sees that it would imprison her in deadening conventionality. In the musician Jake Springland, who offers her a connection with a different world, she finds a man who is, for all his innocence, rather like a prince of darkness. In fact, in her frank acknowledgment of the dark, demonic world, the "human swamp," she resembles Jerry Sasser in *No Place for an Angel,* though, unlike Jerry, she resists disillusionment and ultimately draws strength from her encounter with the evil undercurrents of life. Spencer creates in the character of Julia Garrett the example of one who successfully applies the words of Stein in *Lord Jim.* She actively takes her dream *to* the world; she submits to the "destructive element" and finally comes to possess a self assurance and knowledge of life purified of sentimentality and genteel respectability.

With an intricate plot and complex form that reach beyond the design of *No Place for an Angel, The Snare* is Spencer's most ambitious literary effort and her most important work to date. It is a novel of compelling symbolic power, with a richness of theme and technique that can only be suggested in any brief discussion of it.

Descent into Darkness

Spencer has said that she got the idea for the novel from a newspaper story that ran in the New Orleans *Times-Picayune* in 1952. The strange case involved the reappearance of a man who had been thought murdered; in fact, a young man had earlier been accused and tried for the "murder." Spencer said she clipped the articles because she thought at the time the story would make a good subject for a novel. Five years later, on a trip to New Orleans with her husband, she reviewed the series of articles in the news file, finding a picture of the accused man. "His face was very intense, very intelligent," she said, and she thought "he was somebody really fine mixed up in a sordid situation. Then I thought, well, if a young man like this were down here, he would certainly have a girlfriend. That was how I stumbled onto Julia, who caught hold of my imagination and became the main character. In a way, I backed into her." Spencer went on to explain that because Julia lived in a world that she recognized and understood, she could use the character to "break through into that darker world" that she needed to explore.[2]

Central to the novel's design is Julia's quest to experience life immediately and sensually, as befitting the vision passed on to her by Maurice's father, Henri Devigny. "Old Dev," a lover of Baudelaire, a massive dark figure who shared an Audubon Place mansion with his son and daughter-in-law, initiated Julia into the human swamp. As Julia tells her friend, the *Times-Picayune* reporter Tommy Arnold, "That's what he got me used to. If there's no way out you have to live it."[3] Rather clearly, Dev's sensuous and sexual appetites ensnared the child Julia. A mentor whose physical characteristics suggest a minotaur (gross body, shaggy head, lustful, powerful), Dev is Julia's spiritual father, her natural father having abandoned her to the Devignys upon her mother's death. Shut outside the "magic circle" of Maurice and Isabel's excluding, myopic attachment to each other, Julia and Dev make a separate life. Thus begins Julia's development of a "secret self" that is fascinated, even haunted by the debased, hidden world. Little wonder that she grows to womanhood contemptuous of the New Orleans boys, tied as they are "to a smaller statement of life than she wanted made to her" (97).

The novel opens in medias res, with Julia explaining to Tommy Arnold how she came to be involved with an accused murderer, Jake Springland. With numerous flashbacks filling in Julia's immediate and distant past, the story spirals forward. Julia has long led a double life; in her youth she was protégée of both the dark Dev and the genteel Isabel and Maurice. Later, as a respectable "society girl" engaged to marry the millionaire Martin Parham, she breaks the engagement, moves to a small, run-down apartment, takes a job with an optometrist, and commences an affair with Springland, who eventually leads her into the underworld of drugs and violence. It is in the optometrist's office one winter day in the 1950s that Jake appears incongruously with two strange misfits named Ted Marnie and Wilma Wharton. The mysterious Marnie is part hoodlum, part messiah—a "soul engineer" to Wilma and Jake. Through the bizarre machinations of Marnie, Jake is falsely accused of murdering him, though he is acquitted in a trial that brings him and Julia back together several months after their earlier encounter.

Jake represents for Julia the "something more" that she seeks beyond the vapid facade of polite society, Dev having cultivated in her an affinity for the murky, mysterious depths of life. She is deliberate in her movement away from conventionality and security, unlike Faulkner's Temple Drake, whose descent into the underworld is essentially passive. Julia's idea is that "people draw life from the crooked world. There's a conversation going on with the straight world, all the time" (110). Jake provides Julia's access to this other realm, a world she has always sensed as peculiarly embodied by New Orleans, with its black magic and jazz and swampy terrain. "To Julia, Jake had caught the city's rough corruption with its core of feeling, its peculiar tolerant knowledge. She had circled it for years, but now an outsider had come to discover it, claim it, experience it and give it to her whole" (118–9). She is an "orphan girl in a voodoo city," a mermaid seeking her "element."

Of course, in "Ship Island" New Orleans likewise represents the exotic faraway country, the city where Nancy Lewis seeks respite from deadening everydayness. This city is an important symbol in Spencer's imagination, its vitality tracing back to her own youthful experience of its excitement and variety. In an interview with Hunter McKelva Cole in 1973 she spoke of her memories of New Orleans, "of the favorable and excited reports of it in my family when I was a child." She said that "nobody enjoys New Orleans as much as a small-town Southerner. It's our cosmopolitan, European city. The excellent food, the atmosphere, something of the French past remaining there excite people. Then as soon as I went myself, I felt this same excitement; and so it's been a city of life-long fascination for me."[4]

In the early 1950s Spencer lived on the Mississippi Gulf Coast and frequently visited nearby New Orleans, and by her own account she later visited the city many times during the writing of the novel.[5] One senses that her view of New Orleans, particularly of its place in the symbolic landscape of America, is represented in the comments of the reporter, Tommy Arnold. Drawn to Julia Garrett and the Marnie case, Arnold tries to interest the national media in picking up the local story. He is convinced it will take hold of the country's imagination because he thinks the country at large is fascinated by New Orleans's mystery. "New Orleans was the nation's true pulse beat, but the nation did not know it," he muses. "Voodoo, jazz, sex, and food—who could go further than that toward what was really important to people in the U.S. and A." (81–82).

In part 1 of the novel we follow Julia through her early affair with Jake, a time when she finds a joyous intimacy with her lover and exhilaration in the sex and drugs and music they share. The vision of sensuality that Henri Devigny had bequeathed to Julia at last dims, however, for a number of very human reasons. Ultimately, Julia cannot abandon her thinking self in the relationship with Jake. When she no longer reflects him in an image twice his natural size (to recall Virginia Woolf), he accuses her of "destroying" him. "He could make her give up everything to him but the thing that mattered most—and that was the knowledge that he knew she had, no matter what illusion he decided to believe in, that he wasn't great, that he wasn't going to get where he wanted to go" (147). The year-long orgy—really a sexual idyll—comes to a close with a violent lovemaking scene and Jake's departure.

The following section, "The In-Between Time," moves the narrative quickly forward, with Julia's taking an utterly routine job for a time as a medical librarian in a hospital. "Almost daily, coming and going for four years in her simple linen and cotton dresses, her two good wool suits, her standard beige raincoat," she wonders whether anything lies ahead to break the monotony of her life.

Actually, the routine is partially broken by the appearance of Martin
Parham, who has married and fathered two children during the
interim since their engagement. In an interesting parallel relationship Julia, who "was the whole city of New Orleans" to Martin,
represents the same seductive attractiveness for him as Springland
had for her. For similar psychological reasons, they both find satisfaction in Julia's playing "fancy woman" to Martin's solicitous
patronage. For Julia, the dinners, gifts, and apartment Martin provides are pleasurable, and the freedom from conventionality in being
his mistress brings a slight relief from the tedium of her routine.
With greater intensity, Martin turns to Julia because he is obsessed
with whatever lies beyond the domain of the Parhams, the rich
Parhams of Parham Station, staunch Baptists, conservative, acquisitive, lords of tung and pecan orchards, cattle, oil, of numberless
dollars. Like an animal gulping for air, he flees the Parhams and
his wife—an "uncommonly sweet, pretty, good-humored" girl from
Ridgeland, Mississippi—and finds breath on his occasional visits
to Julia in New Orleans. There is about her a mysterious aloofness,
which Martin imagines to cover some unspeakable secret from her
past, one that attracts and horrifies him. He guesses, rightly, that
Julia's sexual initiation came at the instigation of Henri Devigny,
but his brooding obsession with the act has less to do with Julia
than with his own needs for stimulating fantasies of debauchery.

At the conclusion of this short midsection, Spencer employs a
technique for revealing information and interior thought that she
does not use elsewhere in the novel. Using alternating sections of
diary entries and italicized interior monologues, Spencer depicts
Julia's traumatic childhood experience with Henri Devigny and her
adult reaction to the haunting memory: *"Martin has no belief in the
things or people I know, just in me personally. This is why he can't see me
or know me completely—because he won't accept anybody in connection with
me, starting with Dev. If I write it and show it to him to read, then he
would have to understand it, or recognize it, just because he was reading
it. So I am going to do like this"* (189). What Julia reveals in her diary
is a childhood irremediably shaped by the loss of her parents, the
neglect of Isabel and Maurice, and the complex mesh of love and
abuse at the hands of her surrogate father, Henri Devigny.

At the center of her memory is the day on which Dev took her
with him to the house of his black mistress, the day when, following
a "commotion on the stairs," the woman died suddenly and vio-

lently. What Julia writes for Martin's reading is an account of the aftermath, of the years when Dev devoted himself absolutely to her: "He couldn't be good enough to me, I had all his attention, I was sun, moon, and stars to him, he chose my dresses himself and took me everywhere." What she does not write about, but remembers vividly, is the sexual experience that occurred after the confusion and anguish of the woman's death: *"I'm going to leave out the thing that had most to do with me, for on the way home he started holding me against him, struggling with my body and when we got home he held me to him on the bed and cried and then I don't know what happened. He was convulsed, panting and heaving, and I was not thinking anything at all"* (191). The act of molestation, heightened by the hint of a quasi-incestuous relationship with Devigny, is a source of fascination and horror for Julia and clearly marks her for life. It would appear from her recollection that the incident was not repeated: *"Later I thought, he didn't know what he was doing, he just didn't know. I still think that. He didn't know I was even there, I was just a body he was holding on to"* (192). It is difficult to know, however, whether she is to be understood as repressing other, later experiences or not. In any case, she comes to know deeply and early in life the desperateness of the human condition, with its endless combinations of love and sex and death. Looking back, Julia herself regards her childhood with few regrets. The "hill country" life she might have had with her parents, like the comfortable, provincial world of the Parhams in Mississippi, strikes her as bloodless and lifeless. Her early link with evil shows her "the great life snare." And, though "she saw too much and could have screamed with the seeing," one senses unmistakably that Julia would not replace the seeing with blindness.

In part 2 Spencer portrays the full implication of Julia's bent for dangerous excitement. The section opens eight years after Ted Marnie's "murder," when one morning Martin Parham reads in the New Orleans newspaper that Marnie has been discovered alive and well in California. With this resurrection of Marnie, Spencer suggests that Julia's former life with Springland, with its links with the underworld, is inevitably to be renewed. The objectivity and distance that mark Spencer's scenic design—having the information emanate via Parham via paper—produce an effect like that of a Greek chorus warning of what is to come.

Julia's humdrum life, which for years has only occasionally given outlet to the secret self that yearns for the exotic and forbidden, slowly gives way to the demands of that other self and to the events that speed its reemergence. Parham enters her life again, briefly, before he is killed in an airplane crash, and Tommy Arnold searches her out, certain that the news of Marnie heralds danger for Julia. A drug dealer appears, a man familiar from the days of the Springland episode, and she suddenly knows she has "entered her element. Her nerves woke up. It was as though she had been living the pictured life of an illustrated book and now the book had closed and let her wriggle out newborn" (239). For a short time Julia almost lapses into respectability when she agrees to marry insurance man Joe Delaney, a young widower with a daughter about her own age when she first came to live with the Devignys. But Julia is not ready to be anyone's wife or mother. In fact, she assuages her boredom during the Delaney engagement by stealing purses, dresses, or whatever strikes her fancy.

The later stages of Julia's descent into an abyss of drugs, sensuality, and death bring Springland, Marnie, and Wilma Wharton back into her life. In fact, her memories of Dev seem to propel her toward Marnie in a psychological pattern that the author very deliberately develops. Spencer has herself discussed this pattern, in fact, commenting that "Marnie is a kind of debased image of Henri Devigny, and . . . that association explains her vision. All through the book . . . Devigny keeps resurfacing in her consciousness just as Marnie keeps reappearing in New Orleans after he's thought to be dead." Spencer points out that "Marnie is a shadowy figure" because he is shadowy to Julia; he is a "shadow of her former experience with Devigny, the seducer."[6]

When Springland returns to New Orleans for questioning by the police in connection with the Marnie case, he and Julia resume their affair, though during the intervening years he has married and had children while living in Baton Rouge. For a while the renewal of the old affair is idyllic. Jake is asked by a black jazz group to join them playing at Preservation Hall, Dixieland, and other well-known clubs, a signal he and Julia take to mean that his music is "finally good enough." There is one particularly satisfying moment for Julia, who, living derivatively through Jake's involvement with the musicians, experiences herself a moment of intimate companionship when the band formally invites Jake to join them. The moment brings to her mind Dev's deep attachment to his friends of the Uptowners' Club, men with whom he had shared the deepest sense of community, men with whom he had identified and shared shame and humiliation, friends he had remembered on his deathbed. To Julia the communion with these friends and his family formed the innermost center of Dev's life: "She knew not everything, but enough. She knew he'd kept his communion, had found and kept it, until they died, and then he died, with memories, with the picture of his bride, with the living hand of his son in his, with Baudelaire—and with Julia, 'the child' " (322). For a brief moment Julia also feels the "supreme joy" of communion, when in the room with Jake and the musicians she moves submissively back to the circle of wives and girlfriends surrounding the musicians. She "knows" the truth: that "happiness is communion" (324).

The ecstatic interlude ends abruptly with the appearance of Marnie and Wilma Wharton, who materialize one day in a Cadillac on a street in the French Quarter. Julia never knows whether it is the publicity about her and Springland in a tabloid paper or some deceitful connection between the bandleader and Marnie that brings the pair back into her life. Spencer leaves the narrative ambiguous, although there are hints that the romantic hopefulness of Jake to make it as a musician and of Julia to discover human communion has led them both into Marnie's clutches. Spencer also suggests other motives at work—Julia's "life-thread," as read by a fortune-teller and intuited by Julia, shows that she has not yet "lived out her curse." Also, Marnie is drawn to her because, "God and Demon" that he is, she presents a challenge to him. She is a person "without limits," "without definition," and he sees her as dangerous so long as she moves beyond his power. What he does to exercise his will to control her is kidnap her and Jake, take them to a remote spot in the country, drug them, and force them into horrifying debaucheries that Spencer renders powerfully, though indirectly.

The defilement of body and spirit dispels any lingering illusions Julia has had about the glamour of the crooked world, and it rekindles her old shame and confusion over the experience with Dev. When she painfully recalls her debasement at the hands of Marnie, Jake tries to comfort her: "You weren't any worse than the rest of us," but his words do not comfort. " 'If there was any worse to get,' she murmured, weary and half-faint in the increasing morning heat. 'What self have I got but a body? Oh!' It was gasp and sigh at once. And knowledge. That none can break loose from words spoken or from action done" (342). Julia regards the humiliation of the flesh as both an outrage inflicted upon her and an act she sought at some deep level of being. "There was something in me that wanted to, that wanted it, wanted the worst that could happen." She accepts the inevitable truth a "voice" whispers to her: " 'There is nothing you couldn't do, Julia.' It was the demon's triumph. Demons tell the truth" (343).

At the end of the novel, Julia frees herself from the obsession with an evil, haunted world not so much because it is revolting and disillusioning, but because she is pulled by pregnancy into the ongoing, organic life of renewal. The conception of her child, Jake's son, brings her into the everyday world of ordinary people, where she later makes a modest life for herself and the baby. They live in a spare apartment, visited sometimes by Tommy Arnold, whom Julia refuses to marry—"by refusing marriage," Arnold thinks, "she was stopping his authority" (375). More than any other character Spencer has created, Julia Garrett struggles to find out what kind of human being she is, what her limits are, and then matter-of-factly sets out to live her life with the full knowledge and acceptance of her nature. In the end, "Fatherless and husbandless, she went about the world" (400).

In a short, final section entitled "Battle" Spencer doubles back in time to trace a final testing of Julia's painfully earned equanimity. In a dialogue with Tommy Arnold Julia tells of an event in her recent past more frightening than the experience with Dev or the humiliating night with Marnie and crew. Late-night assaults of her aunt and uncle and bombings of their Audubon Place mansion have convinced Julia that drug dealers, who earlier had tortured her for information about stolen heroin, had misapplied her desperate remark about a "cistern," taking it to be a reference to her aunt and uncle's estate. To protect them, at least to give them back the life they had before her "wild, scary" escapades had come to bedevil them, Julia set out to find and return the drugs and thus appease the mobsters who were threatening them all. Following a hunch, she returned to the country hideaway where Marnie had taken them, remembering that when she had left, she had done so as Jake and Wilma Wharton were making plans to kill Marnie and throw his body in a nearby cistern. When she returned to the place, she made a rope of silk scarfs to lower herself into the pit. There she discovered not only the heroin but the carcass of a buzzard and the ghastly "dead face of an old madman."

In this action—which, significantly, Julia herself initiated—we see the last step of her descent into darkness. She looked into the face of horror, seeing at the bottom of the pit the limits of bestiality. Death is the ultimate obscenity, overshadowing all others. When Julia recounts this mortifying memory of the cistern to Tommy Arnold, he urges her to free herself of the memory, to "wipe it out." Her response reflects her determination not to squander the years she's spent searching to know herself: " 'No, I'll have it, Tommy. All of it. I'll not refuse any part of it.' She sat up, eyes fixed ahead and widening with the discovery she felt banging against her. 'The joy's in that, Tommy. In not refusing' " (402). Julia is a remarkable survivor. Purified of dread and longing, cleansed utterly of sentimentality, she stands as a woman who with great deliberateness accepts her place in the "great life snare."

A Study of Evil

In a 1980 interview Spencer speaks of *The Snare* as "a study of evil" and remarks that, of all her works, it is "in a philosophical sense" her most "intensely thought-out book." Asked whether she saw any parallel between "the moral wasteland of *No Place for an Angel* and the dark and violent world of *The Snare*," she answers with an instructive commentary on the presence and nature of evil in *The Snare:*

Not a parallel exactly. In fact, I think contrast might be a better word. I've never thought of this before, but it strikes me now that the basic difference between these two books is their approach to the question of evil. In *No Place for an Angel,* evil is simply an absence of good, the result of a vacuum of despair. I'm not a student of philosophy; but a friend of mine, who is scholar enough to give me the right context, says that this is evil in Augustinian terms. But I happen to believe that evil is also an active force with an existence of its own, and it occurs to me now that it's this active force of evil that's loose in *The Snare.* That book rests, so the philosophers might say, on a Manichean understanding of evil as an independent power to be dealt with.[7]

Spencer goes on to discuss her belief that "evil is incurable," and to express her intention of showing in the novel that, despite the pervasiveness of evil, "life can still persist and grow into a kind of sainthood." In particular, she notes Julia Garrett's role in embodying her ideas of good and evil, pointing out that the character "arrives at a concept of saintliness as a result of her involvement with evil. . . . Julia has both evil and good in her nature, but the true measure of her character is that she never gives herself wholly to the evil."[8] Much of the narrative power of the novel, as well as its universality, grows out of the author's vision of Julia and the world that encircles her. The strength of the novel, in fact, lies in the engaging, often provocative portrayal of the mysterious Julia. Spencer said in 1972 that she "liked" Julia better than any other woman she'd brought to life,[9] and indeed she has created in this character a woman who can bear the full weight of experience that a richly lived life assimilates.

In *The Snare* Spencer shows many cultural forces at work forming the heroine Julia. The forces of good and evil arise from several traditions influencing her life—her upbringing, her education, her milieu of the South, particularly New Orleans. Spencer suggests something of the literary and philosophical influences on the protagonist in a scene early in the novel when Julia returns to the home of her aunt and uncle to retrieve some favorite books. The book she is most intently seeking is the copy of Baudelaire's poems that Henri Devigny had loved and taught her to read in French. She also picks up, automatically, her missal, "bound in white leatherette." Then she gathers up the several books she had kept by her bed: Charlotte Brontë's *Villette,* "which had given her a firm idea of how life could center around a woman's impressions of it," a book of modern poems from her college days at Tulane, and an old, battered book about folklore in the bayou country, the Cajun country where Dev had spent his youth (24). Without making too much symbolic matter of the books, one can recognize that they nevertheless suggest the range of the search that lies ahead for Julia.

The most determinate influence on Julia is Henri Devigny and, by way of Devigny, Baudelaire's *Les Fleurs du mal (Flowers of Evil).* Explicit references to Baudelaire throughout the novel, as well as pervasive correspondences between Baudelaire's view of life and Spencer's portrayal of Julia's world as a "snare," establish the primacy of the French poet as a literary influence in the novel. The novel's epigraph is from Baudelaire's "L'Irrémédiable" in *Spleen et idéal:* "le Diable / Fait toujours bien tout ce qu'il fait!" The reference here to the devil's handicraft as being always successful points directly to the attractiveness of the seductive world Julia embraces, to the vital, sensual appetite for pleasure that Devigny cultivated in her. The youthful Julia is a Baudelairean creature. When she leaves the house on Audubon Place with her cherished books, she feels flushed with the "self-glory of twenty-four, alive with creature feeling." Riding the streetcar to her apartment, she turns quickly to a remembered passage from Baudelaire's "Harmonie du soir" (Evening harmony): "Voici venir les temps où vibrant sur sa tige / Chaque fleur s'évapore ainsi qu'un encensoir." (The time has come when, on its stem vibrating, / Each flower, like censers, spreads perfumes divine.)[10]

Julia's capacity for sensuality is, of course, a source of her vitality and her danger, and her response to the lush materiality of life as often leads her into pain as into delight. For example, linked with the first lovemaking episode between Jake and Julia is a series of unexpected, painful exchanges—Jake twists Julia's arm behind her, and she is shoved down on the street by a gang of college boys. These experiences, however, intensify her pleasure in the moment. She "would not have wanted anyone to know how much a place with things like these, that sort of street incident, filled in her particular sense of life" (42).

Throughout the novel a Baudelairean attraction-revulsion for things of the flesh motivates Julia's actions. Her paradoxical attitude is expressed in many ways, but chiefly through the complementary relationships with Dev and Marnie. For all the elements of exploitation and perversion, the relationship with Dev represents a loving, sensually satisfying acceptance of life, whereas Marnie, particularly in death, embodies the sickening spectacle of the rotting carcass that is sensualism's final stage. Julia's world seems framed forever by the specter of a transcendent sensuality defined by Devigny and a decadent sensuality manifest in Marnie. She tries to explain her frightening vision of this world to Tommy Arnold in the scene near the end of the novel when she recounts her discovery of Marnie's corpse.

Whenever I close my eyes to sleep, to nap, to rest them, even to blink, I see that face. Sometimes I see Dev's face too, in clouds, dark and thundery or looking out of high windows—the windows over in the house on Audubon Place—or dark on white pillows in that same house, fine old pillow cases trimmed in embroidery, saying, *Je suis comme le roi d'un pays pluvieux . . .* always looking down at me, about to say my name. He up high and Ted Marnie down low. . . . Christ, Tommy, can you think how it is? I mean, for everybody there's a place where the thinking runs out and the world's held in place by something that's not known about really, a mystery, some people say God. For me, there's what I'm telling you. There are those two. (401)

The French scholar Georges Poulet has written incisively of the world view embodied in Baudelaire's *Flowers of Evil,* and a brief summary of a few of his chief points will serve to suggest the parallels between Baudelaire's vision of evil and Spencer's story of a heroine ensnared by a deeply duplicitous world. In an essay entitled "Baudelaire and the Real World" Poulet stresses Baudelaire's belief in the existence of evil, his belief that "its influence alone explains the dual nature common to all men, which none, looking inward, can fail to discern in the depths of his being." To the poet, the sinner is one who is "overborne by the weight of his guilt" and is "cast down to the bottom of a precipice." Many images in Baudelaire focus upon the sinner's slow, steady progress toward evil, as if following an inclined plane downward toward a pit. It is essentially Baudelaire's view of time as an unalterable past that absolutely shapes the future that informs Julia's comment to Martin Parham: "You can't choose your life, you can only discover it" (271). Poulet comments that, in Baudelaire's way of looking at things, "the depth of existence is simply the unfolding, as far as the eye can see, of a single human landscape: a landscape reflecting the same monotonous characteristics, a time-trap in which all men are ensnared."[11]

There are uncountable details of setting, character, and plot in the novel that grow directly or indirectly from the poems of Baudelaire. In addition to "Harmonie du soir," other poems connected with sensuous revelry are specifically mentioned. "La Chevelure" (The hair) provides an important context for Jake and Julia's lovemaking (136); and the atmosphere of "Parfum exotique" (Exotic perfume) surrounds Julia's most vivid memories of Dev. Reiterated imagery of a cat, associated with Julia throughout the novel, recalls several different poems entitled "Cat," as well as persistent cat imagery in many other works by Baudelaire. The lithe body and the mysterious aloofness of the cat are features particularly connected with Julia. Spencer also employs sea imagery, reminiscent of Baudelaire's use of such imagery,[12] to suggest the individual's desire to escape the stultifying, deadening world. Julia's sexual desire is repeatedly expressed in metaphors drawn from sounds of the sea. Her

body's "cries and harsh demands" come as "disembodied and re-
petitive as the sea in a shell" (45); Jake and Julia's lovemaking is
likened to a "hot tussle," in which they are "buried in the warm,
seething tide for days on end" (140). A more melancholy aspect of
Baudelaire's vision is suggested in a poem directly linked with Dev:
"Je suis comme le roi d'un pays pluvieux" (I'm like a king whose
realm is drowned in rain). This first line of part three of Baudelaire's
"Spleen" occurs twice in the novel, important as Dev's dying words,
spoken on a waning August afternoon.

What is central to all these associations between the poems and
the pattern of the novel is Spencer's employment of Baudelaire's
view of the human condition as a vast snare in which the individual
struggles to reconcile a desire for transcendence with a knowledge
that no such transcendence is possible. Julia Garrett's situation is
very nearly that described by Poulet in "Baudelaire and the World
of Imagination": "The point of arrival is a split personality. On the
one hand is the torturer; on the other, the tortured. One's thought
takes revenge on itself for the shame it feels at being what it is."
Julia's refusal to buy peace by "wiping out" her knowledge of her
debasement echoes Baudelaire's view that the only possible resolution to the painful psychological split "consists not in rejecting one's
shame, in hurling it violently in the face of the person one no longer
wants to be, but on the contrary in accepting that shame as the
common fate of all those who suffer."[13] In *Mon coeur mis a nu (My
Heart Laid Bare)*, a volume of critical and autobiographical commentary, Baudelaire writes of the inescapable duality that defines
human nature. His comments reflect the Manichean vision of a
universe split between good and evil, and it seems likely that Baudelaire is the chief source of this view that so centrally shapes *The
Snare*: "In every man, and at all times, there are two simultaneous
yearnings—the one towards God, the other towards Satan. The
invocation of God, or spirituality, is a desire to ascend a step; the
invocation of Satan, or animality, is a delight in descending."[14]

Spencer amplifies—and modifies—in the novel the Baudelairean
conception of evil with references to other literary sources. There
are many details that call to mind Dante's *Inferno*, and indeed Spencer
has said that in writing the conclusion she was "afflicted with a real
horror. I can't say what effect the reader might get, but the imagined
vision of the thing gave me something of the sense of horror of
reading Dante, his approach to the depths of hell, Satan chained at

the bottom of the pit."[15] Spencer's evocation of evil as a steady descent into darkness owes as much or more to Dante, of course, as to Baudelaire. There are also other connections between Julia's apprehension of evil and scenes described in Dante's allegory. For example, after her year-long affair with Jake, Julia has a vision of her world that draws upon several of Dante's circles of hell. "She was staring at the river and all at once it seemed filled with people, with the numberless heads of all the multitudes of the earth, pouring out of the distance and sliding past on the mile-wide stream. . . . Some people were holding to one another, out of desperation or love, then all would vanish, some turning clockwise with the current while others came on and others, inexhaustibly" (148). The muddy stream of heads plagues Julia's imagination, never entirely receding from her thoughts. She does not pass through the Dantean hell to come out on the other side, spared by grace from its horror. It is rather Baudelaire, finally, not the white missal, that frames her refusal to "wipe out" the memory of hell. Julia's journey through paths of evil and the shadow of death brings not the promise of salvation, but an acceptance of the necessity of making one's own reality, of creating oneself by means of choices that are sometimes free, but more often compelled by one's nature and situation.

An important contrast to Julia's avid embracing of the "crooked world," the scary, forbidding, even evil world, is provided in the character of her aunt Isabel. Isabel Devigny is a doll-like woman who has contented herself with an extremely conventional life. She has allowed herself one great passion, her love for her husband, but in many ways she uses the love to shield her from all other encounters. Sensual, passionate people like Julia and Dev frighten her, and threats of violence like those of the menacing drug dealers send her packing. Isabel's life is comfortable and, in many senses, sterile. The couple's son died shortly after childbirth, and Julia, potentially her surrogate child, is relegated to Dev's sphere of control. At the conclusion of the novel Isabel comes to recognize the cost to her of living the sheltered life. "I have life through you," she says to Maurice. "For myself I'm like a piece of china, and I've existed where I was placed to exist. I've no reality, Maurice. And it's too late" (394). What nudges Isabel to this recognition is a visit to Parham Station, to which the Parhams have invited her as a refuge from the bombing threats.

The Parhams illustrate a brand of "goodness" that is, at best, respectability; at worst, their intolerant Protestantism and acquisitive capitalism are the antithesis of life. In fact, the Parhams are one of the evils in the great life snare. To Julia, the Parhams' Mississippi is deadness and denial of life, the place "where you got disapproved of." When she meets Martin's sister Lillian, who is like Walker Percy's Val Vaught in *The Last Gentleman* in having forgone family wealth to work as a missionary in the West, Julia understands the danger the Parhams pose for anyone who wants a life different from theirs. It is after meeting Lillian that she decides to break her engagement with Martin, and it is in knowing that Martin died on his way to visit Lillian that Julia is assured he finally escaped the Parhams' control. Like Julia, Isabel comes to recognize the evil of the narrow, closed-up life when she visits Parham Station. She confides to Maurice: "When I heard them say what they did about Julia, . . . I knew . . . that life was with her. That I can't have life. I can know it when I am near it, but I cannot have it" (394).

In *The Snare* Julia is preeminently the character who "has life." No experience is foreign to her, not even the exotic voodoo and animalism that occupy the religious fringes of her youth. She was reared as a Catholic, but the church is more an assumed than a vital presence in her life. Her several encounters with black voodooism loom with greater intensity in her memory than any attendance at mass, and Dev's youthful back-country belief in the power of animal spirits to inhabit human bodies stays with her as a powerful stimulant to her adult imagination. She treasures a sculpture that represents, as she explains to Tommy Arnold, "a saint very little known, one who thought himself for a time to be an animal altogether— in his soul, I guess, being ugly and secretly wicked in some way. But then he couldn't know this. The sculpture is him believing he is only an animal, not a human soul. He's sitting by a stream thinking this" (369). The sculpture clearly prefigures Julia's position at the end of the novel. She has earned a certain saintliness by virtue of her unsparing, relentless effort to know herself, to know the full extent of her human nature. Her mentors, Dev and Marnie, have unveiled to her the full measure of her bestiality, and yet, in the end, she does not seek to obliterate this image of herself through the diversions of sex and drugs. Rather, she turns to the care of her son and the acceptance of Arnold's friendship.

The final paragraph of the novel weaves together in powerful imagery all the intimations of goodness and evil implicit in Julia's life. The scene portrays her making her way upward to her fourth-floor apartment, an ascending motion symbolic of her movement away from the pit. She carries her sleeping baby in her arms, madonna-like, but equally as present in the tableau is the figure of the cat, making serpentine motions about her feet, reflecting her continuing and inescapable sensuality. "Julia went inside. The neighborhood cat slipped past her when she opened the door. It circled about her ankles, mounting with her. On one floor a pipe was gurgling. The sound faded as she climbed, and then, except for the sleeping child in her arms, she had only the cat, which moved about her footsteps, weaving endlessly" (407). Julia does not erase her potentiality for evil, but neither does she despairingly reject her potentiality for goodness. She accepts both with equanimity.

Critical Reception

In sharp contrast to Spencer's earlier novels *The Snare* received scant critical attention among reviewers in major newspapers and magazines. Those who did review the novel found much to complain of and little to praise. Writing for the *New York Times Book Review,* Madison Jones, a fellow Southern novelist, expressed the warmest reception the book elicited, but Jones thought the structure confusing and flawed. He called *The Snare* Spencer's "largest and most ambitious novel," but he doubted whether the book, "despite some obvious excellence," would advance her reputation. "The Devignys are evidence of her powers of characterization, and there is, best of all, the image of New Orleans itself playing out its essential part in the story. This sense of the living city, rendered in its uniqueness, with its customs and its lights and shades, is probably the novel's solidest single achievement. But the virtues are simply not enough to obscure the flaws."[16] Specifically, Jones found the characterization of Julia vague and unconvincing, and the supporting characters, Jake, Marnie, and Martin Parham, "more like Julia's thoughts than like persons." Even more damaging, he wrote, was the zigzag handling of chronology, "the seemingly numberless cut-backs in time." In his view, the result of Spencer's design was a blunting of effect, a drag on the novel's momentum that produced a "loss of tension," ultimately, "tediousness."

Patrick Cruttwell and Faith Westburg, reviewing the novel in the *Hudson Review,* had a quite different reaction to Spencer's characters. In particular, they found Julia "innocent, determined, naive but not stupid—a convincing creation, for whom one feels the blend of pity, admiration, exasperation and anxiety which one would certainly feel for someone like her in real life." In fact, they wrote that the novel "abounds" with convincing characters, adding parenthetically, "And what a relief!—credible people in a credible world!" Where the novel flagged for them was in Spencer's "evocation of the dangerous world Julia explores," which they found "fuzzy" and "uncertain." In their reading of the novel Spencer never makes clear whether the "snare" is "incurably evil" or "no worse than excitingly unbalanced," and they conclude the review with the suggestion that the novella form, rather than the novel, is better suited to such ambiguities as those Spencer is portraying.[17]

Patricia S. Coyne also censures the novel's thematic ambiguities in the *National Review,* charging that "the author is attempting to make a social statement garnished with artistic pretensions." In a statement heavy with condescension and ridicule Coyne scoffs at the novel's theme: "The theory seems to be that if you are pushed or can push yourself far enough into an atmosphere antithetical to the eternal verities—into, in fact, evil—then you emerge on the other side into freedom." She concludes that "if novels really reflect the condition of society, if art imitates life, we're in trouble."[18] Well, precisely. One suspects Coyne reads *The Snare* all too well and rejects the dualistic world she encounters in it. Spencer herself is similarly troubled by the spectacle of the world Julia Garrett inhabits. She discussed her fears and uncertainties about this world in the interview with Charles Bunting. To her mind, many people find themselves caught in Julia's situation, snared between dangerous vitality on the one hand and a safe emptiness on the other. "We have the inescapable fact of a counter-culture arising and growing like a simultaneous growth along with the square culture." She spoke of her attempt in the novel to explore the lines between the two cultures, "how far one extends into the other and the tensions created and what becomes of the people who are touched, affected; how much danger is there and what can it cause, what can it give?"[19]

Whether because of its unsettling theme or the difficulties implicit in the style and structure of the narrative, *The Snare* has not yet found an appreciative audience. Most of the critics who have discussed it to date have focused on the novel's success or failure to project a compelling, lifelike world, but simple verisimilitude is not the major criterion on which an artistic judgment of the novel will likely rest. Neither is the intricacy of the novel's design in itself a flaw or excellence. Spencer does indeed employ a spiraling, forward-backward plot line, which expresses the protagonists's alternating movements toward the future and backward to the past. She also adopts other techniques that contribute to the obliqueness of the narrative—characterization built partly on the recollection and intuition of the central figure, interior states of mind rendered through imagery. To so describe the structure of *The Snare* is only to say, however, that Spencer makes use of well-established techniques of modern fiction. What future readers of the novel may well come to appreciate is the depth of Spencer's understanding of contemporary American life, reflected in her portrayal of one young woman at midcentury. Many of the same psychological and social forces that she charted in *No Place for an Angel* are present in *The Snare,* but in the later novel Spencer has created in Julia Garrett a character who bears the full weight of these forces, and yet who manages to live her life passionately, with knowledge and courage.

Chapter Nine
The Short Fiction

In 1981 Elizabeth Spencer published a collection of thirty-three works of short fiction that she had written during the years 1944–77. *The Stories of Elizabeth Spencer* included the ten stories of *Ship Island and Other Stories* (1968), the novella *Knights and Dragons* (1965), and twenty-two stories previously published in periodicals but not before collected. In the same year, 1981, the University Press of Mississippi also brought out *Marilee,* a collection of the three stories that share a central protagonist, Marilee Summerall. Spencer's stories exhibit a great range of subjects and settings, reflecting as her novels do her experience of having lived in several different parts of the world. In her preface Spencer observes that in many respects the collection called forth for her a retrospective view of both her personal and her professional life. "Looking back on the times of writing these stories means looking back on the novels that were being written also, either in my head or actually, means looking back, too, on the events and feelings of all those years."

One occasionally finds similarities between the themes and situations of the stories and those of the novels, as in the characters of "The Pincian Gate," for example, who recall Barry Day and Irene Waddell of *No Place for an Angel.* Not surprisingly, one also finds parallels between the stories' content and Spencer's own experience. A few of the stories, such as "The Day Before," are in fact nearly autobiographical. It is remarkable, though, that in view of Spencer's steady work on her novels during these years she also composed a considerable body of short fiction that in most respects is quite distinct from the novels in conception and craft. Indeed, what is most striking here is Spencer's power of imagination, which is reflected in stories that differ from the broad-canvas revelations of the novel. Understanding the demands of the form, she concentrates in the stories more often on the telling image, the gesture that can make a story cohere, than on plot or action. This is simply to say that Spencer's stories are as skillfully crafted and imaginatively put together as are her novels; she is equally dexterous with both the long and short forms of fiction.

Although Spencer began with short fiction early in her career, she did not turn to writing and publishing stories regularly until 1957. She wrote her first story, "The Little Brown Girl," in a writing class with Raymond Goldman at the Watkins Institute in Nashville. In the preface to the collection she gives the year as 1944, but she later corrected the date to 1945.[1] She submitted the story to the *New Yorker* at the time, but it was rejected. In 1950 she published "Pilgrimage" in the *Virginia Quarterly Review,* a story she omits from the collection. It is a first-person narration of a man's return after ten years to the university of his youth and of his measured remembering and judging of his youthful visioning. A static story, it fails to develop much richness of play between the narrator's present state of mind and his remembered university days. When the *New Yorker* accepted "The Little Brown Girl" for publication in 1957, Spencer felt, as she has written in the preface to the collected stories, "the stir of new possibilities for work." Many stories were soon to follow, most often appearing in the *New Yorker,* occasionally in *Redbook* or *McCall's* or, more frequently, in such literary quarterlies as the *Southern Review.*

While it is impossible here to explore the subtleties of theme and technique embodied in all the stories of this collection, which does after all represent a lifetime's work in short fiction, it will be possible to point up something of the range of the stories and to trace some of the recurring themes. Two of the most distinctive and memorable stories have already been discussed in an earlier chapter, and in some ways the theme that links "Ship Island: the Story of a Mermaid" and *Knights and Dragons* will be seen as central to many of the stories in this collection.

The Child's Separation

In their 1980 interview with Spencer the first question E. P. Broadwell and R. W. Hoag put to the author was whether there was "a common theme or other unifying principle" in the collected stories. "That collection spans thirty-three years of story writing," she said, "but, yes, I believe there may be at least one recurrent theme. I think many of the stories are about liberation and the regret you have when you liberate yourself. You see, however much you might want to, you cannot both hold on and be free. And that's the crux in a lot of those stories."[2] Sometimes, of course, writers falter at seeing and describing the broad designs formed by their work, but in this case Spencer's critical eye is sharp indeed. The stories have to do with many kinds of human conflict, but particularly with the interior conflict of the divided self, the ambivalent self that longs for connecting ties to others and for escape and a breaking of the ties. In a lengthy and admiring review of the collection for the *Hudson Review* Clara Claiborne Park identified this theme as "the need to get away," calling it "the pervasive theme of the stories."[3]

Although Spencer deals with many other themes in these stories, it is clear that the tension between connectedness and freedom is common to many of the works. She portrays these alternating impulses as occurring throughout one's life, beginning with the child's first venturing from parents and home. In "The Little Brown Girl" the child Maybeth employs imagination as a way of asserting herself and finding adventure. Trying the patience of her parents with endless questions, she finds companionship with the hired man, Jim Williams, who works in her father's cotton field. One day he mentions to the seven-year-old Maybeth something of his daughter. "He spoke in his making-up voice, but he looked perfectly straight-faced" (*St,* 5). The child courts the fantasy, letting herself half believe in the little brown girl's existence. In part, she's motivated by the wish for a childhood companion, but she also enjoys the mastery implicit in the creating of a playmate in her imagination. Despite her parents' assurance that Jim was only "fooling" about the daughter, she relishes the teasing thoughts of another child, exactly her own size and age, a dark double. One day Maybeth thinks she catches a glimpse of the girl, her imagination finally taking her to the limits of her courage, and she runs for the security of her mother's arms and the comfortable rocking chair.

Seven other stories in the collection involve a child protagonist or an adult narrator who recounts a childhood memory. All but one of these have a Southern setting, and they all involve to some extent the child's dawning recognition of his or her separation from the family and the concomitant sense of loss and freedom. In "The Eclipse" twelve-year-old Weston becomes infatuated with his voice teacher and with his own reputation as the town's finest choirboy. His teacher's tutelage and his reputation for singing gain him a certain independence from his parents, and he basks happily in his situation until Miss Eavers "jilts" him during a trip to New Orleans, where Weston was to audition for a famous boys' choir. He is outraged and miserable when she leaves him at the hotel and goes to lunch with an old acquaintance, a newspaperman in the city. She is to him a kind of surrogate mother and lover—he enjoys her protection, but he fantasizes about leaving home with her, taking her to Chicago where he will become a big nightclub star. The narrative voice of the story is gently ironic, exposing Weston's exuberant romanticism and narcissism with more affection than mockery. We see the childishness of his prank that pays back his teacher for her rejection: he abruptly pulls the emergency brakes on the train as they return home. Doing so wins his father's attention, for he is happy to see his son turn from singing to boyish misbehaving. For a time after Weston returns from his adventure, like the child Maybeth, he is somewhat subdued by the world outside. He has had a brush with the hurt that awaits him when he offers himself and his love to another, a hurt that at first sends him flying back to the family nest. Some days later, however, the security turns to boredom and suffocation, and he at last begins to apprehend the full costs—and gains—of growing up and breaking away.

In the subtle, delicately shaded story, "Presents," a little girl sits amid numberless presents and cousins with an after-Christmas sadness that she doesn't quite understand. Anticipation and excitement have outstripped the day itself, and she's plagued by the half-formed thought that her disappointment may foreshadow similar disappointments in the years ahead. She tells her cousin that she didn't get every present she wished for, but she can't remember what it is she wanted that she didn't get. For solace, Sandy turns to her dog: "They worship one another," her grandmother comments. "You know he was a Christmas present." But the respite from regret that she feels when her beagle is close at hand is short-lived. The family's talk turns to animals, how long or briefly they live—horses, turtles, beagles—and she is struck with an even deeper apprehension about the future. She senses that growing up brings transience and mortality, and, childlike, she is fearful. Spencer writes the story in the third person with the child's view as the controlling consciousness, with the resulting dramatic irony of the reader's seeing clearly what the child only intuits. As in "The Eclipse," the author's control of the tone is deft and sure.

In two other later stories, "A Christian Education" and "Port of Embarkation," the young protagonists come to recognize the vulnerability and limitations of their parents, with somewhat different reactions. In the earlier story an adult narrator recalls an incident when, as a young girl, she was left with her grandfather on a Sunday once when her parents attended a funeral out of town. She accompanied him to the barbershop and drugstore, a trip that would have been strictly forbidden had her religious parents been at home. On their return the truth was quickly out, and the child watched silently as her mother questioned her grandfather about the outing. His deliberate and self-assured answer revealed to the little girl an "immunity of spirit" that allowed him to live his own separate life. It was a spirit, she felt, that had been passed on to her. "After this," the narrator observes, "there was nothing much my parents could finally do about the church and me. They could lock the barn door, but the bright horse of freedom was already loose in my world."

The child whose father has recently departed for his military unit in World War II in "Port of Embarkation" likewise envisions freedom in the image of horses, but the vision, which comes as a dream after she has cried herself to sleep, appears rather as a threatening, chaotic power that leaves her troubled and apprehensive. Her tearful mother, her bullying older brother, and her absent father, who was clearly a protecting, steadying force in the household, present her with changes in the family that seem threatening. The story crystallizes the moment of the twelve-year-old girl's fear of the unknown future, her effort to find comfort from her mother, and her awareness from the example of her troubled older brother that following one's own way is necessary and painful.

In the stories "Moon Rocket" and "On the Gulf" Spencer portrays two children who react in almost opposite ways to the possessive, solicitous ways of the family and to their own bent for adventure. Bill loses himself in elaborate fantasies about moon people and flying saucers, wrapping himself so in his imagined world that he almost forgets about trick-or-treating with his friends on Halloween. When he and his young companion Janey encounter a menacing older boy on a stretch of land in a new subdivision plot, he suddenly senses his vulnerability and exposure when removed from the security of home and friends. Even his make-believe persona, the dauntless Dongoo, offers little protection. "Back of all his painful new knowledge stood two ideas: one was that children in Halloween suits

ought not to be thrown at and knocked down; the other was that
Dongoo, the Rocket Man, ought to Win." Like Weston of "The
Eclipse," Bill begins to see the danger and disappointment that can
proceed from his venturing.

Whereas Bill seeks a private world of the imagination, Mary Dee
in "On the Gulf" takes her place at the center of a household busily
preparing for guests. Like a sponge, she soaks up every nuance of
gesture and intonation that she witnesses. In perfect imitation of
her mother, she quotes, "A girl is known . . . by her hands, her
skin, her carriage, and her hair. We cannot all be beautiful." And
she mimics the maid's sentiments and dialect as readily: "Them old
Meades. . . . I wish they's gone already." In the story the child
has barely reached the stage of questioning her family's values and
manners, but she is clearly a sensitive recorder of the subtle emotional activity going on around her. In the concluding lines her
mother speaks to her sharply: "Don't you know better than to carry
on like that? What are you trying to grow up to be? . . . Stop
listening to us! Stop hearing anything we say!" But Mary Dee is
the kind of child who always listens, hearing everything. In both
of these stories Spencer relies heavily on dialogue and action, and
the characters have a sharp, dramatic presence. A work in a different
mode, however, is the artful story "The Day Before," in which the
first-person narrator relates a childhood memory.

Reading "The Day Before" to an audience in Jackson, Mississippi,
in 1981, Spencer spoke of the story as "autobiographical," adding,
"as the Marilee stories are not." The adult narrator of the story
remembers a significant moment in her girlhood, the time when
she started school, watched over with eager attention by her grandfather and the neighbors next door, an old maid and two bachelor
brothers. What she quickly gains from another child at school on
her first day is the self-reflective consciousness that others see her
and her life differently from the way she sees herself. Of the elderly
neighbors, the new acquaintance flippantly remarks, "They feed
their old dogs out of Havilland china," which came as no news to
the narrator, as she herself observes, for she had often seen the scene
herself. Looking back to the moment when she first beheld her
friends through another's eyes, she recognizes her innocence: "I did
not know what value to give to what I knew, what my ears had
heard, eyes had seen, hands had handled, nor was there anything I
could say about it." What she decides, even at the age of six,

however, is to accept, not censure, what she knows. "I knew if I lived to be a thousand I would never do anything but accept it if an old man fed his dogs out of the best china or if a parrot could quote Shakespeare."

Quite clearly, the narrator's approach to life has been to seek the world beyond the safe domicile and to treasure what she discovers. Such knowledge may in fact unlock life's treasures, as the conclusion suggests. On one of the narrator's recent visits home she played bridge with a friend who had gained possession of a beautiful glass box, which had once belonged to the elderly neighbors of her childhood. The friend had got the box "in a devious way . . . but had never been able to open it." As if her fingers remembered the hidden catch, the narrator touched the locked box and it flew open. She thinks that "something in me was keeping an instinctive faith with what it knew. A great hidden world shimmered for a moment, grew almost visible, just beyond the breaking point of knowledge. Had nothing perhaps ever been lost by that great silent guardian within?"

What Spencer strongly suggests in this story and develops in more detail in other works is the relation that exists between one's early intimacy and security with the family and one's ability later to go one's own way as a separate self, a free person. In "A Christian Education" and "The Day Before" the youthful protagonists have the certainty of support and affection but they also grow up with models of self-assertion or differentness, mainly in the figures of the grandfather and elderly neighbors. This experience in childhood seems to dispose the adult to self-possession and assurance rather than ready acquiescence to the expectations and demands of others. Spencer does not imply, however, that tensions between self and others are always easily resolved, particularly when the principal adversaries are independent-minded young adults and closely knit Southern families.

Holding On and Letting Go

Reviewing the collection of stories in the *Times Literary Supplement*, D. J. Enright observes that in the Mississippi stories the family is "a source of comfort but also of suffocation; it gives you your place in the world but a place determined by others, from which you separate yourself perhaps by necessity but certainly at your peril." He finds the theme "pursued in various guises, in varying degrees

of comedy and of tragedy, with sentimentality always evaded nim-
bly."[4] In a number of stories Spencer explores the theme of the
young adult's effort—typically that of a young woman—to thread
her way between the family's claims and her own desires and ambitions, to find a way of holding on while letting go.

In the memorable story "First Dark," Frances Harvey almost loses
the chance for her own life because of the responsibility she feels
for her invalid mother and, perhaps more to the point, because of
her bemusement by the past. Living in a small Mississippi town
with little excitement, she seems to live in a state of perpetual
revery, in which ghosts of the past are friendlier than prospects for
the future. It is, in fact, a shared ghost story that brings Frances
together with Tom Beavers, a man whose family is not nearly so
high-toned as the Harveys, but who appears on the scene as virtually
her sole romantic prospect. His persistence and her mother's carefully
camouflaged suicide push Frances out of the Harvey house, and she
leaves with Tom, not even looking back. The house remains, "more
beautiful than ever," stately and imperious, as if it had "got rid of
what did not suit it, to be free, at last, to enter with abandon the
land of mourning and shadows and memory."

"First Dark," like many of the stories in this collection, incor-
porates a richly symbolic texture and vividly evokes the place—the
landscape and the society—in which the work is set. In her foreword
Eudora Welty remarks that Spencer can "faultlessly set the social
scene; she takes delight in making her characters reveal themselves
through the most precise and telling particulars." Many reviewers
also located their strongest praise for the collection in Spencer's
acute understanding and depiction of the subtle workings of a class-
conscious society. Clara Park comments that "no other Southern
writer faces so clear-eyed . . . the central reality of the settled life
of a Southern town—the divisibility of human society into classes.
There the sense of place is vertical as well as horizontal; part of
knowing who you are is knowing where you are, not only in knowing
your locality, but also, in the nearly obsolete English sense, knowing
your place."[5] Of course, for Spencer's characters the consciousness
that they not only occupy a place in the family, but form part of a
family who occupies a definite place in the community adds im-
measurably to the complexity of their establishing themselves as
individuals.

Few stories as well illustrate Spencer's grasp of the competing impulses within a person, especially a Southerner, both to identify with and to stand apart from the family as the three Marilee stories, "A Southern Landscape," "Sharon," and "Indian Summer."[6] Spencer writes in her foreword to *Marilee* that "there's a bare possibility" that she may have been like Marilee had she chosen to stay in Mississippi and had not been a writer. Certainly Marilee reflects her creator's sensitive awareness of everything that goes on around her. "If you're anything like me and sometimes turn through the paper reading anything and everything because you're too lazy to get up and do what you ought to be doing, then you already know about my home town." Thus Marilee begins "A Southern Landscape" in a breezy, self-deprecating voice, a voice that Spencer says was the feature her imagination first caught hold of. Marilee's hometown is Port Claiborne, Mississippi,[7] which has a church with a gilded hand for a steeple (as there is in Port Gibson, Mississippi)—a curiosity brought to the attention of her auditor-reader, Marilee conjectures, in Ripley's "Believe It or Not." Anyone coming to visit could easily locate her family's place because, in her words, "Everybody knows us. Not that we *are* anybody—I don't mean that. It's just that we've been there forever."

At the center of Marilee's tale is her high school romance with Foster Hamilton, a boy glamorously older than she, who "came of a real good family, known for being aristocratic and smart." Marilee's mother is convinced that Foster is the "nicest boy that ever walked the earth," but the fact is that he is a drunkard, though certainly no less glamorous for being so. The story, recounted twenty years after the central incident, reveals in the conclusion a Marilee who lives "far away," acutely conscious that "millions of things have happened" in the intervening years. Change and mortality are inescapable, as she sensed in her girlhood when she and Foster drove out to the ruins of Windsor, a colonial mansion that had burned in the 1890s. Vines encasing the enormous columns and crumbling plaster let her know that "what Nature does to Windsor it does to everything, including you and me—there's the horror." What brings solace to Marilee's heart of darkness, an inevitable effect of individualism and personal ambition, is the nurturing memory of her place—in the Summerall family and in Port Claiborne. Like the child of "The Day Before," she possesses this experience through memory, accepting it all, even Foster Hamilton's drinking, the "pure decay" of Windsor, and the gilded hand of the Presbyterian Church. "There have got to be some things you can count on, would be an ordinary way to put it. I'd rather say that I feel the need of a land, of a sure terrain, of a sort of permanent landscape of the heart."

In "Sharon," which takes its title from the name of the family home occupied by Marilee's Uncle Hernan (Hernando de Soto Wirth), she tells of her childhood discovery that the household she so much enjoyed visiting—Sharon—was finally the home not only of her uncle but of Melissa, the black woman who had come in her youth with Hernan's bride from Tennessee. Sharon, filled with beautiful furnishings, had always been thought of by Marilee as a reflection of the long-dead Aunt Eileen. Looking through the window one day, she sees Uncle Hernan and Melissa "talking together and smiling," and she suddenly realizes that Melissa's four children are part of the family. "That blood was ours, mingling and twining with the other. Mama could kick like a mule, fight like a wildcat in a sack, but she would never get it out. It was there for good."

In Marilee's unsparing revelations of the Summeralls and Wirths we witness the character's honest matter-of-factness about the family's strengths and shortcomings, not least of which is pride of name and place. Marilee herself shares many of the family traits, as she recognizes, and we see in her a cherishing of her family identity. Still, we suspect that her keen interest in members who stray beyond the family's tight control may suggest something of Marilee's urge to escape. In "Indian Summer" she speaks of a potential beau, Joe Richard, as having "the air of a divorced man, a name like a Catholic—all this, appealing to me, would be hurdles as high as a steeple to the Summeralls, the McClellands, and the Wirths (except for Uncle Hernan)." In this third Marilee story the narrator tells of another maternal uncle, Rex Wirth, who for years engaged in a struggle against the domination of his wife's family, the McClellands, whose presence is embodied in the farm his wife, Martha, inherited. The place is impressive, with a big two-story house, and possessing it, Rex is a veritable country gentleman. But finally, it is not his own, a galling thought that never leaves him. A dispute with his wife and son about development of the land, which has really to do with a challenge to his authority, sends him packing, and for months he lives with a backwoods family in a cabin near the Mississippi River. "Uncle Rex had been wild in his youth," says Marilee, and his retreat to a place and a woman he had known before his marriage signifies that he retains enough of the wildness and willfulness to stand his ground against the encroachment of the McClellands. Only by leaving, it seems, can he establish sufficient autonomy to make livable a life with Martha on the McClelland place. When he returns home, it is as a man who has reached a compromise between his love of the family and his private desires ("Uncle Rex—what dream did he have?" Marilee wonders). His compromise is represented as only part of a recurring conflict, however, for his son Andrew also faces a challenge to his separateness, brought on by the father's assertion of authority. And Marilee, too, registers with obvious feeling Uncle Hernan's concluding analysis of the heroic struggle between Rex and the family, which one senses has overtones of meaning for her as well: "Rex did what he had to. He settled it with those McClellands, once and for all. It was hard for Rex—remember that. Oh yes, Marilee! For Rex it was mighty hard."

The first-person narrator of "Prelude to a Parking Lot" shares with Marilee Summerall the dilemma of loving and living with a complicated, demanding family while trying to make a life for herself. Her vantage point, like Marilee's in "A Southern Landscape," is some years distant from the main action of the story she recounts. As a married woman with a family of her own, she looks back with equanimity to earlier family conflicts and a failed romance, knowing that once she had made a nervy, courageous decision that brought her emotional independence, of sorts. Telling her story in a sprightly, colloquial voice, she displays a classical recognition and acceptance of her fate, that she is destined to live in the thick of the family forever, but that "forever" for any one individual is a quite momentary stay. Seeing the family home in Nashville, site of so many memories, torn down to make room for a parking lot, she anticipates the comparable future that awaits them all.

The narrators of "Instrument of Destruction" and "A Kiss at the Door" also recall Marilee Summerall as they study their families intently for clues to how one goes about keeping active faith with family and class while letting go enough to follow one's own bent. The young independent woman of "Instrument of Destruction" studies science at the university, but she lives with her aunt, a Southern lady of the old school. The aunt is so rigidly trapped in her role of lady that she cannot—or will not—recognize that her way of life is not only dehumanizing but inescapably doomed. The brief story is rich with implication: the aunt's snobbery dooms her to loneliness; the neighbor child's churlish behavior absolutely contradicts the aunt's assumption that social class predicts behavior; and the narrator's assertiveness, despite her close ties to the family, suggests that she, no less than the child, will eventually prove to be an "instrument of destruction," for she is too forthright and willful to sacrifice her own perceptions or ambitions to accommodate tradition.

Similarly, the first-person narrator of "A Kiss at the Door" wears no lady's mask of refinement, but in some deep way both characters hold to the image of the cultivated or sacrificing lady. In the latter story the narrator searches her memory of her beloved cousin Felice to know whether the cousin's sacrificial existence was the consequence of the family's needs or her own retreat from life. And even if for her family and not from a failed will, "WAS IT WORTH IT?" she asks Felice in her imagination, and finally "were you human?" She guesses that Felice felt life as intensely as she, and so sees her own choice to make a life separate from the family as selfishly indulgent. Nonetheless, she does not recant and bears the worrisome conscience and divided loyalties as *her* necessary burdens. She imagines Felice as a self that she always carries within her: "Her little hand is in mine, feet urgent beside me, voice eager, as I monstrous, not deigning an answer, walk fast in a foreign city."

In the 1975 story "Mr. McMillan," the protagonist Aline tries to describe her Mississippi family to a male friend from Chicago, whom she has arranged to meet in New Orleans. "Of course . . . I love them all," she says, but it is clear from what she says that an abyss separates her values from theirs, her desires from their ambitions for her. "She believed in self-knowledge, even though trying to find it in the bosom of a Mississippi family was like trying to find some object in a gigantic attic, when you really didn't know what you were looking for" (*St,* 335). Still, she knows her search is not singular, for there is, after all, Mr. McMillan, who married and "had a whole life in some little town" in Mississippi for over sixty years, until one day he just calmly walked out, heading for New Orleans. Aline had met Mr. McMillan at the hotel where they resided—kindred spirits, she recognized—and she tells his story to her Northern friend, as if recounting a parable that says little but suggests the world about the impossibility of reconciliation between the yearning individual and the coercive, self-propagating power of the family. In other stories the relationship between holding on and letting go is often maintained in tenuous balance, but in "Mr. McMillan" the choices seem painfully exclusionary.

Desperate Escapes, Radical Searches

Elizabeth Spencer's vision of human nature as comprising an active outer self and a mysterious inner self shares features with that of many modern writers, including her friend Eudora Welty. The doubleness of Mr. McMillan's life, for example, is thematically related to Welty's "Old Mr. Marblehall." But Spencer has been particularly sensitive and adroit in her probing of those moments when the outer and inner selves collide, when the character—usually a woman—is shaken with the discovery that satisfying both one's public role and one's private needs is impossible. The discussion of "Ship Island" and *Knights and Dragons* in chapter 6 traces the embodiment of this theme in these two complex psychological stories.

Another instance of the conflict occurs in the fine early story "The White Azalea." Spencer portrays Miss Theresa Stubblefield on the first day of her first trip to Rome, suddenly called by letter away from enjoyment of the long-awaited visit to Italy to the needs of her aging family in Alabama. Theresa's methodical burial of the letter in a pot of azaleas, which symbolize a lush vitality and innocence, seems a deliberately gentle way to make an escape, but to classics reader Theresa, her act is a heroic gesture indeed: *"Well, I declare!* Theresa thought, astonished at herself, and in that moment it was as though she stood before the statue of some heroic classical woman whose dagger dripped with stony blood" (*St,* 69).

In a later story, "I, Maureen," the protagonist's escape is almost as wrenching and violent as that Theresa Stubblefield imagines. Maureen Partham, in a Cinderella-like marriage to the wealthy, upper-class Denis Partham of the Montreal Lakeshore set, discovers she can have her sanity and life only by abandoning the Partham world, including husband and children. Her situation calls to mind Julia Garrett of *The Snare,* who guessed what suffocation and emotional death would likely proceed from marriage to Martin Parham and so refused to marry him. Maureen lives the alternate scenario. This is a haunting story of psychological dissolution and pain, one of Spencer's very finest stories. The near-accidental death of Maureen's husband is the act that exacerbates her need for escape, although her initial vision of dangerous entrapment had come several weeks earlier, in a casual moment when her sight had momentarily been blocked as she was sunbathing on the family pier. "A bit of blue-green glass arching into the sun's rays, caught and trapped an angle of that light, refracting it to me. It struck, a match for lightning. My vision simply for a moment was by this brilliance extinguished; and in the plunge of darkness that ensued I could only see the glass rock reverse its course and speed toward me. It entered my truest self, my consciousness, reverberating with silent brilliance. From that point on I date my new beginning" (*St,* 344).

Maureen tries later, after her first suicide attempt, to explain the vision to her psychiatrist, but without much success. Her experience is like Catherine's in *No Place for an Angel;* the doctors can hardly listen to her in their haste to classify her symptoms, to fit her madness to a pattern. Despite the doctors' and family's efforts, Maureen finally can find no middle distance where she can recover sanity within her conventional life, and so she leaves them all, even her son and daughter, and takes up residence in a small apartment in East Montreal. She is like a fish, or mermaid, "thrown barely alive back into water," which in her case is a section of the city with small shops and accents of many nationalities. She finds a job in a photographer's shop, makes a home for herself in a small, spare apartment, and later takes a lover, a man whom she cares about and who satisfies her sexually and emotionally, but who does not demand the sacrifice of her identity.

Despite repeated attempts of the family members to draw Maureen back into the Partham life, she refuses to return, though in one episode she does reveal her deep love for her son and her willingness to make sacrifices for him. Desperately ill with peritonitis, he lies in the hospital, waiting each night for her to come from her job to spend a long night's vigil with him. She seems to her son like some spirit that makes his recovery possible. To her husband, Denis, though, her mystical power over the son and, above all, her insistence on living a life apart from them all are unwanted frustrations. "I don't know why you ever had to turn into a spirit at all! Just a woman, a wife, a mother, a human being—! That's all I ever wanted!" Denis cries out to her. And her reply, "Believe me, Denis . . . *I don't know either,"* states her sad destiny. Like Kate Chopin's Edna Pontellier in *The Awakening,* Maureen finds her disaffection with the conventional woman's life disruptive and painful, but she can neither will herself into submission nor will away her need for separateness. Like Chopin's character, she would sacrifice her life for her children, but she will not give up her identity for them. The life she chooses and makes for herself may be paltry and unimpressive, but it allows her to possess a core of self that is sturdy and free. She insists on being known as "I, Maureen," and in that insistence we find her desperate escape from the enclosed world of selflessness and invisibility.

It is perhaps more accurate to say of characters like Mr. McMillan and Maureen Partham that they undertook radical searches than that they sought desperate escapes. In other stories and with other characters the retreat from stultifying, deadening, or lonely lives may similarly follow a path that eventually leads to new beginnings and unexpected fulfillments, or it may take the way of inner recoil, a way of pulling back from the human world into daydreams and obsessions with mystery. In "The Absence," for example, Bonnie Richards tries to fold herself away from life, like an object in a drawer, during the lonely absence of her husband. In a more light-hearted story, "The Bufords," Miss Jackson flees from her schoolchildren, particularly the overwhelming brood of Bufords, to become a secret other self. "This was her secret, and when she went out, this was what happened: she turned into Lelia, from the time she was dressing in the afternoon until after midnight, when she got in. The next morning, she would be Miss Jackson again." And in "Wisteria," which is reminiscent of Katherine Mansfield's stories, the divorced, middle-aged Evaline wills away the emptiness of her life by giving parties, imagining acquaintances are friends and seeing only amiability and cheeriness.

Despite some implications of future disillusionment and unhappiness for such characters as Evaline and Bonnie Richards, their means of escape are not nearly so self-destructive as that of a character like Judith Kane. Narrated by a young woman onlooker who is at first intimidated and later victimized by the mysterious central figure, "Judith Kane" presents a powerful study of crippling self-consciousness. Spencer has spoken of the story as a "study of evil,"[8] referring to the destructive narcissism of the beautiful Judith. To be sure, she is "la belle dame sans merci," the beautiful lady without mercy, who feels compelled to bewitch or possess every man she meets. But Spencer allows us to see too much of Judith from the inside, to see her struggles with the insecurities that give rise to the narcissism, to make us believe in her as a personification of evil. The narrator's acute self-consciousness and need for privacy are a mirror reflection of Judith's preoccupation with finding a mate who matches her perfection. Both women live under a kind of spell of their own making; both are fearful of and fascinated by sexuality. In admitting her affection for the graduate student she has come to know during the summer, however, the narrator takes a step toward freeing herself from her debilitating self-consciousness. Judith, on the other hand, is stuck in her disturbed craziness, unable to allay her fears except by dominating a man. As Spencer reveals in an incident that forms a story within the story—the episode of Yancey Clements's window peeping at Judith's nakedness—Judith feels herself alive only when she sees herself reflected in another's eyes. Deprived of the reflection, Judith Kane becomes a witchlike shell of a woman. The narrator understands all this about Judith years later when she recalls her story, and in the telling of it she indirectly reveals her own recovery—or escape—from destructive dependency and self-absorption.

In other stories characters search to assuage anxiety or alleviate boredom in less ominous ways. The protagonist of "The Finder" allows his gift of second sight, an ability to envision the whereabouts of lost objects such as marbles, books, and rings, to set him apart from family and friends of Dalton, Mississippi. Gavin Anderson's curiosity and gift bring the strange and unusual into his life, off-setting the sameness of small-town life, and though occasionally troubled by thoughts that his psychic power might be the "Devil's gift," he clearly relishes his differentness—at least for a time. Not until he feels his marriage threatened and his relationship with the Anderson clan strained does he forswear the gift and the extramarital affair it has led him into. He has played with wildness and evil, he thinks, to the point that he has almost lost home and hearth. Still, he cannot stifle his fascination with whatever life it is that lies beyond the pale of respectability and safety. Driving home with his wife, having ended his affair with the flamboyant Mrs. Beris, he is possessed by fantasy. Something other than the steady Gavin Anderson emerges, another imagined self—the Natchez Trace high-wayman who two generations earlier had been the lover of Mrs. Beris's grandmother. The story leaves the reader uncertain whether his is a pathological or innocuous fantasy, but what is clear is that

Gavin Anderson cannot, however much he tries or wishes, forsake his wild, passionate self.

Two final stories in which we see characters retreating from everydayness or searching for fulfillment are "Go South in Winter" and "The Search," both stories that Spencer has said she sought deliberately to remove from Southern settings.[9] In the first story Mrs. Landis's daydreamy melding of a pleasurable memory of her son's youth and a radio broadcast's report on the death of some man named Landis produces a strange reaction. The protagonist halfway enters into a grief she knows is not hers, with pain and tears that send her from sunbathing on the beach back to her hotel room for the afternoon. But the daydream furnishes her a vehicle for deep feeling and dissolves her detachment, and in doing so refreshes her and returns her to "safe surfaces." In "The Search" Spencer portrays a husband and wife who for several years have searched fruitlessly for their daughter, a young woman who eloped with a college sweetheart to Canada and then vanished. The story's action marks their recognition that the search has become hopeless and that its continuation will finally undermine their life together and their sanity, especially the wife's. She has felt her identity most deeply connected to motherhood, and so has sought her daughter as desperately as one might fight off death. In a symbolic gesture she relinquishes the search and her daughter, seeing finally that the pursuit of a hopeless search offers neither fulfillment nor relief from anguish.

Modern Marriages

Some of Spencer's most sensitive and subtle stories treat the relation between husband and wife and the adjustments and compromises couples make to maintain a marriage. "Fishing Lake," "Adult Holiday," and "A Bad Cold" all center on a moment of conflict or strain when all the shared years past seem suddenly tested again, in each instance a casual moment that comes upon the couples without warning and elapses quickly, leaving them with subtly strengthened ties. In a story tinged with satire Judy Owens comes to understand much about her husband, his scholarly idol Thompson, and her own marriage in "The Visit." Although Judy "finished only two years of college" and her husband often finds it necessary to "put her right about things," it is she who fully takes in the significant details of their visit to the Thompson villa. One suspects that the concluding image of the story foreshadows the consequence of Judy's seeing so much—dislocation and change from their old relationship. "From the corner of her eye, Judy saw a huge boulder, dislodged by their wheels, float out into a white gorge with the leisure of a dream."

Marriage, like the relationship between child and parent, offers a vivid metaphor of one of the most basic conflicts experienced by a human being, the tension between one's longing for autonomy and for connectedness with another. For many of Spencer's characters, such as Julia Garrett of *The Snare*, the yearning for independence is linked with a curiosity about the underside of life, the allurement of the wild, untamed, and exciting. Julia sees marriage as a loss of freedom she will not accept, and though she bears a child and happily makes a home for the two of them, she refuses to marry Tommy Arnold. Maureen Partham discovers she has no identity apart from that of Denis's wife and her children's mother, and she literally loses her mind until she recovers her self—I, Maureen. Judith Kane fears commitment and marriage not so much because she is so in love with herself that she can find no one who satisfies her expectations, but because she knows so well her inextricable needs for both the debased Yancey Clements and the noble Scott Crawford. She has to have them both, at least the two sides of experience they represent. Similarly, the dutiful, family-loving Gavin Anderson finds himself drawn toward the exotic Mrs. Beris. Try though he will, he cannot purge himself of his fascination with romance and danger.

In one of her strongest stories, the recent "The Girl Who Loved Horses," Spencer creates a daring, willful woman who is slightly reminiscent of Ary Morgan in *This Crooked Way*. Her pride, desire for power, and fascination with sex are all imaged in her love of horses. As a girl, Deborah Dale had loved the danger and exhilaration of riding her calico pell-mell across a remote pasture, and when her worried parents asked, "Why do you ride a horse so fast, Deedee?" she answered, "I just like to." She marries Clyde Mecklin because he, too, likes horses and because when he "kissed her her ears drummed, and it came back to her once more, not thought of in years, the drumming hoofs of the calico, and the ghosting father, behind, invisible, observant, off on the bare distant November rise." For a while life seems to serve Deborah very well; she has her horses,

Clyde, and fast automobiles that satisfy her. Only her mother's desire for grandchildren is unassuaged. Emma Dale cannot understand why her daughter will risk life and limb breaking horses or speeding in a car, but to the question, "Why do you like to drive so fast?" Deborah can only answer, "I don't know." This is the same answer Judith Kane gives to the young narrator's question of how Judith could want both Yancey Clements and Scott Crawford.

The carefully wrought balance in Deborah's young married life proves to be precarious, however, for it turns out that wildness and marriage are finally not compatible, or, rather, that one cannot continuously sustain one's contrary needs. Threatened with rape by a young hired man who is nearly a physical double of Clyde, and later kidnapped and threatened again, Deborah experiences a level of fear and mastery she never before knew. She also discovers how deeply attracted she has always been to the mysterious, hidden self lurking beneath the surfaces of her husband and her father. Spencer subtly pairs the figures of Clyde and the hired man, Deborah's father and a wandering tramp to suggest the doubleness of personality that answers her complementary needs. Deborah's frightening encounter with rape and death seems to exorcise her wild demon, and she returns home with a somber sense of a new beginning. She has met the challenge of sexually menacing men and unbroken horses, and she is ready for a different challenge. "I want my children now," she says to Clyde, "her anger, her victory, held up like a blade against his stubborn willfullness." She speaks with finality and resignation, like Julia Garrett at the conclusion of *The Snare*. She is ready to leave behind the youthful self and take up the burdens of the family.

In this absorbing, intricate story, which is the final entry in *The Stories of Elizabeth Spencer,* the author reveals the broad dimensions of the human need for separateness, for escape from dominating, suffocating ties. She also shows here, as elsewhere throughout the collection, the individual's need for reconciliation and sacrifice. In these thirty-three stories Spencer portrays a remarkable variety of characters in a wide range of settings and circumstances. What most of the characters share, finally, is curiosity and vitality—most are searchers and wanderers. Like Marilee's Uncle Rex, most of them come home, though some, like Marilee herself in "A Southern Landscape," come only so far as memory brings them. Such free spirits as she cling to their freedom and independence, but they still feel "the need of a land, of a sure terrain, of a sort of permanent landscape of the heart."

Chapter Ten
After the Storm

The 1984 publication of Elizabeth Spencer's eighth novel, *The Salt Line*, marked her return for the first time since *The Voice at the Back Door* to a novel with a Mississippi landscape and a central male protagonist. In many ways the book embodies a subtle and sophisticated recapitulation of themes Spencer has explored since her earliest works. As in the early Mississippi novels, she is concerned here with the relation of the individual to the past, particularly to family and community traditions that prove vital or antithetical to growth and renewal. Like Kinloch Armstrong, Amos Dudley, and Duncan Harper, Arnie Carrington of *The Salt Line* grew up in the Mississippi hills, though it is not so much native land that he shares with the others as an earnest willingness to act in behalf of his principles. He is by profession, however, a man of thought, an English professor devoted to the life and works of the romantic poet Lord Byron. Spencer thus portrays him as a complex man of action who is also an intellectual, a scholar who is a sensual romanticist.

We see in Arnie a man older and wiser than the chief characters of the early novels, a man in his sixties, trying to maintain hopefulness and purposefulness even after betrayal and loss. Living on the Gulf Coast in the early 1970s, he has lived through difficult times: the campus upheavals of the 1960s, which indirectly cost him his professorship; the 1969 hurricane, Camille, which devastated the Mississippi coast; and finally the death of his wife. Arnie's years of struggle for autonomy and independence are largely behind him, and what he faces is his turn in the human cycle to be the guardian, the preserver of tradition, the caretaker of whatever of the past is to be maintained for future generations.

The Salt Line has affinities with *The Snare* and, especially, with *No Place for an Angel,* for thematically it presents a kind of sequel to these novels. Arnie's situation at the opening parallels that of Catherine and Julia at the conclusion: having survived life's storms, literally and metaphorically, he is at the point of setting out upon a final stretch of life. He engages the question that frames Robert

Frost's poem "The Oven Bird": what to make of "a diminished thing," how to live late years, heading toward death. Spencer's Arnie Carrington is an appealing and compelling character who tries to "gather everything up" that he knows about love and death, thought and action. Nonetheless, he sometimes acts foolishly and mistakenly, despite his age, intelligence, and humaneness.

Spencer has created in Arnie a deeply human man who registers the force of his violent, skeptical times. At one point he is overwhelmed by a "tiredness" that extends backward "through the many strains and tensions his generation had endured, all the way back to Pearl Harbor and the monotony of radios, reiterated shock news on a Sunday morning in December—opening gun of the American Age."[1] In Arnie's struggle to persevere in such an age, a gray world indeed, we find one of Spencer's most hopeful affirmations of contemporary life.

An Island Refuge

The Salt Line opens just at the moment when Arnie Carrington's past intrudes upon the refuge he has tried to establish for himself on the Gulf Coast. "On a Monday morning in October, Arnie Carrington went into a drugstore in Gulfport, Mississippi, and saw the one person he least wanted to see, Lex Graham. Lex was not supposed to be in that area at all." In the brief paragraph Spencer establishes the central characters and the setting, insinuates past conflicts, and sets up the first move in a suspenseful plot that moves intricately but surely to final revelations about Lex and Arnie. In his generally positive review of the novel for the New York Times Anatole Broyard reiterated the praise Spencer has so often received in the past for her mastery of the craft of fiction, a theme also picked up by Christopher Porterfield in his review in Time. Ironically, Broyard views her skill in creating a well-made novel to be so rare among current writers as to constitute nearly an obtrusive style: "Because it's not so much in evidence anymore, craft in a novel paradoxically reminds us of the author's presence, instead of obliterating it. This moves so naturally and so well, we think, that it must be a fiction. Life isn't as tidy, as well plotted, as that."[2]

Arnie Carrington's life is not really a tidy one, however, nor is Spencer's portrayal of it, except in the sense that she writes a clear and lucid prose. One does have the sense that Spencer is always in control of her material, but the design of the novel is flexible and expansive, allowing for the development of a number of characters not only through straightforward narrative but through the countless subtle ways of image and symbol. The four-part structure of the novel traces a year in Carrington's life, from the October morning when he first spies Lex Graham to the following September. Arnie's four-year residence on the Coast has commenced when he resigned his position on the English faculty at Hartsville University, a state institution that lies about an hour's ride northward—a fictitious setting, as is the small coastal town of Notchaki where Arnie resides, though Spencer quite clearly draws upon her knowledge of the geographical area and of academic life in general for her details.

A charismatic teacher and a promising scholar, with one book published on Byron and another underway, Carrington had been drawn into various protest movements on campus in the 1960s: "Contentions, disputes . . . over causes he'd thought he could help win. Blacks enrolled at the university, scandal over veterans' housing, Vietnam protest" (25). Placards bearing the phrase "Carrington Cares" bore witness to the students' esteem and to a fame that, unfortunately, would turn quickly to notoriety with the shifts in the national political scene and in local academic politics. Among others, his colleague Lex Graham, bearing old grudges of professional jealousy and, more important, suspecting rightly that his wife Dorothy and Arnie had for a time been lovers, sets him up for censure, bringing groundless charges of an affair with a student. Arnie's victimization is not particularly remarkable—an agent of change who with the next new wave becomes the displaced old guard—but his ungrudging, almost cheerful willingness to make a new beginning is unusual, and the spirit and vitality he musters in the face of adversity make him one of Spencer's most memorable characters.

To a large extent, it is his wife Evelyn's uncommon wit and courage that account for Arnie's capacity for renewal. "What do you do when something's over?" he wonders, as he drives from Hartsville, having deposited his scrawled resignation in intercampus mail. "You finish your book," Evelyn tells him. "Everyone should be so lucky. You have a book to finish" (111). He seeks the refuge of the Coast because it is the place that since childhood has represented for him escape from oppressiveness. "If anything bugged you, head to the Coast. There was sun and peaceful sort of light, great tranquillity, a kind of inner breathing came on, the wind made the old trees whisper and stirred the long moss hanging to the ground. To open your eyes on a new day was happiness" (37). Once past the "salt line," an imaginary line where one first caught smell of the salty Gulf, he could find safety.

But, of course, Arnie finds that there is no such island, no such brave new world where one is magically immune from unhappiness and mortality. A hurricane comes to destroy much of the Coast's beauty, and Evelyn's painful bout with cancer even constrains him finally to hasten the death of her whom he most loves. Quixotically, he turns in his despair to the one compelling cause that seems worth living for, the restoration of the Coast to some of its former grace and beauty, the way he remembered it from childhood, Arnie's protest against neon and golden arches. He tells his architect friend, Joe Yates, "I'm keeping faith with what I remember. I'm giving it back if I can. Somewhere else, I'd do something different. But I'm not there—not somewhere else—I'm here. A guardian" (38).

Unfortunately, Arnie's guardianship does not go well for either him or his cause. He seems for a time a failed Prospero, "king of a ruined country," he thinks, for his plans collapse, his money dwindles, and, most distressing, he suffers from a sexual impotence that has afflicted him since Evelyn's death. His efforts to restore his and the area's vitality are self-defeating, even defensive and reactionary. He refuses to sell a small offshore island he owns, for he fears Evelyn's grave, located on the island, will be desecrated by the proposed purchaser, newcomer Frank Matteo, whom Arnie suspects has Mafia connections and wants the island for drug deliveries. Rebuffing Matteo but desperate for money, Arnie writes Lex Graham, recent inheritor of his father's fortune, in an effort to enlist Lex's financial sponsorship of some of his business enterprises. It is a move that unleashes the past upon Arnie—and Lex—and it leads ultimately to both potency and destruction.

The male characters of *The Salt Line* dominate the action, but their gestures and defenses result in little more than an increasing of their pain and vulnerability. It is through the agency of women and the human connections uniquely available through families that the men find whatever islands of refuge exist for human beings. The memory of Evelyn sustains Arnie through the years of his intensest grief. He regularly visits her grave, where to him she is recoverable as some hovering spirit with which he seeks communion, though at last his hold to the past turns morbid and life-threatening. In a mysterious chain of events, as if Evelyn's protecting spirit were in control of actions designed to return him to the living, Arnie is freed of his morbidity, his impotence, and ultimately of Lex's menace.

Accepting Arnie's invitation to survey the island, Lex is bitten by an exotic viper, presumably brought there in a drug cache from Southeast Asia, though much about the island scene suggests that Evelyn's ghost exists in more than Arnie's imagination. Interestingly, the short review of the novel that appeared in the *Atlantic* concluded that "in an oblique way, this is a ghost story, and a very fine one."[3] But Spencer leaves the possibility of Evelyn's presence in spirit as only that—a possibility. We know only that a presence, manifest in a swarm of butterflies, then in an illusory appearance of a naked woman, seems to lead Lex to the destined snakebite and the resulting severe illness that draws his family to the Coast, a chain reaction of events that eventuates in the embittered Lex's leaving the Coast permanently.

Dorothy Graham and daughter Lucinda occupy much of Lex's thought, and he acts, often irrationally, in response to his unrealistic images of them, images upon which he has based most of his pride of manhood. An eighteenth-century scholar, Lex is a man obsessed with order and control, a perverted model of the Enlightenment, whose rigidity subjects him to certain disappointment. "Poor Lex" was Evelyn Carrington's phrase, and she used it with sympathy. Dorothy and Lucinda are Lex's proudest possessions, the most prized of the furnishings that decorate his house. With his newly inherited fortune, he wants to purchase a mansion on the Coast to showcase Lucinda with style. Spiritually impoverished, he is most at home tooling back and forth between destinations in his beige Mercedes. No wonder Dorothy and Lucinda both gravitate to the more immediate and earthy realm of Arnie Carrington. Dorothy's is an especially sad case. Her marriage is as surely ended as if she were widowed, but she lacks the active will or courage to leave Lex. Instead, she takes leave of her sanity and thereby, ironically, restores Lex's role as husband. Her interminable need for mental treatment and her crazy wanderings from her home to distant nightspots make Lex a guardian, giving him the focus and clear function he so desperately requires.

Lucinda Graham is a projection of her father's pride, and indeed she exists in the novel only through the eyes of Lex and Arnie. For Lex she is like one of his portraits of eighteenth-century belles, a portrait come to life. For Arnie, she is an embodiment of youth and beauty, with the power of a loving daughter or youthful lover to restore his spirit and happiness. As Lex lies feverish and stricken in the hospital, Lucinda leaves his side for a walk with Arnie to the nearby lighthouse. They talk of Byron, Lucinda having done a school report on the poet, and then of Arnie's house, with its great Buddha statue, washed up after the hurricane, which presides over a make-shift garden and a flock of white ducks. Arnie's conversation dazzles Lucinda, and in turn she gives him a rapt, admiring attention that swells his ego. There are many details in *The Salt Line* that recall Shakespeare's *The Tempest*—the storm, the island, the arrival of the protagonist's betrayer—but Lucinda, seen through Arnie's eyes, particularly recalls Miranda of the play. Lucinda's delight in the world that she glimpses through Arnie not only gratifies him but restores his "power."

Although Spencer is deliberately ambiguous in the lighthouse episode about the nature of the intimacy between Arnie and Lucinda, the passage is quite clear in revealing the magical sexual empow-erment that Arnie feels. The language subtly underscores Arnie's romantic penchant for idealizing and aggrandizing life:

His heart constricted, almost with pain, before it burst forth, blooming with utter wonderment. And straight on the heels of that came power, like a flash of fire. The old lighthouse on its green lawn must have teetered from the force of magic within. He called her name, softly, and she turned at once, face flushing with sudden bright expectancy, and in a word, which burst out . . . she was his, all else thrown aside, claimed forever. . . . "Understand me," he was wildly pleading, rough hand to soft cheek. "Please do! I was never any age but yours!" (149–50)

Sexually aroused, he goes immediately to Barbra K., a black woman who "from time to time had tried to help him," and for the first time he consummates the two-year-old affair. Hours later, having returned home, Arnie is surprised by the arrival of Dorothy Graham, who has read in Lucinda's sketchy account of the lighthouse visit with Arnie what she takes to be a message to her to come to his bed. "She meant, then, not to conquer but to end it, finish in a flash of glory, where surrender has the air of victory" (168).

Barbra K., Lucinda, and Dorothy Graham all enable Arnie to recover his sexual potency, but it is another woman, Mavis Henley, who helps him recover his capacity for caring involvement with people. Mavis, victim of two bad marriages and a failing love affair with Frank Matteo, is down and out when she and Arnie strike up a friendship in Matteo's restaurant early in the novel. Weakened by her unhappiness and a recent abortion Matteo has insisted upon, Mavis is in even more need of reclamation and restoration than is Arnie's hurricane-damaged real estate. Their relationship, born of mutual trust and need, draws Arnie into the organic, human enterprise, in which the guardianship and preservation that most matter are the provisions for a future generation.

Mavis and Arnie are not lovers, though most of the community suspect that they are, oblivious to Arnie's grief for Evelyn or Mavis's love for Matteo. After a brief reunion with Matteo results in a new pregnancy for Mavis, most assume the child is Arnie's, particularly since he sees to her care, helping her set up a small art supplies business and seeing her daily as she comes to visit him and care for the flock of ducks. In ways that matter, of course, they are a family, she a daughter, wife, surrogate lover, and Arnie, a father-husband. During the spring and summer of her developing pregnancy, Arnie is reunited with his own son, the child of a first marriage, a young man who has tried to start a new business in Texas but who, like his father, has fallen on hard financial times. During this time Arnie also returns to his book about Byron's last days, a biography of the poet in Greece during the last months of his life. But good times seem always to be followed by bad, especially in families, whether they are natural or acquired ones.

A shocking, bloody massacre of the white ducks in Arnie's garden brings terror one day to Mavis and recharges Arnie's old helpless rage against the uncertainty and destructiveness that seem to stalk him. In rebellion, he goes immediately to Matteo, charging the violence to a group of young people who include Matteo's nephew—"hippies," all having come to the Coast for the summer and taken up residence in an old vacant house. Culpable in many acts that have offended the genteel population of Notchaki, they are nonetheless innocent of the assault on the ducks. With much of the same motive that had led Lex Graham to force Arnie from Hartsville University, Arnie turns on the "weasels," as Joe Yates has named them, making scapegoats of them and Matteo for Mavis's troubles, his troubles, the world's troubles. Matteo, whose complicated life story is developed in a lengthy section of part three of the novel, turns out to be a troubled and yet appealing character, for all his underworld connections. Entrapped by family responsibilities and divided sympathies, he rages in frustration at his nephew and the gang of youths, and finally burns the house in a rampage that leaves one of them dead, another injured.

In the final part of the novel Spencer fully develops the ironies implicit in much of the preceding action, showing how divergent are aims and results, how false and misleading are appearances. Arnie at last approaches financial solvency by selling his island to Frank Matteo, a sale encouraged by Joe Yates, who without Arnie's full knowledge has arranged to have the island taken over by the federal government. The cultivated Southern gentleman, rather than the newcomer mobster, is thus the manipulator. The self-pitying, rigid man of order, Lex, turns out to be the murderer of ducks, and Matteo, seemingly so tight-lipped and controlling at the beginning of the novel, is not only hoodwinked in the island deal and spurned as a result by his Mafia "connection" in Florida, but then is haplessly assaulted by a tornado on his way back to Mississippi.

The final scene of the novel brings together Arnie, Barbra K., Joe Yates, and Frank Matteo in the hospital where Lex Graham had once lain stricken and earlier Evelyn Carrington had died. The premature birth of Mavis's child, coming after so much violence and misunderstanding, epitomizes the renewal and restored order that the group of friends and acquaintances seek and finally experience. For the first time Arnie notices how much Barbra K. resembles Evelyn, and he thinks, "We can go to the island one day. . . . But no need to go there, really, with her here, ashore" (301). Like godparents, they with Joe Yates await the news of the birth, wondering whether Matteo will acknowledge his child.

The closing action of the novel is problematic, reinforcing Spencer's portrayal throughout the book of a world that constantly oscillates between order and chaos, restoration and destruction, familial love and loneliness. Matteo does relinquish his carefully wrought callousness, eagerly greeting the news of his son's birth and Arnie's command to go to Mavis. " 'You think I don't want to? Seeing my son. Why that's all there is! . . . You think that's not everything there is?' he challenged. 'You think for a minute that's not all?' " (302). But in his desperate reiteration of the question, the last lines of the novel, we sense Matteo's fright and tentativeness about giving up his separateness to take his place as husband and father. Nevertheless, the mantle of responsibility has passed to him, the "damned crook, this dark projection in their lives," Arnie thinks, hoping Matteo will prove to be worthy and reliable in his new role as guardian. In any event, Arnie faces the uncertain future with no choice at all but to accept what comes, including Frank Matteo. Arnie himself feels "ancient" as he sits in the hospital waiting room, and when he momentarily blanks out, falling to the floor, it is Frank who lifts him up and helps him to his chair. To Arnie's credit, he serenely accepts the fall and the helping hand. In doing so, he defines and exemplifies the best life mortals can make of the human condition.

Arnie Carrington finds his dream of an island refuge, a haven encircled by the salt line, to be an illusion. He discovers that life's invasions will not be forestalled by lines or walls or water. Whenever such a realization has come upon him, intermittently throughout the novel, Arnie has sought solace for his unhappiness and despair by turning to meditation before the Buddha in his garden, but even the Buddha is taken from him, removed to a museum in New Orleans. The Buddha, symbolic of the transcendent spirit, and the white ducks, so typical of the mundane and mortal, suggest the splendid and comic proportions of human beings. As a respectful lover of both the heroic and comic tendencies that men and women harbor, Arnie makes a journey one day to visit the Buddha, locked away in the museum's storage department, in his efforts to attain the serenity and spiritual wholeness that accommodate both tendencies. It is a spring day shortly after the slaughter of the ducks, and Arnie is deeply troubled with both old griefs and new thoughts of death. Spencer communicates the pathos of his appeal to the Buddha in a powerful, slightly ironic understatement:

"Two ducks are left. It's why I came, to tell you about it. And ask: How can we gather everything up? Everything we know? And preferably not as corpses." His sign at this was profound, occurring on the moment of rising. He bent to touch the bronze knee and a tear fell for everything from wives to ducks to poets dead in Greece. It landed on the Buddha's slippered foot and he wiped it off with the end of his tie, patted the solemn knee, and went away. (277)

What Spencer gives us in the character of Arnie Carrington is a life intensely felt, and thought, and lived. She does not imply that human frailty or sorrow can be mediated by appeal to some other, heavenly world, but she does suggest that the human spirit is sufficient, with its boundless capacity for love and hope, to sustain us in this life.

A Lifetime of Fiction

In eight novels and nearly forty short stories written over a span of forty years, Elizabeth Spencer has established herself as a writer admired for her literary craftsmanship. Occasionally, reviewers have qualified their praise with comments or implications that the author's mastery of craft has somehow come at the cost of substance, though it seems odd indeed to discredit craft as a flaw of vision. In some of the later works, especially *The Snare,* the dense texture of the prose has elicited the opposite response, that the rich detail of the book is so subtle and indirect that craft and clarity suffer. For the most part, however, Spencer's fiction has received strongly favorable reviews in the most respected literary magazines and newspapers in the country ever since the publication of *Fire in the Morning* in 1948.

In light of her literary reputation, it is puzzling that her fiction has so seldom attracted the attention of literary critics, particularly academic critics, for more penetrating and detailed analysis than is possible in reviews. To some degree the explanation may lie in the fact that Spencer has written largely in the tradition of realism. Though she has experimented with multiple narrators, interior monologue, intricate chronologies, symbolic imagery, and many other devices of psychological revelation of character, in the main she has stayed with the traditional forms. She has given her readers a canon of fiction notable for strong, memorable characters, for suspenseful, coherent plots that belong to the best tradition of the novel, and for a narrative style that is vigorous but amazingly smooth and supple. In her writing she has drawn deeply from her own personal experience, which has included years in Europe and Canada as well as the American South. She has also brought to the fiction her seasoned, informed observations about contemporary men and women whose lives are quite different from hers. In surveying all of Spencer's fiction, one is perhaps most struck with the variety of it—the presence of a great range of characters and settings and the broad exploration of themes that touch upon an infinite array of human conflict.

In the early novels, the Mississippi novels, Spencer re-creates the hill country of Mississippi in the first part of the twentieth century. In a milieu that includes both frontier individualism and a tribalism that enforces conformity and racism, she traces also the impulses within a person and a community that express the need for love and a desire for justice. Indeed, few works of fiction or nonfiction approach the keen accuracy of *The Voice at the Back Door* in portraying the lives of blacks and whites in a small Southern town. In a 1983 retrospective review of this novel John Malcolm Brinnin writes of its power and truth, showing as it does "a way of life obscured by outrage and oversimplified by headlines." He continues, "No other work of literature or any exercise in polemics made me better understand that the term 'civil rights movement' was but a paltry designation for a vast shift in awareness that had already occurred and awaited only the sacrifices of martyrs, black and white, to cause it to be written into law." Brinnin concludes that Spencer wrote of what she knew firsthand "with the kind of bare documentary exactitude which time lifts into metaphor—as though, from the mythological murk of Faulkner territory, she had emerged holding up a crisp photograph negative on which black is visible only in relation to white, and vice versa."[4]

Whereas in these early novels Spencer depicts the individual in a traditional society trying to strike a workable compromise between independent conscience and societal tradition, the later novels examine more pointedly the sacrifice of self that such compromises often entail, especially when the "individual" is a woman. In *No Place for an Angel* the choice seems bleakly to be either an independence that leads to loneliness or a sacrifice of the self. The fragmentation of modern life and the relentless quest of the individualistic ego undermine the efforts of those like Catherine Latham who long for a life where compromise is possible. In *The Snare* Spencer portrays a young woman who craves to know more of life than the genteel, daylight world reveals, and who in her search for knowledge and autonomy stumbles into the dark elements of the underworld. Shunning tradition and taboo, Julia Garrett forges an identity entirely for herself, based upon what she knows—deeply and profoundly—about her nature as the human animal.

But, in these later novels, Spencer provokes us to think of the consequences for humanity of radical individualism, a dominant strain in the American mind, and of unremitting self-consciousness, the characteristic mode of modernism. Finally, she suggests, the autonomous will devoted solely to the separate self will not sustain life. She portrays in the later works a Western society battered by social conflict and almost bereft of any sustaining tradition or shared values, a society threatened with sterility and morbidity by the abandonment of familial commitment and communal responsibility. To be sure, there is a needful time and place for youth's separation and independence, but if life is to be ongoing, Spencer implies, someone must finally be prepared to say, as Deborah does in "The Girl Who Loved Horses," "I want my children now." Implicit in the conclusion of *The Snare* and in the recent novel *The Salt Line* is the acceptance of such responsibility, signifying at least the partial forfeiture of self that is inescapable and utterly necessary to human survival.

In her 1972 essay "Storytelling, Old and New," Spencer noted that "the modern theme of self-exploration with heavy emphasis on the private sexual nature and fantasy has been done to the point of weariness." In her conclusion she clearly had in mind not only the wearisomeness but the danger posed by a society or a fiction dominated by self-obsessed, self-enclosed persons. "Can we think of ourselves again in communion with others, in communities either small, medium or large, which may be torn apart disastrously or find a common note, an accord? One word for it, maybe, is love."[5]

The 1984 novel *The Salt Line* focuses upon the search of a group of individuals for the common note that will connect and sustain them as a community of men and women. Here the central female characters play quite traditional roles as accepters and nurturers of troubled men. In fact, the danger posed for Mavis Henley seems not so much a loss of separateness as a loss of connection. What she needs as a pregnant woman soon to deliver a child is support, emotional and financial—the same things that Arnie Carrington needs. What is remarkable about Spencer's portrayal here of Mavis and Arnie, who to all outward appearances seem an odd couple indeed, is their similarity. Spencer's vision is androgynous, revealing in both man and woman the capacity for sacrifice and nurturance and the need for love. The characterization of Arnie Carrington is perhaps most unusual in that he unites qualities we often associate exclusively with either fatherliness or motherliness, masculinity or femininity. For all his manly sexuality and impulse toward territoriality, Arnie expresses a sensitive, solicitous tenderness for others. He represents Spencer's essentially hopeful view of the possibilities for life in the waning years of the twentieth century.

As woman and writer, Elizabeth Spencer has lived in the mainstream of contemporary life. Never having lost the sensibilities of a small-town Southerner, she has vastly deepened her understanding of the world through her years of study and residence in Italy and Canada. She told Charles Bunting in 1972, three months before the publication of *The Snare,* that she would like to write "two or three more large novels," continuing what she had started with *No Place for an Angel* and *The Snare.* "I feel more in focus with modern experience as a whole than I used to," she said.[6] One can only hope that *The Salt Line* does not signify a *Tempest*-like farewell to fiction, and that there will be more novels to come from Elizabeth Spencer. Her considerable talent, her gift for revealing detail and apt metaphor, and her wise understanding of the world she writes of give assurance of Spencer's growing reputation among twentieth-century writers.

Notes and References

Chapter One

1. "Storytelling, Old and New," *Writer* 85 (January 1972):9.
2. "Emerging as a Writer in Faulkner's Mississippi," in *Faulkner and the Southern Renaissance,* ed. Doreen Fowler and Ann J. Abadie (Jackson, Miss., 1982), 120–37; hereafter cited in text as *EW* followed by page number.
3. Charles T. Bunting, " 'In That Time and at That Place': The Literary World of Elizabeth Spencer," *Mississippi Quarterly* 28 (Fall 1975):438.
4. I have drawn biographical information from a wide variety of sources, including conversations and correspondence with Elizabeth Spencer. In addition to Spencer and to sources cited in notes, I have relied upon Laura Barge's "Biographical Note," which forms the first section of her invaluable "An Elizabeth Spencer Checklist, 1948 to 1976," *Mississippi Quarterly* 29 (Fall 1976):569–90.
5. John G. Jones, "Elizabeth Spencer," *Mississippi Writers Talking* (Jackson, Miss., 1982), 101.
6. Jones, "Spencer," 105.
7. Eudora Welty, foreword to *The Stories of Elizabeth Spencer* (Garden City, N.Y.: Doubleday, 1981), xvii.
8. Charlotte Capers, "An Evening with Eudora Welty and Elizabeth Spencer," *Delta Review* 4 (November 1967):70–72.
9. Louise Davis, "Girl with a Typewriter Drawl," *Nashville Tennessean Magazine,* 16 April 1961, 15.
10. Two different literary historians have placed Spencer in the "second generation" school of Vanderbilt writers. John M. Bradbury, *Renaissance in the South* (Chapel Hill, N.C., 1963), 117–8, discusses Spencer and Peter Taylor as having the "firmest reputations" among the "New Traditionalists." See also Richard Meeker, "The Youngest Generation of Southern Fiction Writers," in *Southern Writers: Appraisals in Our Time,* ed. R. C. Simonini, Jr. (Charlottesville, Va., 1964), 175–76.
11. Bunting, "Literary World," 440.
12. Elizabeth Pell Broadwell and Ronald Wesley Hoag, "A Conversation with Elizabeth Spencer," *Southern Review* 18 (Winter 1982):115.
13. Bunting, "Literary World," 455–56.
14. *Stark Young: A Life in the Arts—Letters, 1900–1962,* ed. John Pilkington (Baton Rouge: Louisiana State University Press, 1975), 2:1125.

15. Jan Nordby Gretlund, "An Interview with Eudora Welty," in *Conversations with Eudora Welty,* ed. Peggy Whitman Prenshaw (Jackson: University Press of Mississippi, 1984), 194.

16. Broadwell and Hoag, "A Conversation," 115.

17. Jones, "Spencer," 119.

18. Broadwell and Hoag, "A Conversation," 113. In a more recent interview Spencer has commented that her mother generally supported her writing, while her father "wanted the whole nonsense stopped." Laurie L. Brown, "Interviews with Seven Contemporary Writers," in *Women Writers of the Contemporary South,* ed. Peggy Whitman Prenshaw (Jackson, Miss., 1984), 6.

19. Josephine Haley, "An Interview with Elizabeth Spencer," *Notes on Mississippi Writers* 1 (Fall 1968):53.

20. Hunter McKelva Cole, "Elizabeth Spencer at Sycamore Fair," *Notes on Mississippi Writers* 6 (Winter 1974):82.

21. Brown, "Interviews," 12.

22. Kenneth R. Tolliver, "Elizabeth Spencer: Writer in Perspective," *Delta Review* 2 (July–August 1965):43.

23. The comment occurs in a letter received from Elizabeth Spencer, 26 September 1983.

24. See Spencer's comments in "Elizabeth Spencer," *Contemporary Novelists,* ed. James Vinson (New York, 1972), 1163–64.

Chapter Two

1. Hubert Creekmore, "Submerged Antagonisms," *New York Times Book Review,* 12 September 1948, 14, 16.

2. *Fire in the Morning* (1948; reprint, New York: McGraw-Hill, 1968), 24–25; hereafter page references cited in the text.

3. Broadwell and Hoag, "A Conversation," 119.

4. Ibid., 120.

5. Davis, "Girl with a Typewriter Drawl," 20.

6. Broadwell and Hoag, "A Conversation," 121.

7. Creekmore, "Submerged Antagonisms," 16.

8. Bunting, "Literary World," 442.

9. Djuna Barnes, *Nightwood* (1937; reprint, New York: New Directions, 1961), 86.

10. "Elizabeth Spencer's Three Mississippi Novels," *South Atlantic Quarterly* 63 (Summer 1964):352–53.

11. R. W. Flint, "Recent Fiction," *Hudson Review* 1 (Winter 1949):590.

12. Worth Tuttle Hedden, "With Passion, Suspense, Humor," *New York Herald Tribune Book Review,* 5 September 1948, 3.

13. Harrison Smith, "New Faces, Old Story," *Saturday Review,* 6 November 1948, 30.

14. Jesse Edward Cross, "Spencer," *Library Journal,* 1 September 1948, 1194.

15. *"Fire in the Morning,"* *New Yorker,* 30 October 1948, 110.

16. "Buried Evil," *Time,* 27 September 1948, 100–101.

17. Burger, "Mississippi Novels," 351.

18. Flint, "Recent Fiction," 590.

19. Henrietta Buckmaster, "People Within a Place," *Christian Science Monitor,* 28 October 1948, 20.

Chapter Three

1. Bunting, "Literary World," 440.

2. Broadwell and Hoag, "A Conversation," 118.

3. Jones, "Spencer," 100.

4. Bunting, "Literary World," 441.

5. *This Crooked Way* (1952; reprint, New York: McGraw-Hill, 1968), 7; hereafter page references cited in the text.

6. *The Complete Stories of Flannery O'Connor* (New York: Farrar, Straus & Giroux, 1971), 173–74.

7. Broadwell and Hoag, "A Conversation," 118.

8. Donald G. Mathews, *Religion in the Old South* (Chicago: University of Chicago Press, 1977), 39–41.

9. Martha Banta, *Failure and Success in America: A Literary Debate,* (Princeton, N.J.: Princeton University Press, 1978), 24–25.

10. Bunting, "Literary World," 440–41.

11. F. Cudworth Flint, "Fiction Chronicle," *Sewanee Review* 60 (October–December 1952):711.

12. Burger, "Mississippi Novels," 357.

13. See Bradbury, *Renaissance in the South,* 118.

14. Bunting, "Literary World," 437.

15. Ibid., 436–37.

16. Frances Gaither, "Amos Dudley and God," *New York Times Book Review,* 9 March 1952, 5.

17. Cid Ricketts Sumner, "Delta Characters," *Saturday Review of Literature,* 8 March 1952, 16.

18. "Seaboard to Shire," *Times (London) Literary Supplement,* 1 August 1952, 497.

19. Worth Tuttle Hedden, "A Thirty-Year Family Story Set in the Mississippi Delta Country," *New York Herald Tribune Book Review,* 16 March 1952, 5.

20. Anthony West, "Books," *New Yorker,* 22 March 1952, 70.

21. Nancy Baker, "Success Road May Also Lead to Ruination," *Chicago Sunday Tribune,* 20 April 1952, 15.

22. "Troubles in the Delta," *Time,* 24 March 1952, 108; Harvey Swados, "Faithful Disciple?" *Nation* 174 (7 June 1952):561.

23. Daniel Joseph Singal, *The War Within: From Victorian to Modernist Thought in the South, 1919–1945* (Chapel Hill, N.C.: University of North Carolina Press, 1982), 3–33.

Chapter Four

1. Introduction to *The Voice at the Back Door* (New York, 1965), xviii; hereafter page references to the introduction cited by roman numerals in the text. Subsequent references to the novel are to the first edition (New York, 1956).

2. Jones, "Spencer," 117.

3. Haley, "An Interview," 51.

4. Broadwell and Hoag, "A Conversation," 116.

5. Brendan Gill, "Books: All Praise," *New Yorker,* 15 December 1956, 180.

6. Orville Prescott, "Books of the Times," *New York Times,* 19 October 1956, 25.

7. Francis Hackett, "Portents from the New South," *New Republic,* 19 November 1956, 30.

8. See Borden Deal, "Edge of Violence," *New York Times Book Review,* 21 October 1956, 5, and Robert Tallant, "Call to Conscience," *Saturday Review of Literature,* 20 October 1956, 18.

9. Caroline Tunstall, "Southern Tense, Revealing," *New York Herald Tribune Book Review,* 28 October 1956, 13.

10. Lillian Smith, *Killers of the Dream* (New York: W. W. Norton, 1949), 137. See also John Dollard's discussion of "The Sexual Gain," in *Caste and Class in a Southern Town* (1937; reprint, Garden City, N.Y.: Doubleday Anchor, 1957), 134–72.

11. See Broadwell and Hoag, "A Conversation," 117.

12. Anne Goodwyn Jones, *Tomorrow Is Another Day: The Woman Writer in the South, 1859–1936* (Baton Rouge: Louisiana State University Press, 1981), 5. See also Nancy F. Cott, *The Bonds of Womanhood: "Woman's Sphere" in New England, 1780–1835* (New Haven: Yale University Press, 1977), 11.

13. Dorothy Van Ghent, "New Books in Review," *Yale Review,* 46 (Winter 1956), 287.

14. Bunting, "Literary World," 442–3.

15. Dollard, *Caste and Class,* viii.

16. Bunting, "Literary World," 443.

17. David G. Pugh, *"The Voice at the Back Door:* Elizabeth Spencer Looks into Mississippi," in *The Fifties: Fiction, Poetry, Drama,* ed. Warren French (Deland, Fla., 1970), 105.

18. Van Ghent, "New Books," 288.

Chapter Five

1. Bunting, "Literary World," 450.

2. Ibid.

3. Broadwell and Hoag, "A Conversation," 129.

4. Josephine Hendin, *Vulnerable People: A View of American Fiction since 1945* (New York: Oxford University Press, 1978), 222.

5. *The Light in the Piazza* (New York, 1960), 61; hereafter page references cited in the text.

6. Isa Kapp, "Literary Love Affair with Italy," *New Leader,* 20 March 1961, 27.

7. Granville Hicks, "Morality Play in Two Acts," *Saturday Review of Literature,* 26 November 1960, 18.

8. Spencer speaks of her first encounter with Forster's fiction, and of her particular admiration of *Where Angels Fear To Tread* in *E. M. Forster: Centenary Revaluations,* ed. Judith Scherer Herz and Robert K. Martin (Toronto: University of Toronto Press, 1982), 288.

9. Broadwell and Hoag, "A Conversation," 122.

10. Ibid., 123.

11. Elizabeth Janeway, "For Better and Worse," *New York Times Book Review,* 20 November 1960, 6, 18.

12. Broadwell and Hoag, "A Conversation," 123.

13. Bunting, "Literary World," 448.

14. Hilton Anderson, "Elizabeth Spencer's Two Italian Novellas," *Notes on Mississippi Writers* 13 (1981):18–19.

15. Broadwell and Hoag, "A Conversation," 124.

16. Haley, "An Interview," 53.

17. Ibid.

18. Bunting, "Literary World," 449.

19. William Hogan, "Elizabeth Spencer's Controversial Novella," *San Francisco Chronicle,* 21 November 1960, 41, reported a movie sale of $200,000, but in a personal letter, 16 January 1984, Spencer states that the amount was $75,000.

20. Orville Prescott, "Books of the Times," *New York Times,* 21 November 1960, 27.

21. Susan M. Black, "A Dream in Italy," *New Republic,* 5 December 1960, 20.

22. Shirley Spieckerman, *New Mexico Quarterly,* 30 (Winter 1960):414; Phoebe Adams, *Atlantic Monthly,* 207 (February 1961):113.

23. "No Magnolias in Florence," *Time,* 21 November 1960, 108.

24. Max Cosman, "Notable Novelette," *Commonweal,* 13 January 1961, 417.

25. Virgilia Peterson, "In Florence, a Curious Encounter," *New York Herald Tribune Book Review,* 27 November 1960, 30.

26. See Richard Foster, "What Is Fiction For?" *Hudson Review,* 14 (Spring 1961):142–43; Nolan Miller, "Three of the Best," *Antioch Review* 21 (Spring 1961):119, 123–25; George Steiner, *Yale Review* 50 (March 1961):424; Zoilus, "Too Graceful to be True," *Kenyon Review* 23 (Winter 1961):185–86.

27. Jones, "Spencer," 120.

Chapter Six

1. Rachel M. Brownstein, *Becoming a Heroine* (New York: Viking, 1982), xix.

2. Bunting, "Literary World," 459.

3. Jones, "Spencer," 121.

4. *The Stories of Elizabeth Spencer* (Garden City, N.Y., 1981), 85; hereafter cited in the text as *St* followed by page number; references to this work also occur in chapter 9.

5. Broadwell and Hoag, "A Conversation," 125.

6. Bunting, "Literary World," 460.

7. See Jones, "Spencer," 121.

8. Dorothy Dinnerstein, *The Mermaid and the Minotaur: Sexual Arrangements and Human Malaise* (1976; reprint, New York: Harper Colophon, 1977), 4–5.

9. Barge, "An Elizabeth Spencer Checklist," 574.

10. Jones, "Spencer," 127.

11. Broadwell and Hoag, "A Conversation," 124.

12. Ibid.

13. Granville Hicks, "Official Business in Rome," *Saturday Review,* 26 June 1965, 25–26.

14. Orville Prescott, "Books of the Times: All Aggravation and Ambiguity," *New York Times,* 30 June 1965, 35.

15. Rosemary E. Jones, "Knights and Dragons," *Commonweal,* 22 October 1965, 106–7.

16. Arthur Mizener, "Shadow and Sun," *New York Times Book Review,* 11 July 1965, 5. In a brief but discerning review Patrick Cruttwell describes the novella as *"elegant* and *civilized,"* in "Fiction Chronicle," *Hudson Review* 18 (Autumn 1965):445–46.

17. Stanley Kauffmann, "Sense and Sensibility," *New Republic,* 26 June 1965, 27–28.

18. Broadwell and Hoag, "A Conversation," 123–24.

19. Jones, "Spencer," 127.

20. Bunting, "Literary World," 454.

Chapter Seven

1. Granville Hicks, "Lives Like Assorted Pastries," *Saturday Review,* 21 October 1967, 29–30.

2. Carlos Baker, *"Two American Marriages,"* New York Times Book *Review,* 22 October 1967, 8.

3. Walter Sullivan, "Fiction in a Dry Season: Some Signs of "Hope," *Sewanee Review* 77 (Winter 1969):163–64.

4. Bunting, "Literary World," 453.

5. *No Place for an Angel* (New York, 1967), 253; hereafter page references cited in the text.

6. Broadwell and Hoag, "A Conversation," 125.

7. Haley, "An Interview," 46.

8. Broadwell and Hoag, "A Conversation," 126.

9. Haley, "An Interview," 51.

10. Broadwell and Hoag, "A Conversation," 125–26.

11. Joseph Conrad, *Lord Jim* (1899; reprint, New York: Doubleday, Page, 1926), 214.

12. Northrop Frye, *Anatomy of Criticism* (1957; reprint, New York: Atheneum, 1966), 237.

Chapter Eight

1. Hendin, *Vulnerable People,* 222.

2. Broadwell and Hoag, "A Conversation," 128.

3. *The Snare* (New York, 1972), 78; hereafter page references cited in the text.

4. Cole, "Elizabeth Spencer," 83.

5. Bunting, "Literary World," 451.

6. Broadwell and Hoag, "A Conversation," 127.

7. Ibid., 126.

8. Ibid., 127.

9. Bunting, "Literary World," 453.

10. *The Flowers of Evil and Other Poems of Charles Baudelaire,* trans. Francis Duke (Charlottesville: University of Virginia Press, 1961).

11. Georges Poulet, "Baudelaire and the Real World," *Baudelaire: The Artist and His World,* trans. Robert Allen and James Emmons (Geneva: Editions d'Art Albert Skira, 1969), 129–34.

12. See John Middleton Murray, "Baudelaire," in *Baudelaire: A Collection of Critical Essays,* ed. Henri Peyre (Englewood Cliffs, N.J.: Prentice-Hall, 1962), 102–3.

13. Poulet, *Baudelaire,* 140–42.

14. Charles Baudelaire, *My Heart Laid Bare,* ed. Peter Quennell, trans. Norman Cameron (London: Weidenfeld & Nicolson, 1950), 181.

15. Broadwell and Hoag, "A Conversation," 127.

16. Madison Jones, "The Snare," *New York Times Book Review,* 17 December 1972, 6, 20.

17. Patrick Cruttwell and Faith Westburg, "Fiction Chronicle," *Hudson Review* 26 (Summer 1973):421–22. Reviewing the novel in the *Georgia Review* 28 (Winter 1974):755–57, Rayburn Moore also found Spencer's treatment of evil to be "rather vague and amorphous."

18. Patricia S. Coyne, "Ennui and Evil," *National Review,* 30 March 1973, 374.

19. Bunting, "Literary World," 452.

Chapter Nine

1. In response to a question about the date, she wrote, "Actually, though I have said differently from a lapse of memory, the story must have been rejected in 1945, for I now recall I wrote it in Raymond Goldman's class," Spencer to Prenshaw, 2 February 1984.

2. Broadwell and Hoag, "A Conversation," 111.

3. Clara Claiborne Park, "A Personal Road," *Hudson Review* 34 (Winter 1981–82):604. See also Robert Buffington, "Ways Religious, Tedious, Fabulous, and Labyrinthine," *Sewanee Review* 90 (Spring 1982):272–73, who notes the "apparently impossible demands by family and society" that confront many of the characters in the stories.

4. D. J. Enright, "The Landscape of the Heart," *Times* (London) *Literary Supplement,* 15 July 1983, 745.

5. Park, "A Personal Road," 602.

6. See Karen Evoy, *"Marilee:* 'A Permanent Landscape of the Heart,' " *Mississippi Quarterly* 36 (Fall 1983):569–78, for a discussion of the unity of *Marilee.* Evoy notes that the three stories portray three separate journeys in time, each of which allows Marilee "to renew the ties with her family and home town . . . in an attempted retrieval of the very past that was lost through the rites of adulthood (i.e., growing up and leaving home)," 571.

7. See Hunter M. Cole, "Windsor in Spencer and Welty: A Real and an Imaginary Landscape," *Notes on Mississippi Writers* 7 (Spring 1974):2–11, for a discussion of the geographical area around Port Gibson, Mississippi, that Spencer draws upon in her description of Port Claiborne.

8. See Jones, "Elizabeth Spencer," 122.

9. Broadwell and Hoag, "A Conversation," 117.

Chapter Ten

1. *The Salt Line* (Garden City, N.Y., 1984), 230; hereafter page references cited in the text.

2. Anatole Broyard, "The Well-Made Novel," *New York Times,* 7 January 1984, 16; see also Christopher Porterfield, "Perplexities," *Time,* 13 February 1984, 70.

3. Phoebe-Lou Adams, "Short Reviews," *Atlantic* 253 (February 1984):104.

4. John Malcolm Brinnin, "Black and White in Redneck Country," *Washington Post Book World,* 15 May 1983, 10.

5. "Storytelling, Old and New," 30.

6. Bunting, "Literary World," 458–59.

Selected Bibliography

PRIMARY SOURCES

1. Novels

Fire in the Morning. New York: Dodd, Mead, 1948. Reprint. New York: McGraw-Hill, 1968.

This Crooked Way. New York: Dodd, Mead, 1952. Reprint. New York: McGraw-Hill, 1968.

The Voice at the Back Door. New York: McGraw-Hill, 1956. Reprints. New York: Pocket Books, 1958; New York: New American Library (Signet), 1964; New York: Time, 1965, with a new introduction by the author; New York: Time-Life, 1982.

The Light in the Piazza. New York: McGraw-Hill, 1960. Originally published in the *New Yorker,* 18 June 1960, 41–107. Reprint. New York: Pocket Books, 1962.

Knights and Dragons. New York: McGraw-Hill, 1965. Originally published in *Redbook,* July, 1965, 129–52. (See also *The Stories of Elizabeth Spencer,* Section 2 below.)

No Place for an Angel. New York: McGraw-Hill, 1967.

The Snare. New York: McGraw-Hill, 1972.

The Salt Line. Garden City, N.Y.: Doubleday, 1984.

2. Collected Short Stories

Ship Island and Other Stories. New York: McGraw-Hill, 1968. Reprinted in *The Stories of Elizabeth Spencer.* Garden City, N.Y.: Doubleday, 1981. References in the text are to the Doubleday edition. Includes three new stories, "Judith Kane," "Wisteria," and "The Day Before," and the following previously published stories: "The Little Brown Girl," *New Yorker* 33 (20 July 1957):27–29; "First Dark," *New Yorker* 35 (20 June 1959):31–40; "A Southern Landscape," *New Yorker* 36 (26 March 1960):28–34; "The White Azalea," *Texas Quarterly* 4 (Winter 1961):112–17; "The Visit," *Prairie Schooner* 38 (Summer 1964):95–108; "The Fishing Lake," *New Yorker* 40 (29 August 1964):24–25; "Ship Island," *New Yorker* 40 (12 September 1964):52–94.

The Stories of Elizabeth Spencer. Garden City, N.Y.: Doubleday, 1981. Reprinted. New York: Penguin, 1983. Includes *Ship Island and Other*

Stories, Knights and Dragons, and the following previously published stories: "The Eclipse," *New Yorker* 34 (12 July 1958):25–30; "Moon Rocket," *McCall's* 88 (October 1960:80–81, 178, 182, 184; "The Adult Holiday," *New Yorker* 41 (12 June 1965):35–36; "The Pincian Gate," *New Yorker* 42 (16 April 1966):50–52; "The Absence," *New Yorker* 42 (10 September 1966):53–54; "The Bufords," as "Those Bufords," *McCall's* 94 (January 1967):76–77, 124, 126; "A Bad Cold," *New Yorker* 43 (27 May 1967):38–39; "On the Gulf," *Delta Review* 5 (February 1968):44–46; "Sharon," *New Yorker* 46 (9 May 1970):36–39; "The Finder," *New Yorker* 46 (23 January 1971):30–39; "Presents," *Shenandoah* 22 (Winter 1971):68–73; "Instruments of Destruction," *Mississippi Review* 1 (January 1972):47–53; "A Kiss at the Door," *Southern Review* 8 (July 1972):676–80; "A Christian Education," *Atlantic Monthly* 233 (March 1974):73–74; "Mr. McMillan," *Southern Review* 11 (Winter 1975):205–11; "Prelude to a Parking Lot," *Southern Review* 12 (Summer 1976):454–69; "I, Maureen," *76: New Canadian Stories,* Ottawa: Oberon Press, 1976, 70–99; "Port of Embarkation," *Atlantic* 239 (January 1977):69–71; "Indian Summer," *Southern Review* 14 (Summer 1978):560–79; "Go South in Winter," *Journal of Canadian Fiction* 23 (1979):44–47; "The Search," *Chatelaine,* April 1979, 62, 78, 80, 83; "The Girl Who Loved Horses," *Ontario Review,* no. 10 (Spring–Summer 1979):5–20.

Marilee. Jackson: University Press of Mississippi, 1981. Includes "A Southern Landscape," "Sharon," "Indian Summer," and a foreword by the author.

3. Uncollected Short Stories (arranged chronologically)

"Pilgrimage." *Virginia Quarterly Review* 26 (Summer 1950):393–404.

"A Beautiful Day for a Wedding." *Redbook* 119 (September 1962):48–49, 98–102.

"The Atwater Fiancee." *Montrealer* 37 (September 1963):24–26.

"The Name of the Game." *McCall's* 99 (September 1972):94–95, 112, 114, 117–18.

"Jean-Pierre." *New Yorker* 42 (17 August 1981):30–40.

4. Selected Essays, Articles, and Reviews (arranged chronologically)

"Film Premiere of 'Intruder' Described by Novelist Spencer." Review of film, *Intruder in the Dust. Delta Democrat Times,* 16 October 1949, 18.

"Author and Critic Predicts Second Foote Book May Mark Emergence of New Leading Novelist." Review of Shelby Foote's *Follow Me Down. Delta Democrat Times,* 25 June 1950, 17.

"Foote's Third Novel Scores with Theme Centered on Money." Review of
   Shelby Foote's *Love in a Dry Season*. *Delta Democrat Times*, 23 September
   1951, 18.
"Valley Hill." *Delta Review* 1 (Autumn 1964):18–23.
"On Writing Fiction." *Notes on Mississippi Writers* 3 (Fall 1970):71–72.
"Storytelling, Old and New." *Writer* 85 (January 1972):9–10, 30.
"Elizabeth Spencer Comments." In *Contemporary Novelists*, edited by James
   Vinson, 1163–64. New York: St. Martin's Press, 1972.
"Douglas Book Is 'Good and Courageous.' " Review of Ellen Douglas's
   Apostles of Light. *Delta Democrat Times*, 11 March 1973, 25.
"State of Grace." *Vancouver Sun Weekend Magazine*, 12 August 1978, 18–
   20. On Tennessee, in special number, "The Last Days of Elvis Presley."
"Eudora Welty: An Introduction." *Eudora Welty Newsletter* 3 (April 1979):2–
   3.
"Emerging As a Writer in Faulkner's Mississippi." In *Faulkner and the
   Southern Renaissance*, edited by Doreen Fowler and Ann Abadie, 120–
   37. Jackson: University Press of Mississippi, 1982.
"Writers' Panel." In *E. M. Forster: Centenary Revaluations*, edited by Judith
   Scherer Herz and Robert K. Martin, 288–307. Toronto: University
   of Toronto Press, 1982.
"Experiment Is Out, Concern Is In." Review of *Best American Short Stories
   1982*. *New York Times Book Review*, 21 November 1982, 7, 49.

5. Unpublished thesis
"Irish Mythology in the Early Poetry of William Butler Yeats." Master's
   thesis, Vanderbilt University, 1943.

6. Manuscript Collection
University of Kentucky Library, Lexington, Kentucky. National Library
   of Canada, Ottawa.

SECONDARY SOURCES

1. Bibliography
Barge, Laura. "An Elizabeth Spencer Checklist, 1948 to 1976." *Mississippi
   Quarterly* 29 (Fall 1976):569–90. An invaluable guide. In addition
   to general bibliographical and biographical information, Barge gives
   foreign editions of Spencer's works, translations, information about
   the manuscripts, and a detailed listing of book reviews.
Pilkington, John. "Elizabeth Spencer." In *A Bibliographical Guide to the
   Study of Southern Literature*, edited by Louis D. Rubin, Jr., 294–95.
   Baton Rouge: Louisiana State University Press, 1969.

2. Biography

Capers, Charlotte. "An Evening with Eudora Welty and Elizabeth Spencer." *Delta Review* 4 (November 1967):70–72.

Davis, Louise. "Girl with a Typewriter Drawl." *Nashville Tennessean Magazine,* 16 April 1961, 14–15, 20.

"Elizabeth Spencer." *Mississippi English Newsletter* 6 (November 1972):1–2.

Tolliver, Kenneth R. "Elizabeth Spencer: Writer in Perspective." *Delta Review* 2 (July–August 1965):43, 70.

3. Interviews

Broadwell, Elizabeth Pell, and Ronald Wesley Hoag. "A Conversation with Elizabeth Spencer." *Southern Review* 18 (Winter 1982):111–30.

Brown, Laurie L. "Interviews with Seven Contemporary Writers." In *Women Writers of the Contemporary South,* edited by Peggy Whitman Prenshaw, 3–22. Jackson: University Press of Mississippi, 1984.

Bunting, Charles T. " 'In That Time and at That Place': The Literary World of Elizabeth Spencer." *Mississippi Quarterly* 28 (Fall 1975):435–60.

Cole, Hunter McKelva. "Elizabeth Spencer at Sycamore Fair." *Notes on Mississippi Writers* 6 (Winter 1974):81–86.

Haley, Josephine. "An Interview with Elizabeth Spencer." *Notes on Mississippi Writers* 1 (Fall 1968):42–55.

Jones, John Griffin. "Elizabeth Spencer." *Mississippi Writers Talking.* Jackson: University Press of Mississippi, 1982, 95–129.

4. Selected Criticism

Anderson, Hilton. *Elizabeth Spencer.* Jackson: Mississippi Library Commission, 1976. A survey discussion of Spencer's works through *The Snare.*

———. "Elizabeth Spencer's Two Italian Novellas." *Notes on Mississippi Writers* 13 (1981):18–35. Discusses *The Light in the Piazza* and *Knights and Dragons.*

Bradbury, John M. *Renaissance in the South: A Critical History of Literature, 1920–1960.* Chapel Hill: University of North Carolina Press, 1963, 117–19. Brief survey of works through *The Light in the Piazza.*

Brinnin, John Malcolm. "Black and White in Redneck Country." *Washington Post Book World,* 15 May 1983, 10. A retrospective review of *The Voice at the Back Door.*

Burger, Nash K. "Elizabeth Spencer's Three Mississippi Novels." *South Atlantic Quarterly* 63 (Summer 1964):351–62. Discusses Spencer's first three novels.

Cole, Hunter McKelva. "Windsor in Spencer and Welty: A Real and an Imaginary Landscape." *Notes on Mississippi Writers* 7 (Spring 1974):2–11. Discusses setting of "A Southern Landscape."

Enright, D. J. "The Landscape of the Heart." *Times* (London) *Literary Supplement,* 15 July 1983, 745. Detailed review of the collected stories.

Evoy, Karen. *"Marilee:* 'A Permanent Landscape of the Heart.' " *Mississippi Quarterly* 36 (Fall 1983):569–78.

French, Warren. "Elizabeth Spencer." In *Contemporary Novelists,* edited by James Vinson, 1164–65. New York: St. Martin's Press, 1972.

Hoffman, Frederick J. *The Art of Southern Fiction.* Carbondale: University of Southern Illinois Press, 1967, 113–14. Brief discussion of *The Voice at the Back Door.*

Johnson, Regina Nichols. "The Sense of Community in the Fiction of Elizabeth Spencer." Master's thesis, University of Alabama-Huntsville, 1977.

Meeker, Richard K. "The Youngest Generation of Southern Fiction Writers." In *Southern Writers: Appraisals in Our Time,* edited by R. C. Simonini, Jr., 175–76. Charlottesville: University of Virginia Press, 1964.

Park, Clara Claiborne. "A Personal Road." *Hudson Review* 34 (Winter 1981–82):601–5. Detailed review of the collected stories.

Prenshaw, Peggy Whitman. "Elizabeth Spencer." In *American Novelists since World War II,* 2d ser., edited by James E. Kibler, Jr., 320–27. Vol. 6 of *Dictionary of Literary Biography.* Detroit: Gale Research, 1980.

Pugh, David G. *"The Voice at the Back Door:* Elizabeth Spencer Looks into Mississippi." In *The Fifties: Fiction, Poetry, Drama,* edited by Warren French, 103–10. Deland, Fla.: Everett, Edwards, 1970.

Sullivan, Walter. "The Continuing Renascence: Southern Fiction in the Fifties." In *South: Modern Southern Literature in Its Cultural Setting,* edited by Louis D. Rubin, Jr., and Robert D. Jacobs, 376–91. Garden City, N.Y.: Doubleday Dolphin, 1961. Briefly discusses *The Voice at the Back Door.*

Index

Adams, Phoebe, 76
Atlantic Monthly, 76, 155
Austen, Jane, 8, 9

Baker, Carlos, 91
Baker, Nancy, 47
Banta, Martha: *Failure and Success in America: A Literary Debate,* 36
Barge, Laura, 83
Barnes, Djuna: *Nightwood,* 28–29
Baudelaire, Charles, 119, 123, 124, 125, 126; *Les Fleurs du mal,* 122
Beauvoir, Simone de, 89
Belhaven College, 6, 7
Black, Susan M., 76
Boccaccio: *The Decameron,* 69
Boorstein, Daniel: *The Image,* 97
Bowen, Elizabeth, 10
Brinnin, John Malcolm, 161
Brontë, Charlotte: *Villette,* 122
Brown vs. *Board of Education,* 50
Browning, Robert: *The Ring and the Book,* 38
Brownstein, Rachel M.: *Becoming a Heroine,* 78
Broyard, Anatole, 152
Buckmaster, Henrietta, 30
Burger, Nash K., 29, 45

Capers, Charlotte, 7
Cash, W. J.: *The Mind of the South,* 48
Cather, Willa, 8
Chekhov, Anton, 8
Chicago Sunday Tribune, 47
Chopin, Kate: *The Awakening,* 144–45
Citizen's Council, 50
Clay, David, 9, 10, 11, 16
Clay, Justine, 11
Commonweal, 76, 87
Conrad, Joseph, 8, 103; *Lord Jim,* 103, 112
Cosman, Max, 76
Coyne, Patricia S., 129
Cozzens, James Gould: *The Just and the Unjust,* 51
Crane, Stephen: *The Red Badge of Courage,* 87; "The Open Boat," 87
Creekmore, Hubert, 16

Cruttwell, Patrick, 129

Dante, 126; *Inferno,* 125
Davidson, Donald, 7, 9, 48
Dinnerstein, Dorothy, 84: *The Mermaid and the Minotaur: Sexual Arrangement and Human Malaise,* 82
Dollard, John: *Caste and Class in a Southern Town,* 62

Eliot, George, 9
Eliot, T.S.: *The Waste Land,* 97
Enright, D. J., 137

Faulkner, William, 1, 3, 7, 8, 9, 10, 11, 18, 20, 23, 29, 30, 35, 48, 52, 64, 114; *Absalom, Absalom!,* 35–36, 47; *As I Lay Dying,* 20, 38; *Go Down Moses,* 23; *Intruder in the Dust,* 30; *Light in August,* 37; *The Reivers,* 4; *The Sound and the Fury,* 64
Fitzgerald, F. Scott, 99; Gatsby (*The Great Gatsby*), 35–36
Flint, F. C., 42, 45
Flint, R. W., 29, 30
Foote, Shelby: *Follow Me Down,* 38
Forster, E. M., 69
Frye, Northrop: *Anatomy of Criticism,* 110

Ghent, Dorothy Van, 61
Gill, Brendan, 51, 52
Goldman, Raymond, 9, 132
Guggenheim Fellowship, 10, 49
Guggenheim Foundation, 11, 13

Hackett, Francis, 52
Hardy, Thomas, 8, 28, 109
Hedden, Worth Tuttle, 29, 47
Hellman, Lillian, 16
Hemingway, Ernest, 8, 104
Hendin, Josephine, 68, 112
Hicks, Granville, 76, 87, 91
Hudson Review, 129, 133

James, Henry, 69, 73, 83, 85; "The Jolly Corner," 70
Janeway, Elizabeth, 72

Jones, Anne Goodwyn: *Tomorrow Is Another Day*, 60
Jones, Madison, 128
Jones, Rosemary E., 87, 88
Joyce, James, 9

Kapp, Isa, 76
Kauffmann, Stanley, 88, 91
Keats, John, 28
Kenyon Review, 13

Library Journal, 30

McCall's, 132
McGraw-Hill Fiction Award, 76
Mansfield, Katherine, 8, 145
Mathews, Donald G., 35
Melville, Herman, 36, 96
Mills, C. Wright, 103; *The Power Elite*, 101
Mizener, Arthur, 88
Morris, Willie: *North toward Home*, 51

Nation, 47
National Review, 129
New Mexico Quarterly, 76
New Republic, 52, 76, 88
New York Herald Tribune Book Review, 52
New York Times, 51, 76, 152
New York Times Book Review, 16, 72, 88, 91, 128
New Yorker, 12, 30, 47, 75, 76, 132

O. Henry prize, 13
O'Connor, Flannery, 1; "The River," 34
Owsley, Frank: *Plain Folk of the Old South*, 48

Park, Clara Claiborne, 133, 138
Percy, Walker, 101; *The Last Gentleman*, 61, 127
Peterson, Virgilia, 76
Porter, Katherine Anne, 8, 10
Porterfield, Christopher, 152
Poulet, Georges, 124, 125
Prescott, Orville, 51, 76, 87
Proust, Marcel, 9
Pugh, David G., 64

Ransom, John Crowe, 10
Redbook, 83, 132
Reisman, David: *The Lonely Crowd*, 101
Rusher, John, 11

Sewanee Review, 34, 42, 91

Shakespeare, William: *The Tempest*, 156
Singal, D. J., 48
Smith, Harrison, 29
Smith, Lillian: *Killers of the Dream*, 54
Southern Review, 132
Spencer, Elizabeth, birth, 2–3; childhood in Carrollton, Miss., 2–4; education, 4–9; family's reading, 4–5; literary technique, 26–29, 38–39, 42–46, 62–64, 72–74, 81–82, 83–85, 88–89, 92, 95–96, 102, 109–10, 130–31, 160; marriage, 2, 11; oral tradition, 4, 6; teaching, 9–10, 32; travel to Italy, 2, 10–12, 15, 49; residence in Canada, 2, 12, 15

WORKS—NON-FICTION:
"Emerging as a Writer in Faulkner's Mississippi," 1, 3–6, 8
"Storytelling, Old and New," 162
"Valley Hill," 3

WORKS—SHORT STORIES:
"Absence, The," 145
"Adult Holiday, The," 147
"Bad Cold, A," 147
"Bufords, The," 145
"Christian Education, A," 3, 135, 137
"Day Before, The," 3, 131, 136–37
"Eclipse, The," 133–34
"Finder, The," 146–47
"First Dark," 13, 138
"Fishing Lake, The," 147
"Girl Who Loved Horses, The," 148–49, 162
"Go South in the Winter," 147
"I, Maureen," 14, 143–45
"Indian Summer," 139–41
"Instrument of Destruction," 141–42
"Judith Kane," 145–46
"Kiss at the Door, A," 141–42
"Little Brown Girl, The," 3, 132–33
Marilee, 14, 131, 139–40
"Moon Rocket," 135
"Mr. McMillan," 142–43
"On the Gulf," 135–36
"Pilgrimage," 132
"Pincian Gate, The," 131
"Port of Embarkation," 135
"Prelude to a Parking Lot," 141
"Presents," 134
"Search, The," 147
"Sharon," 139–40

Ship Island and Other Stories, 13–14, 78, 131

"Ship Island: The Story of a Mermaid," 10, 13, 68, 78–83, 90, 112, 114, 132, 143

"Southern Landscape, A," 139, 141, 149

Stories of Elizabeth Spencer, The, 6, 12, 14, 78, 83, 131–50

"Visit, The," 147–48

"White Azalea, The," 143

"Wisteria," 145

WORKS—NOVELS AND NOVELLAS:

Fire in the Morning, 3–4, 9–10, 16–31, 32–33, 41, 47, 49, 55, 59, 70, 160

Knights and Dragons, 12–14, 67, 78, 83–90, 94, 106, 112, 131–32, 143

Light in the Piazza, The, 12, 13, 51, 66–77, 78, 83, 84, 87

No Place for an Angel, 13, 67, 78, 90, 91–111, 112, 121, 130, 131, 144, 151, 161, 163

Salt Line, The, 10, 14–15, 151–60, 162, 163

Snare, The, 13–14, 67, 78–79, 112–30, 143, 148, 151, 160–61, 162, 163

This Crooked Way, 10, 32–48, 51, 102, 148

Voice at the Back Door, The, 2, 4, 11, 49–65, 66, 86–87, 94, 151, 161

Spieckerman, Shirley, 76

Sullivan, Walter, 91
Sumner, Cid Ricketts, 47

Taine, H. A., 61
Tennessean (Nashville), 7, 9, 26
Tennyson, Alfred, 28
Till, Emmett, 50
Time, 30, 47, 76, 152
Times Literary Supplement, 47, 137
Times Picayune (New Orleans), 113
Tunstall, Caroline, 52
Turgenev, Ivan, 8

Vanderbilt University, 1, 6, 7, 9, 18, 26, 48
Virginia Quarterly Review, 10, 132

Warren, Robert Penn, 9, 16, 18; *All the King's Men,* 16, 47, 48; "Blackberry Winter," 33
Watkins Institute, 9, 132
Welty, Eudora, 6, 7, 10, 13, 16, 88, 138, 143; *The Golden Apples,* 73–74; "The Wide Net," 33–34
West, Anthony, 51
Westburg, Faith, 129
Whyte, William H., Jr.: *The Organization Man,* 101
Woolf, Virginia, 8, 9, 88, 89, 91, 115

Yale Review, 61
Yeats, William Butler, 7, 9
Young, Stark, 10

813.54
Sp745

118 219